CW00821051

John Laws is John Laws.

Christopher Stewart has worked in newspapers, radio, and television in Queensland, New South Wales and the ACT, including as News Director of Sydney's 2SM and Chief of Staff with National Nine News. He headed the Australian Government's largest public affairs organisations in Social Security, Defence, and Foreign Affairs and Trade, and served three years as Counsellor in the Australian Embassy in Tokyo directing Australia's public relations activities throughout North Asia. For two years, he was Australia's chief negotiator on international social security treaties. In 2000-1 he spent six months in Solomon Islands first as an adviser to the Office of the Prime Minister during the ceasefire period that followed civil unrest in that country, then as an adviser to the Peace Monitoring Council during disarmament and reconstruction. He has held several senior executive positions in the private sector and now works in Brisbane and lives on the Gold Coast.

Christopher is proudly Australian but also cherishes his Irish heritage. He began writing the stories in this book 15 years ago.

JOHN LAWS

and CHRISTOPHER STEWART

There's always more to the story

Pan Macmillan Australia

First published 2004 in Macmillan by Pan Macmillan Australia Pty Limited
St Martins Tower, 31 Market Street, Sydney

National Library of Australia
Cataloguing-in-Publication data:

Laws, John, 1935– .
There's always more to the story: John Laws' favourite Australian stories.

Bibliography
ISBN 1 4050 36281.

1. Australia – Social life and customs. 2. Australia – Biography. 3. Australia – History. I. Stewart, Christopher Robert, 1953– . II. Title.

994

Set in 12.5/15 pt Bembo by Midland Typesetters
Printed in Australia by McPherson's Printing Group

Cover design: Deborah Parry Graphics
Front cover photographs: Portrait of Arthur Hoey Davis (Steele Rudd) taken at Supreme Court, Brisbane, 1903, by Paul C. Poulsen, National Library of Australia PIC/7217/1-2. Fly-past at Parliament House, 1927, National Archives of Australia, A3560, 3049.
Back cover photographs: Portrait of Arthur Orton, 1834–1898, National Library of Australia PIC S10700, and the CSS *Shenandoah* sketched at anchor in Hobson's Bay near Melbourne, La Trobe Picture Collection, State Library of Victoria.

ADA LEADS THE WAY

There's an old saying that if you have one lawyer in town they'll go broke, but have two lawyers in town and they'll both make a fortune – mostly by writing to each other.

At the heart of that jibe is the truth – the legal profession thrives on disagreeing with each other, and in trying to convince everyone else that issues are so complicated they can only be resolved by 'the law'.

Take, for example, the curious rule of 'precedent' that obliges judges and magistrates to follow the decisions made by more senior judges or courts in similar cases. This is a story about how the legal profession in New South Wales used 'precedent' to perpetrate a shameful discrimination.

PROFESSOR PITT CORBETT was the most respected legal academic in Australia in 1898. He was head of the Sydney University Law School, had impeccable academic credentials and was very well connected in government and business circles in New South Wales.

So Ada Evans knew it was not a good sign when she was summoned to his room. The professor was fuming; he had recently returned from an overseas trip and saw for the first time the student list for the coming year. He wanted to find out from Ada what her name was doing on that list.

Professor Corbett told her that it was preposterous she should presume to be suitable for law. For a start, women did not have the necessary physique. He suggested she might think about a more suitable career, such as one in medicine, and leave law to men.

However, Ada was not going to be bullied or dissuaded. She had already had to battle her way through an Arts degree at the university three years earlier. She politely, but firmly, declined to withdraw. Professor Pitt Corbett was now even more angry. However, there was nothing he could do because the university had recently introduced a policy of equal access for women.

Ada Evans stood her ground and four years later, in 1902, became Australia's first female law graduate. It seemed she had won the battle with Professor Pitt Corbett and his colleagues in the legal profession. Or had she? There's a great deal more to this story.

Ada Evans may have used the university system to frustrate Professor Corbett and gain her law degree, but the legal profession had prepared a very unpleasant surprise for her once she graduated.

A law degree was one thing, but to practise, you had to be admitted to the Bar as a solicitor or barrister. That meant registering with a law firm as a 'student at law' – the legal equivalent of an apprenticeship.

When Ada tried to register, she was denied on the basis that there was no 'precedent' of a woman being approved. Cunningly, this was not denying her admission to the Bar, but simply saying that the Bar could not allow her to proceed to acquire the necessary qualification for the moment because it needed some guidance. Yet there was no indication where that guidance would come from. Despite protests to London and the New South Wales Parliament by Ada's friends and supporters, the decision stood.

Three years later, the Melbourne Bar admitted Ms Flos Greig without any apparent concern for a lack of precedent. But still the Sydney lawyers resisted change.

For 16 years, Ada Evans took the fight up to the all-male legal profession. And still the answer remained: 'But there is no precedent.' Finally, in 1918, the *Women's Legal Status Act* was passed into law in New South Wales and Ada was allowed to register. She completed her three years of training and was admitted to the Bar of the Supreme Court of New South Wales. On 12 May 1921, 19 years after graduating from Sydney University, Ada Emily Evans had achieved her goal.

But to everyone's surprise, she declined to take her place at the Bar. This woman of 47 had spent almost half her life pursuing the dream of becoming a barrister. She had overcome the prejudice and discrimination of the all-male legal fraternity in New South Wales, and in doing so, had changed the law for all women who followed her. However, she said that it had been such a long battle she feared she would not be at her best when she approached the Bar and she did not wish 'women's standing in the profession to be undermined by a show of incompetence'.

With her last shot, she had struck at the heart of her detractors. She displayed even more dignity in victory than she had displayed for so many years in apparent defeat.

Ada Evans retired to the New South Wales town of Bowral, where she died in 1947. To this day the New South Wales Law Society refers to the past 80 years as the period 'After Ada'.

AFFABLE ALFRED

I think everyone knows my opinion of politicians. I've often said that if you are in politics you must either be a liar or a hypocrite – you've got a choice, but it has to be one of these.

But I have to admit that I have met a handful of politicians over the years who are truthful and principled. Ted Mack, the former independent from North Sydney, was one, and I think Senator Bob Brown from Tasmania is as well – even though I don't agree with much of his politics.

We included this story because it is about political principles – in more than one respect.

ALFRED DEAKIN WAS Australia's second, fifth and seventh prime minister. The eloquent and intellectual Melbourne barrister and journalist first made his name as an advocate of Federation. But he is probably best remembered as the champion of the infamous White Australia Policy that was designed to prevent 'coloured' people and Asians from entering Australia.

Alfred Deakin was born in Fitzroy, Melbourne, in August 1856. He matriculated from the Church of

Alfred Deakin (on the right) was quick to recognise the potential of inventions such as the motor car for Australia. He is pictured here around 1910.

England Grammar School then graduated in law from Melbourne University, even though he had no interest in being a lawyer. His real interests were history, literature, religion, philosophy and science. As his law career inevitably faltered for lack of motivation, he moved into journalism as a columnist with *The Age* newspaper from 1878 until 1883.

His research and writing led him to two new interests at about the same time – politics and spiritualism. While he was preparing to participate in Victorian politics, he was also exploring Eastern mysticism and religions, and participating in seances. He eventually became President of the Spiritualist Association, where he met his future wife, Pattie.

Deakin also believed that through seances he was able to consult with some of the greatest political and philosophical minds of all time – he claimed to have talked with Sophocles, John Stuart Mill and a number of deceased premiers of Victoria. However, his most frequent adviser was the long-dead John Bunyan, author of *The Pilgrim's Progress*. Deakin published a book called *A New Pilgrim's Progress* in 1877; he claimed that Bunyan had passed the ideas and words on to him from 'the other side'.

Alfred Deakin served in several Victorian governments and was responsible for significant labour reforms, including the Victorian Factory Acts of 1885 and 1893 that ended child labour, and introduced workers' compensation and limited working hours for women and children. He also drove an innovative national agenda in the absence of a Federal Parliament. His pet project was the Riverina irrigation project in southern New South Wales. He spent several months in the United States of America studying the subject before writing the policy for Australia.

But there can be no doubt that Alfred Deakin's most significant contribution was in delivering Federation after months in London negotiating the final detail with the British Government.

In his ministerial roles in the new national government that followed, Alfred Deakin sponsored laws on trade protection, expansion of the defence forces, labour reform and welfare. He was a passionate advocate for the poor and disadvantaged. He was also responsible for the establishment of the High Court, the Conciliation and Arbitration Court and the Australian Public Service.

However, Alfred Deakin engineered some controversial legislation as well. In particular there was the White Australia immigration policy that ensured Australia would be perceived as a white outpost in the Asia-Pacific region for decades to come.

Deakin first became Prime Minister in 1903 when Edmund Barton moved to fill a vacancy on the High Court. In three terms – two with the support of the Labor Party – Deakin served a total of five troubled years in the country's top job. But there's always more to the story.

Alfred Deakin was a scrupulously honest man with strong views on political principles. That is why he was respected by all sides of politics. He was one of the few politicians of his time to decline honours and awards, including a knighthood. He said he was only doing the job for which he was paid.

When Deakin was 22, friends convinced him to stand for election to the Victorian Parliament. With just two weeks' notice, he mounted a campaign that carried him into the Legislative Assembly with a 97-vote victory. In July 1879, he was sworn in and took his place in the House. When he rose to give his maiden speech, he stunned everyone present, including his own party, by resigning. Deakin told the Assembly that he had learned there had been a shortage of ballot papers at one polling booth. Even though the additional ballot papers would not have changed the outcome of the by-election, Alfred Deakin saw this as an issue of principle and as far as he was concerned the result was invalid. The by-election was held again and Deakin lost.

Principles were also the central issue in perhaps the most extraordinary aspect of Alfred Deakin's political career. For 14 years, including his time as Prime Minister and as opposition leader, Deakin wrote an anonymous column in the London *Morning Post* commenting on Australian politics. Only his family knew the truth; his wife, Pattie, would address the envelopes containing the copy for the columns in her handwriting to ensure no-one linked the contents to Alfred.

The *Morning Post*'s support for the Deakin government was, at times, crucial in shoring up support for it at home and in England. For this reason, many commentators have argued since that Deakin acted improperly and unethically in not declaring a conflict of interest. However, Alfred Deakin said he saw no problem with the arrangement because he always maintained a balanced perspective in his commentary. Indeed, many of his columns were strongly critical of his own actions; in some cases they were almost disrespectful. For instance, after a poor showing in the 1903 election, his column said that 'Mr Deakin may well view the position before him with rueful solicitude'. Alfred Deakin dealt with criticism of his alleged 'deceit' towards the Australian people by ignoring it.

When 'Affable Alfred' Deakin retired from Parliament in 1913, three years after losing government, his health was quickly deteriorating with what was most likely Alzheimer's disease. His famous memory failing, he became an invalid and died in 1919 at the age of 63.

AFTER YOU

The more I discover about our history the more I realise what a distorted version of events we were given during our years at school. We weren't taught history – we were taught someone's interpretation of what happened.

Most Australians of my generation came into the 60s and 70s loaded with prejudice. This was not because we had malice in our hearts, but because we had been taught to believe certain things about our past.

Questioning our history and challenging traditional beliefs is both wise and healthy for society. Not only does it encourage each of us to learn more about our heritage, it also helps to create a more accurate record for generations to come.

WE ALL LEARNED at school that Captain James Cook was the first white man to set foot on the east coast of Australia. Well, it is not true. The first Englishman to step ashore was 16-year-old Isaac Smith, a young crewman on Cook's ship, HM Barque *Endeavour*.

It was 6 am on Thursday 20 April 1770 when Second Lieutenant Zachary Hicks first sighted the coast of Australia. Lieutenant James Cook was excited.

The romantic way early artists portrayed James Cook's landing at Botany Bay.

He had been dispatched from England in August 1768 with secret orders to find the Great South Land. In August 1769, he discovered the North Island of New Zealand and now he had found the large landmass that he suspected lay to the north.

On 29 April 1770, Cook anchored the *Endeavour* off the southern point of what he called Sting Rays Harbour – James Banks later renamed it Botany Bay – and prepared to go ashore to claim the land for England. Cook went in the first of two longboats, together with Banks and Able Seaman Isaac Smith, who had become Cook's assistant mapmaker.

As the landing party neared the shore, they saw Aborigines waving at them. At first, Cook thought they were beckoning the visitors to come ashore, but then they began throwing spears and Cook fired two musket shots in their direction to scare them away.

When the boat touched the sand of the beach, James Cook turned to young Isaac Smith and said, 'Isaac, you shall land first.' And so, when a plaque was erected in 1948 at Kurnell to mark the spot where Cook's party came ashore, Isaac Smith was honoured as the first Englishman to set foot in New South Wales.

But, of course, there's more to the story. There are plenty of theories as to why James Cook allowed a 16-year-old able seaman to precede him ashore at Botany Bay. It is possible that it was so that Smith could hold the boat steady for Cook to make a dignified and dry-stocking landing. Or it might have been in case the Aborigines again attacked with spears. Or perhaps it was because Captain Cook was so impressed with young Smith's drafting skills that he saw a lot of himself in the boy; after all, James Cook had built a career on his success in surveying and mapmaking.

But the most likely reason Isaac Smith was first ashore at Kurnell was quite simply that Cook's wife, Elizabeth, had asked her husband to allow Isaac some special honour during their long cruise because he was her favourite cousin. In fact, Isaac was only on the *Endeavour* at Mrs Cook's request.

Regardless of Mrs Cook's intervention, Isaac Smith proved a valuable member of the *Endeavour*'s crew. He produced several important maps and charts of New Zealand and Australia, as well as a dictionary of 30

Aboriginal words. He was promoted to midshipman after the *Endeavour* left Australia, and went on to become a Rear Admiral in a distinguished Royal Navy career.

Admiral Isaac Smith died in 1831, alone in a house left to him by his brother. It was the gatehouse to Merton Abbey, the former home of England's greatest naval hero, Lord Nelson. However, he only moved to this house shortly before he died. For the previous 20 years – after he retired from the navy – Isaac Smith lived with his cousin, Elizabeth, who had been widowed when James Cook was killed in the Hawaiian Islands in 1779.

Elizabeth Cook died at the age of 93 on 13 May 1835. She had outlived all six of her children. Shortly before her death, Elizabeth fulfilled a request made by her husband before he sailed on his final voyage; the request was that before she died, she was to destroy all his personal papers.

ARTHUR ORTON

If you tell a lie without intending to hurt anyone, is it still wrong?

That might seem a ridiculous question; but what if you were so desperate to survive, or to provide for your family, that you told a little lie you thought couldn't possibly hurt anyone? Then one lie led to another, and so on until it got out of hand.

Your conscience tells you to get out of the situation that you have created for yourself as quickly as possible, but you discover that if you don't go on with the deceit, you will break the heart of the person to whom you originally lied.

The kindest thing you can do is continue with the lie. What would you do?

This story is about just such a dilemma.

AS FAR AS everyone in Wagga Wagga, New South Wales, knew, Thomas Castro was a butcher who had migrated from England. No-one imagined he might be the heir to a fortune and aristocratic titles in both England and France. But, in 1865, Castro stepped forward to announce that he was Sir Roger Charles Tichborne, the Eleventh Baronet of Tichborne, a descendent of the French Bourbon Conti dynasty and heir to a fortune.

Sir Roger Tichborne had disappeared 13 years earlier during an adventurous world trip ahead of his intended marriage. He was 24 years old when he sailed from Rio de Janeiro for New York on a coastal ship named the *Bella*. The ship capsized at sea with the apparent loss of all 40 passengers and crew.

Tichborne's mother, the Dowager Lady Henrietta, refused to accept that her son was dead, believing he had been rescued but was suffering from amnesia. As years went by she clung to hope, believing even the wildest stories of survivor sightings. One of these suggested that Roger's ship had not sunk, but had been hijacked and sailed to Australia, where it was renamed.

In 1865, 12 years after Roger's disappearance and well after insurance policies had been paid out, Lady Henrietta ordered advertisements to be placed in newspapers around the world in English, French and Spanish, asking for information on her son's whereabouts. She also contacted a man named Cubitt about whom she had read in a London newspaper. Cubitt ran a private missing persons' bureau in Melbourne. It was he who decided to place an advertisement in the Wagga newspaper.

Soon a Wagga solicitor and old friend of Cubitt, named Gibbes, contacted him to say that he had seen Sir Roger Tichborne in Wagga. He was living under the assumed name of Thomas Castro and was a client of Gibbes.

Thomas Castro was a bankrupt butcher who had told wild stories of being a rich Englishman living under an assumed identity. At first he laughed at the suggestion from Gibbes that he resembled the missing Tichborne, but eventually he changed his tune.

Cubitt wrote to Lady Henrietta to tell her the good news. She was delighted, but the rest of the family were suspicious. They arranged for a former family servant, who had retired to Sydney, to meet Castro. To everyone's surprise, except Lady Henrietta's, the servant confirmed the man was, indeed, Sir Roger Tichborne. A frail and elderly Dowager Tichborne immediately telegraphed funds for her long-lost son to travel to England. Castro took his wife and child with him, arriving in London on Christmas Day 1866.

It was now that the greatest suspicions were aroused in the family. They were confronted with a man weighing more than 130 kilograms with a strong cockney accent and poor manners, who spoke no French and recalled none of the stories of his youth his family were putting to him. Sir Roger Tichborne, a painfully thin and weak man, was raised and educated in Paris with French as his first language. He spoke English with a thick accent. He had served as an officer in the army and lived a privileged life on a large pension. He was a refined gentleman.

Dozens of former friends, teachers and relatives were brought to meet Castro. Not one thought that he was Roger Tichborne, even though he knew a great deal about the family. However, the dowager refused to listen to any of the doubters. 'This is my son,' she proclaimed vehemently as she granted him a large allowance and a sizeable estate.

It was only after Lady Tichborne's death and three years of trials instigated by the family, who had been deprived of their inheritance, that Castro's claims fell apart. A school friend told the court that Roger had tattooed the initials RCT on his arm – Castro had no tattoo. Castro had said he was rescued from the sinking of the *Bella* by a ship called the *Osprey* – there was no such ship registered anywhere in the world. And, finally, the prosecution produced a man named Charles Orton, who had told them that the man claiming to be Roger Tichborne was, in fact, his brother Arthur Orton from Wapping.

Eventually, in 1874, a court found that the claimant of the title of Sir Roger Tichborne was a fraud. It sentenced Arthur Orton to 14 years in prison despite his insistence to the end that he was, indeed, Roger Tichborne. But there is, as always, more to the story.

Arthur Orton served four years in prison before the Tichborne family mysteriously asked for his release. They said justice had been served by the family fortune going to the rightful heirs.

Although he became known as one of the world's most famous imposters, it seems Arthur Orton could have been what you might call an 'accidental fraud'. He was born the youngest of 12 children to an honest, hardworking Wapping butcher. At 15, he was sent to sea by his father to learn a trade. He hated the life and

A portrait of Wagga Wagga butcher Arthur Orton, who claimed to be the missing heir to a French fortune.

jumped ship in Chile, where he lived with a family named Castro.

After a year, Arthur returned to England to work in the butcher shop with his father. But when he had saved enough money, he bought a ticket for Australia and left in search of adventure. Instead, he lost his money and fell into a life of horse and cattle stealing to supplement the income from his butcher shop in Wagga. He was struggling to survive when the opportunity to become Sir Roger Tichborne was presented to him.

When he emerged from prison, Arthur Orton declared that he wanted to confess to the lie. He sold his story to *People* magazine in 1895. In the article he said that he only ever intended to get enough money from the Tichborne family to enable his wife and child to travel to Panama, where his brother had a successful business. He had carried off his deceit for so long because as the Tichborne family, friends and former servants tried to expose him, they actually gave him more and more information he could use to confirm his identity as Sir Roger. The whole thing just got out of hand, according to Orton.

Coincidentally, Arthur Orton, imposter, died on April Fools' Day 1898. He was buried in an unmarked pauper's grave in Paddington Cemetery in London.

At last the mystery of the missing Tichborne heir was over. Or was it? Someone is yet to explain who arranged for the inscription on Arthur Orton's simple coffin. It read:

Sir Roger Charles Doughty Tichborne
Born 5 January 1829–died 1 April 1898.

THE ASSASSIN

A commentator said recently of the ongoing conflict in the Middle East that the real tragedy of war is the innocent civilian casualties.

I disagree. I believe the tragedy of war is that humans kill and maim other humans – civilians and soldiers – to settle what always begins as a disagreement.

The reality is that our armed forces exist to engage and kill the enemy. That is their purpose and their duty. We train them to avoid mortal combat wherever possible and hope that they can use the threat of force as a deterrent.

But when the situation comes down to kill or be killed, there is little choice.

That's how it was in 1915 at Gallipoli.

YOU HAD TO be a damn fine horseman, marksman and bushman to survive in Central Queensland in the early 1900s. If you couldn't eat off the land, work cattle in dense bushland and spend months alone, you might as well head south to Brisbane.

Billy Sing, from Clermont, was one of the best bushmen around Proserpine and he was also the best shot in

AWM PO1778.004

Billy Sing (left) talks with the British Commander at Gallipoli, General Birdwood (back to camera) who later asked to spend time as Sing's spotter.

the Proserpine Rifle Club. In October 1914, just eight weeks after war had been declared in Europe, Billy Sing signed up as a volunteer for the First Australian Infantry Force. He was sent off to Brisbane for training with the 5th Light Horse – a Queensland regiment – and was on his way to Egypt by Christmas that year.

When the first infantry battalions landed at Gallipoli on 25 April 1915, the 5th Light Horse were still being held in reserve in Egypt. But with a rapidly rising casualty toll after four weeks, they were put on notice in May and were soon on their way by sea to the Dardenelles. When the light horsemen arrived at Suvla Bay, they were told they would be dispersed among the infantry units dug in on the hillsides and cliffs, to learn the tactics of trench warfare.

With Billy's marksmanship it was inevitable that he would be given the job of sniper. Every day for the next six months, he would rise before the sun and move quietly to a concealed sniping position. There he would lie motionless until after sunset, in the freezing cold of winter or the stinking heat of summer, with a spotter alongside him peering through a telescope for the slightest glimpse of a Turkish target. Billy would only move to slide his rifle out of the nest to take a shot. Some days he would not fire at all. One day he claimed nine victims.

Billy Sing became such a celebrity among the ANZAC troops that even the British commander at Gallipoli, General Birdwood, asked to spend time with him acting as his spotter. The rising tally of Billy's kills lifted morale among the soldiers pinned down by merciless Turkish fire. He became their hero and their revenge.

This Queensland bushman and his bolt-action Lee Enfield .303 rifle sent a shiver through the Turkish army. The Turks too had come to know of Billy Sing and his nicknames 'The Assassin' and 'The Murderer'. Turkish commanders sent their own best sniper, a man known to the Australians as 'Abdul the Terrible', specifically to find and kill Billy Sing. But Billy got him first.

As the Turkish death toll from Billy's sniping began

to reach 200, Turk artillery barrages were ordered on Bolton's Ridge, where he was thought to be hiding. But again they could not stop him. Only once was Billy Sing wounded at Gallipoli – when a Turkish sniper fired a shot that hit Billy's spotter. The bullet deflected into Billy's shoulder after passing through his offsider's hands and face. Private Sing was out of action for just one week.

By October 1915, Billy Sing had an official tally of 150 and an unofficial tally of 201 victims, and he was singled out for special mention in a signal from General Birdwood.

Meanwhile, the stories of Billy Sing's skill were beginning to feature in stories appearing in newspapers in England and the United States of America. In 1916, after the withdrawal of the ANZACs from Gallipoli, Billy Sing received his first official recognition when he was Mentioned in Despatches by the Commander of the Allied Forces, Sir Ian Hamilton. Shortly afterwards he was awarded one of our highest bravery awards, the Distinguished Conduct Medal for conspicuous gallantry at Gallipoli. It is an incredible tale, but you haven't heard all of the story yet; there's always more.

While it might seem inhuman to be decorating a man for ruthlessly killing others, the fact is that the sniping that Billy and the other Australian marksmen carried out kept Turkish troops pinned down, saving hundreds of Australian lives. It also neutralised the Turkish snipers who were picking off ANZAC forces trapped on the hillside of the cove.

After evacuation from Gallipoli, Billy Sing transferred from the Light Horse to the 31st Infantry Battalion and shipped out to France in August 1916. He was wounded several times during the next 18 months. During recuperation in Scotland, he met and married a waitress named Elizabeth Stewart, leaving her soon afterwards to return to the trenches in France.

Snipers were not used in the European battlefields the way they had been at Gallipoli, but Billy still proved himself invaluable. He was mentioned a number of times in reports by Allied commanders, who praised his gallant service.

In one operation, Billy led an Australian team to search out and kill German snipers who had been taking a heavy toll on Australian and Belgian troops at Polygon Wood in Belgium. He was recommended for the Military Medal for that operation; it was not approved, despite the Belgians awarding him the Croix de Guerre for the same action.

The irony of this story is that Billy Sing was not supposed to be at Gallipoli or in Belgium – he shouldn't have even been in the Australian Army. In those days only people of European blood were considered suitable for Australia's armed forces. Billy Sing was Chinese. He was accepted only after an army recruitment officer 'overlooked' the section of his application form nominating parents' nationality. Billy Sing was just one of many Australians of Chinese descent who served with distinction in the Australian forces during World War I.

The most highly decorated was Private Caleb James

Shang from Cairns. He was awarded the Distinguished Conduct Medal and Bar, and the Military Medal for conspicuous gallantry in France in 1917 and 1918.

Billy Sing eventually brought his Scottish bride back to Proserpine in late 1918 to a hero's welcome from the town. However, Elizabeth didn't take to life in Central Queensland and soon left Billy. He worked around Clermont and the nearby goldfields before moving to Brisbane in 1942.

William Edward Sing died in May 1943, at the age of 57, in his room at a boarding house in West End. His only asset was his weekly pay packet from labouring.

AUSTRALIA'S HELEN KELLER

Whenever my mate Dale calls me during the program it gives me a lift. He has a way of making me laugh.

There are people who listen to my program just to hear Dale tell a story or sing one of his songs. And when his birthday or Christmas comes around, we are swamped by callers wanting to send him presents.

He may not be able to do some of the things that other people do, but anyone who thinks that Dale is handicapped, disabled or disadvantaged is just not paying attention. Dale has been given a wonderful gift that he just loves sharing with everyone – the ability to make us smile and laugh, and to feel good about things.

Good on you, Dale.

THERE WERE NOT many women attending Australian universities in 1890. But that didn't worry Matilda Ann Aston. She was not your average young Australian woman and she certainly didn't care much for convention and precedent.

Matilda was born at Carisbrook, a small farming town in country Victoria, in 1873. Her father was the town bootmaker and 'Tilly' was the youngest of eight children. Life was tough and tragedy never far away in the bush in those days. By the time Tilly was born, her parents, Edward and Ann, had already lost two children – Elizabeth, at the age of one, and a son named George, who drowned in a creek. When Tilly was just eight years old, her father died and Ann Aston was left without financial support.

One day, a lay preacher visited Carisbrook and convinced the Aston family that little Tilly should leave home and go to Melbourne for schooling. With the help of the Church, Tilly went to live with a family in the city and excelled during her 11 years at school. She matriculated, and at the age of 16 entered Melbourne University to study for an Arts degree. But Tilly encountered problems with the course and when the strain of trying to keep up became too great she was forced to withdraw halfway through her second year, in 1894. The unfamiliar experience of failure left her disappointed and slightly angry.

While she considered what she would do now that her dreams had been shattered, she earned money tutoring children in piano and singing and discovered that she related well to young students. She also began writing; first some poetry, then novels, including *The Woolinappers* in 1905 and *The Straight-Goer* in 1908.

In 1913, when she was 40 years old, Tilly Aston decided she wanted to be a teacher and she enrolled in a training course. She was so successful that within a year she was appointed head of her old school in Melbourne.

All the while, she did her best to support her family back in Carisbrook. During World War I she waved goodbye to six nephews as they left on troopships for Gallipoli and France. When three were killed, Tilly turned to her poetry to express her grief. She wrote a poem that was to become a classic – *A Woman to the Shrine*. After the war, Tilly continued to write while teaching. She published *Maiden Verses* in 1919 and then *Singable Songs* in 1923.

However, once again, bad luck played a hand in Matilda Aston's life. What should have been a minor fall caused her serious injury and she was forced out of teaching in 1925, just 12 years after she started. But Tilly Aston wasn't about to let injury tie her down. She was receiving a small pension from the education department, so she launched herself into unpaid community work, establishing libraries, founding community associations, and generally encouraging Australians like herself to strive for goals. Twice she was awarded the King's Medal for distinguished citizenship.

She also continued writing and in 1935 won a Commonwealth Grant. Later that year she published *Songs of Light*, then *Gold from Old Diggings* in 1937, *Old Timers* in 1938 and *The Inner Garden* in 1940. In all, Tilly Aston produced nine books of verse and prose, including some of the most vivid descriptions ever penned of country Victoria, where she grew up.

During World War II, when in her seventies, Tilly rounded up a band of women in similar circumstances to herself to knit woollen garments for the soldiers fighting in the trenches of Europe. The Red Cross honoured her voluntary work with a medal. Matilda Ann Aston died in her home town of Carisbrook in 1947 aged 74. But there's always more to the story.

In 1937, Matilda Aston recorded a message for a niece. It was a very personal message that she wanted her sister's child to keep to remember her aunt.

In that message Tilly said: '. . . whatever effect my life attainments may have upon others, there has been a fair amount of personal satisfaction in my victories over circumstance.'

One of the sweetest of victories was Tilly Aston's appointment in 1913 as head of the Melbourne school in which she was educated—the School for the Blind. Against strong opposition, Tilly became the first blind teacher of the blind. The woman who became known as 'Australia's Helen Keller' was born with impaired vision. By the time she was seven, Tilly had lost her eyesight completely. It was by sheer coincidence that a former coalminer named Thomas James came to Carisbrook and heard of Tilly. He had been blinded in a mining accident years earlier and had gone on to learn Braille and to teach the blind. It was Thomas James who convinced the Aston family to send Matilda to Melbourne.

When Tilly matriculated to Melbourne University in 1892, she became the first blind person in Australia to attempt a university degree. The problem that forced her to withdraw in her second year was a lack of text-books in Braille. Despite the help of a tutor who built

VISION AUSTRALIA FOUNDATION

Matilda Aston enthrals a young audience with a story from one of her Braille books.

a crude machine for Tilly to copy books into Braille, she could not keep up with the coursework.

When she left Melbourne University, Tilly gathered together a group of friends to discuss how they could correct the shortage of Braille textbooks for university students. Out of that meeting in 1894, the Victorian Association of Braille Writers was formed, and from that came the Braille Library. Matilda Aston went on to form the Association for the Advancement of the Blind, now known as Vision Australia Foundation.

Tilly was a remarkable woman with vision that extended far beyond eyesight. For instance, those Red Cross volunteers she rounded up during World War II to knit the socks and scarves were all blind. They didn't need eyesight to make a contribution to the war effort.

And through her vivid prose and verse, Tilly Aston proved that she didn't live in darkness just because she couldn't see. She lived in the vision of the beautiful country Victorian surroundings of her childhood – beauty that she saw for just seven years, but which stayed with her forever.

In that 1937 recorded message to her niece, Matilda Aston said:

> As I have drifted or struggled along through life, I have gradually acquired many things. Always I have greatly desired to be happy and to spread the same infection around me. This wish has been amply fulfilled.

There is little doubt those who benefited from Matilda Ann Aston's work in the decades since would agree.

AVIATORS EXTRAORDINAIRE

Until I started working on this book I thought I had lived a pretty interesting life. But compared with some of the stories we've assembled here, my biography might look pretty boring.

We may only be a relatively young country, but we have already established an incredibly colourful history, and it is still being written.

Here is a story about two men who each wrote himself into our history before they met each other, and then went on to even greater achievement together.

SAPPER CHARLES JACKSON from Melbourne appears twice on the list of Australians wounded at Gallipoli in 1915. He was lucky – although he was one of the 19,000 diggers wounded, he was not among the 8700 killed.

The second time he was wounded, he was shipped back to Australia and discharged – not because of his injuries, but because of his age. The army had discovered that when Charles enlisted, he was only 16 and even after six months in Gallipoli and Egypt, he was still only 17. Undeterred, the young man was back in the army and fighting in France soon after he turned 18.

After being wounded for a third time, he was selected for officer school where, as part of his training, Charles flew as an observer in reconnaissance aircraft. He took an instant liking to flying and nominated for pilot training. At the age of 20, already with three years battlefield experience in Gallipoli and France under his belt, and having been wounded three times, Charles qualified as a pilot with the Australian Flying Corps.

Coincidentally, another young Australian soldier named Charles who survived Gallipoli had also been plucked from the trenches in France to undergo officer training in England. He, too, qualified as a pilot, but he was transferred to the British Royal Flying Corps.

In 1917, after just three months in the air, this Charles was awarded the Military Cross for bravery in downing a German aircraft then strafing a German troop column to prevent it moving against Allied positions. Like the other Charles, he was just 20 years old.

Soon after he received the MC, he was attacked by three German fighter planes while returning from a mission. Despite getting 180 bullet holes in his aircraft, and having three of his toes shot off, Charles managed to evade the enemy and land his aircraft safely. He was in hospital for months and returned to flying only as an instructor in England. But, as we know, there's always more to the story.

When 16-year-old Sapper Charles Jackson was

wounded for the second time at Gallipoli, the army discovered that not only was he underage, but that he was using a false name. His full correct name was Charles Thomas Phillipe Ulm – not Jackson.

When Charles Ulm qualified as a pilot towards the end of 1917, he expected to see action quickly, but to his frustration and disappointment, he spent the rest of the war as an instructor.

He returned to Australia in 1919 after the war ended, at about the same time as that other Australian pilot named Charles – Charles Edward Kingsford Smith. The two had a lot in common. Both men were 22 and they were looking for ways to use the flying skills they had acquired in Europe. In 1926, they would meet in Sydney and become close friends and flying partners.

Charles Kingsford Smith and Charles Ulm became household names in Australia and around the world by setting record after record in aviation, including circumnavigating Australia in just 10 days and five hours, in 1927, then the following year crossing the Pacific from the United States of America to Australia in three hops – from San Francisco to Honolulu, Honolulu to Fiji, and Fiji to Sydney. On the leg from Honolulu to Suva, they were in the air for 33 hours.

Ulm and Kingsford Smith did everything together. They formed Australian National Airways in 1928, and in December 1930, when Smith married his second wife, Mary Powell, it was Charles Ulm who stood as his best man. But their friendship fell apart in 1932,

Charles Kingsford Smith (left) with Charles Ulm soon after their record-breaking 1928 Trans-Pacific flight.

when ANA went into liquidation at the same time that Charles Kingsford Smith published an autobiography in which Ulm felt he was not given fair credit for his contribution to Smith's achievements. To add insult to injury, Charles Kingsford Smith was also knighted that year. Charles Ulm and Charles Kingsford Smith went their separate ways, and both went on to set trans-Tasman and trans-Pacific aviation records in their own right.

On 5 December 1934, Charles Ulm disappeared while attempting to break the trans-Pacific record. He had used every cent he owned, as well as cashing in his life insurance policy, to buy a brand-new aircraft and recruit a crew for the record attempt. As they approached Honolulu in the middle of the night and in bad weather, Ulm and his crew lost their bearings and ran out of fuel. They radioed that they had crash-landed in the ocean but were floating. No trace was ever found of them or the aircraft, despite one of the most extensive air–sea searches undertaken in the Pacific to that time. Charles Ulm was just 37 years old.

When he heard that his former friend was missing, presumed dead, Sir Charles Kingsford Smith was said to be inconsolable. But, 12 months later he, too, would vanish while attempting to break a record. His aircraft crashed on 8 November somewhere between Allahabad and Singapore, while flying from England to Australia. Sir Charles Kingsford Smith was 38 years old.

'BARTY'

When I take a break from my radio program, I often take an overseas trip or a cruise. 'How can you claim to be in touch with the things that matter to Australians when you spend half your time in Europe or America?' comes the inevitable criticism.

Obviously these small-minded people don't listen to my program, because if they did they would know that the John Laws Morning Show *is not about what I think; it is about what you, the listeners, have on your minds. I just provide the opportunity for you to be heard.*

My contribution is mostly listening, occasionally giving my opinion, playing a little of my favourite music and, whenever I get the chance, indulging in what I love most – good old-fashioned storytelling and bush poetry.

That's why I couldn't resist including the tale of 'Barty' here – he was one hell of a storyteller! Barty's story also proves how your perspective can improve when you spend time outside looking in.

ANDREW PATERSON LIVED with his widowed grandmother at Gladesville in Sydney from the age of ten, when he started his senior education at Sydney Grammar School in 1874.

Sydney must have seemed a long way from where he was born, near Orange; from Buckinbah station, where he spent his first seven years; and Illalong station, near Yass, where his family had then settled. And Sydney Grammar was very different from the little public school at Binalong where he learned his early lessons. But Andrew was the eldest child in the family and Andrew Bogle and his wife, Rose, were determined that their first-born, 'Barty', was going to get a good start in life. They wanted him to be a lawyer.

Andrew craved excitement and adventure; he made quite a name for himself in rowing, polo, cricket and tennis while also scoring high marks in the classroom. However, it was at weekends that he got to indulge his love of horses, when he rode as an amateur jockey at the Randwick and Rosehill gallops, winning the majority of his races. Andrew loved horse riding. Every chance he got, he made his way from Sydney to Yass and worked with his father on the property, riding all day and listening at night to the drovers and the teamsters telling their stories about life in the outback.

Andrew finished school at 16 and was articled to a Sydney firm of solicitors, Spain and Salway, while he completed his studies at Sydney University. He was admitted to the Bar as a solicitor on 28 August 1886, and formed a partnership called Street and Paterson.

While still a law student, he wrote a number of

poems that were published in *The Bulletin* and the *Sydney Mail* newspaper. The writing helped him overcome the frustration of being separated from the bush. The first piece published, in 1885, was a poem to the Australian troops in the Sudan.

Before long he was in demand with editors and publishers, who could not wait to publish his writings for an appreciative Sydney audience.

But, in 1899, at the height of his fame, Andrew left Australia, once again in search of adventure. He convinced his friends, the Fairfax family who owned the *Sydney Morning Herald*, to send him as a special correspondent to report on the Boer War in South Africa. Sir James Fairfax gave him money and two horses for the assignment. From Africa, Andrew went to China in 1901 to report on the Boxer Rebellion, but arrived after the uprising had ended.

By 1902 it was obvious to Andrew and to everyone he knew that he was not going to continue in law. He decided that journalism was far more exciting and challenging, and so he began a tour of Australia, writing stories and poetry about what he saw. While visiting Tenterfield station in northern New South Wales, he met Alice Emily Walker. He married her the following year at the station.

Alice and Andrew lived at Woollahra for six years while Andrew was editor of the *Sydney Evening News*, but in 1908 they settled with their two children on a property called Coodra, near Yass, on the Upper Murrumbidgee. Unfortunately, Andrew struck financial

A portrait of Andrew Paterson from about 1890.

difficulties and had to sell the property and take up wheat farming at Grenfell.

In 1914, when war broke out in Europe, Andrew could not resist the call to adventure. He left for London, expecting to be snapped up as an experienced war correspondent. But no-one wanted his services. Rather than return to his family in Australia, he enlisted as an ambulance driver and was sent to the front lines of France. He eventually finished the war as a major in the Australian Mounted Infantry in Egypt.

In the final two years of the war, Alice left 13-year-old Grace and 11-year-old Hugh with her parents and joined Andrew in the Middle East, where she worked as a volunteer in a military hospital in Ismailia.

After the war Andrew and Alice returned to Australia, where Andrew became editor of the *Sydney Sportsman* and a regular writer for *Smith's Weekly* and various radio programs. But there's always more to the story.

Andrew Paterson retired as a journalist in 1930, then spent most of his time with his children and grandchildren in Sydney. But he continued writing until his death on 6 February 1941, just ten days short of his 77th birthday.

For Andrew, the highlights of his life were almost certainly his adventures abroad in foreign wars. He met many interesting characters, including his lifelong friend, Rudyard Kipling, who was also reporting on the Boer War.

But for Australians, Andrew's most important and memorable achievement was the writing he did before the Boer War. This was when he penned 'Clancy of the Overflow', 'The Man from Snowy River', and 'Waltzing Matilda'. In those days the young solicitor, war correspondent, battlefield ambulance driver and author, wrote not under his real name of Andrew Barton Paterson, but under pseudonyms – sometimes 'B' but most often 'The Banjo'. 'Banjo' Paterson took his name from his childhood best friend, a racehorse called Banjo on his parents' property at Illalong.

Banjo Paterson is remembered not only for his poetry and other writing but for his passionate campaigns for social justice in Australia, especially for the working class. In everything he wrote, he seemed to find a way to prick the conscience and the spirit of a nation.

BEYOND REASONABLE DOUBT?

Remember that song 'The Tears of a Clown'? Well, some of the saddest people I have met during my career have been famous comedians. It is remarkable how many are insecure and haunted by feelings of inferiority.

Most struggle with the constant pressure to be funny, while some have dark secrets or memories that have been suppressed by their clowning and humour.

A number end up with drug or alcohol dependence, or both, in trying to cope with the contradictions of their inner and outer personalities. Robin Williams and Billy Connolly are two who have confronted their demons, dealt with them, and discovered that they were even funnier without the cocaine or whisky.

Sometimes you just don't know what is going on in people's minds.

AMONG AUSTRALIA'S MOST controversial criminal trials during the 20th century was that of our last bushrangers, brothers Patrick and James Kenniff, in Queensland in 1902. They were both convicted of double murder and sentenced to death by hanging. James's sentence was later commuted to life imprisonment, but Patrick was hanged in Brisbane's Boggo Road Gaol on 12 January 1903.

James (Jimmy) and Patrick (Paddy) Kenniff were raised in New South Wales and had been jailed a number of times for horse and cattle stealing. In the early 1890s, they moved into Queensland with a plan to start fresh as honest stockmen. But it wasn't long before they were in trouble again for stealing horses. In 1895, Paddy was sentenced to four years and Jimmy three years imprisonment on St Helena Island in the middle of Moreton Bay. They were released two years later for good behaviour.

The brothers returned to the Maranoa district, this time with their father, to run a grazing property called Ralph. But when more than a thousand head of cattle went missing from the neighbouring property, Carnarvon, the manager, Albert Dahlke, accused them of duffing. Although nothing could be proven, the owners of Carnarvon bought the Kenniffs out of their lease and ordered them from the area.

In December 1897, the Kenniff boys stole 40 horses from Carnarvon then took them to Toowoomba by train and sold them off. However, during their celebratory drinking spree, Paddy Kenniff cashed a cheque in a pub; the cheque was one the boys had taken when they held up a small store to create a diversion at Yuelba, where they were loading the horses onto the train. The police soon had a description and knew they were chasing the Kenniffs for the horse stealing and the hold-up at the shop.

For the next two years, Paddy and Jimmy Kenniff stole horses and cattle from Carnarvon and other properties to the west. They were eventually arrested in 1899, but when Jimmy faced a court in Charleville and Paddy a court in Roma, juries in both towns acquitted them of the duffing charges. However, Paddy was sentenced to three years for the hold-up at the store. He was released in November 1901.

No sooner had he returned to join his brother than police issued a warrant for the pair's arrest for horse stealing. A police posse led by Constable George Doyle of the Upper Warrego Police Station set out to arrest them. He took with him the manager of Carnarvon station, Albert Dahlke, who hated the Kenniffs, and an Aboriginal tracker, Sam Johnson.

On Easter Sunday morning 1902, the party went to Lethbridge's Pocket in the Carnarvon Ranges, where the Kenniffs were known to camp. Sam Johnson spotted the two Kenniff boys and a chase ensued. Constable Doyle and Albert Dahlke caught Jimmy Kenniff and tied him up, but Paddy escaped. Sam Johnson was sent by Constable Doyle to recover the packhorse that the searchers had abandoned when the chase started. When he returned, Doyle, Dahlke and Jimmy Kenniff were gone. Sam Johnson fled when Paddy and Jimmy rode towards him on their horses shouting and waving guns.

A police search party returned to the scene and found bullet marks in trees near the site. They also found the remains of three fires, some clotted blood, bone fragments and stained rocks. When Constable

Doyle's horse was found, the pack bags contained charcoal, later identified as burnt human remains.

The Government offered a large reward for the capture of Jimmy and Paddy Kenniff for the murder of Constable Doyle and Albert Dahlke. For three months, more than 50 police hunted the bushrangers. They were eventually arrested without a fight on the banks of the Maranoa River, south of Mitchell. Paddy and Jimmy were taken under police guard to Rockhampton and committed for trial in Brisbane's Supreme Court on two counts each of wilful murder. Largely on the sketchy evidence of Aboriginal tracker Sam Johnson, the pair were convicted of the murders and sentenced to death by the Chief Justice, Sir Samuel Griffith.

The Queensland Government later decided to commute Jimmy Kenniff's sentence to life after the Full Bench of the Court considered the evidence, and one judge held that it was not beyond reasonable doubt that Jimmy participated in murder given that he was restrained when last seen with the victims. He served 16 years in prison and returned to Queensland after his release. He died in 1940.

Patrick was hanged before any appeal against his sentence could be lodged. But there's more to this story.

Patrick Kenniff's controversial hanging weighed heavily on the minds of those who conducted his execution – especially the Brisbane Under-Sheriff, Arthur Davis, who ultimately gave the order to the

Brisbane Under-Sheriff Arthur Hoey Davis with his horse outside the Supreme Court in 1903.

hangman. There was already public disquiet about the conduct of the court case and the haste with which the sentence was carried out. Shortly after Patrick Kenniff died, a number of legal experts declared that the trial had been a miscarriage of justice and that Patrick Kenniff should not have been convicted of murder and executed.

That was the final straw for Under-Sheriff Davis – he decided to resign to concentrate on another career far away from the law and the courts, as a writer. Using the name Steele Rudd, Davis had already successfully published a series of humorous sketches called *On Our*

Selection. Its central characters, Dad and Dave, were to become famous in movies, cartoons and radio shows.

Students of Steele Rudd would know what strain Davis felt from the Kenniff hanging. His story *The Miserable Clerk* makes a none-too-subtle reference to the irreverence often shown at a hanging in Boggo Road Gaol. Arthur Davis refused to discuss the Kenniff hanging again for years. He died in 1935.

THE BIG SHOW

Australian entertainment is going through a high point at the moment with some exciting young performers forging international reputations, and big-name artists lining up to tour here. But it's not the first time we've seen this happen; the 50s and 60s were just as exciting and maybe even more so.

My family get tired of me saying, 'I saw him perform at the old Sydney Stadium in 1959,' or 'I interviewed her in 1958 after she made that movie with Clark Gable.' But it's true – I saw or met many of the big names of music and movies at that time.

There weren't too many American or British stars who didn't visit Australia in those days, even though it took a couple of weeks out of their schedule for them to get here.

And almost all the big stars who visited came back again.

THERE WASN'T AN empty seat in the West Melbourne Stadium on the evening of 4 February 1958. Promoter Lee Gordon was claiming it was his best ever line-up for a *Big Show* and rock-and-roll-mad teenagers lapped it up.

For two years in a row, Gordon had treated

Australian fans to big-name American stars with his 'Lee Gordon World Hit Parade' – in 1957 it was Bill Haley and his Comets, and Little Richard. This time is was Jodie Sands, Paul Anka and Jerry Lee Lewis. And best of all for Australian music, the crowds also got to see home-grown talent like Johnny O'Keefe, Lonnie Lee and Col Joye showcased on the same bill.

The *Big Show* was on a breakneck schedule to fit in with the stars' American commitments. There were ten shows staged in six days, starting at Sydney Stadium on 30 January, then Newcastle the following night, back to Sydney on 1 February, then up to Brisbane's Cloudland Ballroom on the 3rd, West Melbourne Stadium on the 4th, and finally back to Brisbane for another two nights at Cloudland on the 6th and 8th.

Local star Johnny O'Keefe opened the *Big Show* that year with his current hit 'Wild One' and, as usual, JO'K had them dancing in the aisles before the headline stars had even appeared. Following O'Keefe onto the stage was one of the most popular American stars of the 50s, Jodie Sands, who had recorded a string of hits including 'Love Me Again', 'The Way I Love You', 'With All My Heart' and 'Some Day'.

Paul Anka was at the top of the Australian charts at the time of the *Big Show* tour in 1958 with 'Diana' and he had just released 'You Are My Destiny' in the USA, where it was already rocketing up the charts.

The performer everybody had come to see was rocker Jerry Lee Lewis, who was second on the US charts and top of the UK charts with 'Great Balls of

Fire'. Jerry Lee had everyone up on the seats and, according to the *Melbourne Herald* newspaper, 'the stadium shook'.

However, when the show was over, there was no question that all of these seasoned performers had been upstaged by an up-and-coming 22-year-old singer from Texas who stood almost motionless on stage, but mesmerised everyone with his electric guitar technique and singing. His name was Buddy Holly, and in January and February 1958 he gave Australian fans a taste of some of his current hit songs, including 'Maybe Baby', 'Peggy Sue', 'Oh Boy,' 'Everyday' and 'I'm Gonna Love You Too'.

Holly and his band, the Crickets, had come fresh from appearances on the *Ed Sullivan* television show and a barnstorming tour of the United States. It was the first time Buddy, Jerry Allison and Joe B Maudlin had left continental USA. Buddy Holly was going to be a rock-and-roll music legend; it was just a matter of how big.

When he returned from the tour of Australia, Buddy Holly went into the recording studios to do his only solo album, called simply *Buddy Holly*. He had put the finishing touches on some of the songs for the album during the Australian tour, including a new number called 'Rave On'.

One of the Crickets, Jerry Allison, also went straight into the studios when he got home from Australia to record his first solo record. The 'A' side was a Top 100 hit called 'Real Wild Child' – it was a cover version of the song that John O'Keefe had opened the Australian tour shows with, except he called it 'Wild One'. The song JO'K and his band wrote became a US chart hit at Number 85.

But there's always more to the story. The *Big Show* of 1958 was just one of many rock-and-roll tours of Australia in the 50s by famous names such as Little Richard, Frank Sinatra and Bobby Darrin. A year to the day after Jerry Lee Lewis and Buddy Holly rocked Melbourne, Chuck Berry was top of the bill as Lee Gordon's *Big Show* gave Sydney another dose of the same rock-and-roll medicine. As the crowd spilled out of Sydney Stadium that night they picked up the early edition of the Sydney *Telegraph* dated 5 February 1959. One after another they stopped in disbelief. The excitement of the concert turned to tears as they read the front-page story in the *Telegraph*. Three of rock-and-roll's biggest stars had been killed in an air crash. The names jumped off the paper—The Big Bopper, Ritchie Valens and, most painfully, the young Texan who they'd cheered 12 months earlier, Buddy Holly.

One awful thing about Buddy Holly's death was that he was offered the chance to return to Australia in 1959 for another *Big Show* tour and for a while he considered the invitation seriously. However, he decided he was too busy building his American fan base to include the 1959 Australian tour in his schedule. If he had accepted, he would have been on-stage in Sydney instead of taking off in a light aircraft during a snowstorm at Clear Lake, Iowa, that day the music died.

By eerie coincidence, a year before he died in a plane crash, his tour to Australia was almost cancelled when his aircraft had to abort its take-off from Honolulu at the last minute because of engine failure.

BLACK MAGIC

Discrimination didn't start with this generation or the last one. Women, black people, the poor and uneducated, and followers of particular religions have been the victims of bias and prejudice for centuries.

However, the inspirational stories we present in this book demonstrate that for all of our history, there have been people who let nothing stand in the way of their dreams.

Some will say that they were exceptions to the rule. I agree, they were exceptional – exceptional Australians who proved by their actions that character, dignity, courage and loyalty do not belong to one gender, one colour, one religion or one social class.

IT WAS ALWAYS a treat for the Waters children when their mother Grace read them stories about famous flyers like Sir Charles Kingsford Smith and Bert Hinkler. Afterwards, the fourth child, Leonard, would often carve a crude propellor from a piece of wood, attach it to the end of a stick and run round and round the backyard at Euraba in northern New South Wales, dreaming that he was a pilot flying among the clouds.

In 1924 every little boy wanted to be a pilot like Smithy or Hinkler.

But the Depression brought Leonard's dream of flying to a sudden end; at 14, he had to leave school to help his father work the Nindigully station, near St George in Queensland. He turned out to be a pretty good shearer, even as a teenager.

Then came war. As every fit young man in Australia enlisted, Len Waters waited his time, anxiously watching the calendar for his 18th birthday to come round in 1942. By now Australia was under threat from a Japanese invasion from the north.

Within weeks of turning 18, Len Waters made his way to the nearest enlistment centre and joined the Royal Australian Air Force as a flight mechanic. He was a whiz with engines and even though he lacked formal training, he was prepared to take any job so long as it meant that his dream of being a pilot stayed alive. The RAAF was desperate for volunteers after suffering heavy casualties in Europe.

Len studied hard at nights and weekends with flight manuals and morse code books, and within a year was one of 375 applicants competing for scarce aircrew places at the No. 1 Elementary Flying Training School at Narrandera, in New South Wales. After the aptitude and selection tests were completed, he was disappointed to be offered a wireless operator/gunner position in bombers – the job with the highest fatality rate in the airforce. Determined that he was going to be a pilot, Len Waters took a gamble and declined the offer.

The gamble paid off when the selection board decided he was such a good candidate that it would offer him one of the 48 sought-after places in pilot training.

After pilot training at Narrandera, Len went on to Uranquinty, also in New South Wales, before graduating as a Sergeant Pilot. He then had a short period of preparation with an operational training unit in Mildura, Victoria, before being posted in November 1944 to No. 78 Squadron flying American-built Kittyhawk P-40M fighters against the Japanese in New Guinea and Indonesia.

In quick time he was promoted to Flight Sergeant and then Warrant Officer, flying 95 operational sorties in ground attack and reconnaissance missions over New Guinea and the Dutch East Indies. He received several commendations for bravery and on one mission flew three hours back to his base with a Japanese anti-aircraft shell lodged in the fuselage behind his seat. He said later that it was one of the best landings he ever made.

Len Waters was discharged at the end of the war and returned home in January 1946, with plans to start his own airline in western Queensland. Four weeks after returning he married his girlfriend, Gladys Saunders, and set about raising financial backing for his business. But he couldn't raise the money and had no choice but to go back to shearing. He never flew again.

Len Waters died in an accident at Cunnamulla in 1993, aged 69. By coincidence, it was 24 August – the same date that he had enlisted in the RAAF to become a pilot. But there's always more to the story.

AWM PO1659.001

Warrant Officer Len Waters in the cockpit of his Kittyhawk fighter.

Warrant Officer Waters was described by colleagues as more than a handy pilot. He was well known by Australian ground troops in the area because of fearless low flying in his distinctive aircraft, which was named *Black Magic*.

Little did they know how appropriate that name *Black Magic* was for its pilot – Len Waters was the only Aboriginal fighter pilot in the RAAF.

Leonard Victor was one of 11 Waters children born on Euraba Mission, located between Boomi and Garrah. His parents had no money for education, but

Len's father, Donald, was able to teach his son almost everything about the family's old Ford. It was that mechanical skill that got Len Waters into the RAAF. Once in the door, a lack of education didn't stop Flight Sergeant Waters, especially when he was in the cockpit of his fighter. By the end of the war he was commanding flights that included commissioned officers with professional backgrounds and private school educations.

By the way, the name of Len Waters' Kittyhawk in Borneo was not his choice – it was sheer coincidence that he was assigned to an aircraft that had been flown previously by a pilot named John Blackmore. As Len Waters said later: 'Was that fate or what? What an omen.'

BOXER REBELLION

Why do we keep up this charade of calling our armed forces the 'Australian Defence Force'? It is the same politically correct tripe that changed our police 'forces' to 'services'.

I'm sure the criminals are dead scared of having 'service' used against them. In the same way, playing with words doesn't stop terrorists, dictatorships or invaders. What stops them is equal or greater force, and usually armed force.

Since our earliest days we have been sending troops from Australia to help with emergencies and wars all over the world. Most of the conflicts we joined involved a threat to a stable and democratic world, but with the exception of Pacific battles to stop the Japanese pushing south in 1942, it would be hard to argue any were in defence of Australia.

Let's stop the rubbish and be proud that we have strong police forces and armed forces.

THE FIRST DAY of 1901 dawned bright and warm for three-and-a-half million citizens of the newly federated Australian states. It was a Tuesday, but many went to church that day to pray for their new nation and their promising future.

Half a world away, in the depths of a bitter Chinese winter, another group of Australians also huddled in prayer . . . prayer that they would soon be going home to share in the celebrations. These were the 462 sailors from New South Wales and Victoria who were part of an 8000-strong multinational force sent into China to put down the Boxer Rebellion. They could not have imagined, when they voted for Federation 18 months earlier, that they would spend this day in someone else's country, on the other side of the world, putting down a revolution.

The uprising in China was an unwelcome international incident. Amid ever-increasing exploitation of China by foreigners, resentment had festered, leading to attacks on foreign-owned property and the killing of foreigners and their supporters. Secret Chinese societies had formed to plot the expulsion of the Westerners. Foremost among these was a society whose name translated to 'Righteous and Harmonious Fists'. The foreign media dubbed this group 'The Boxers'.

When Russia, Germany, Austria, India and England committed troops to put down the uprising and protect their interests in China, the British realised they were stretched beyond their capacity because of commitments in South Africa, where they were already fighting the Boers. The Australian colonies were asked to help in China, even though they also had committed heavily to the Boer conflict.

With most of the regular forces in South Africa, it fell to volunteer reservists of the colonial navies to make up the China contingent. There were 200 men from the Victorian Navy, 262 from the New South Wales Navy, and 96 officers and men crewing the South Australian Navy's gunboat, *Protector*. The first Australian detachment left Sydney on 8 August 1900.

The Victorians and New South Welshmen arrived at the mouth of the Pei-Ho River on 9 September 1900, then marched across land to Tientsin, where they left the Victorians to protect foreign nationals, including a future president of the United States of America, Herbert Hoover, and his wife. The Victorians joined multinational forces searching for, and destroying, rebel headquarters in the province.

Meanwhile, the New South Wales detachment linked up with British troops and together they stormed Peking (Beijing) on 20 October to relieve the foreign embassies that had been under siege. This action was the basis for the Hollywood movie *55 Days at Peking*. The New South Wales contingent was then stationed in Peking to protect foreign nationals from the Chinese rebels and to carry out raids on Boxer strongholds near the city.

As they huddled in the bitter Chinese snow, both detachments probably wished they were aboard the gunboat *Protector*. She was already steaming home to sunny Adelaide with her crew of 96 after finishing a tour of duty as a picket and mail ship for the British naval forces blockading rivers and estuaries. By the time they were ordered home, the Victorian and New South Wales naval reservists had lost six men to sickness,

AWM PO0417.003

Some of the New South Wales naval contingent and their commandeered transport in Peking in 1901.

suicide or injury, but none as a direct result of enemy action. But there's more to the story of Australia's involvement in the Boxer Rebellion. There's always more.

Even though they missed the Federation celebrations at home, the China contingent had survived a Chinese winter, and a bloody rebellion. Now it was time to go home to their full-time jobs.

By coincidence, the China contingent arrived in Sydney on 25 April – a date that would become even more significant in Australian military history 14 years later with the landings at Anzac Cove. However, the reservists who returned from China did not receive the welcome home they expected. A smallpox scare put them all into quarantine as soon as their ship arrived in Sydney Harbour. Most sailors were not allowed home to their families for another two weeks.

The contingents from New South Wales, Victoria and South Australia played a minor, but colourful, role in putting down the Boxer Rebellion. They carried out patrols, provided protection to foreigners and to embassies, performed the roles of policemen and firemen in Beijing, and provided firing squads in Tientsin for the execution of Chinese found guilty of supporting the Boxer rebels.

BUSHRANGER SAM

If you want to see how differently we all interpret our history, ask people around you what they think of when you say the word 'bushranger'.

Some will simply say Ned Kelly. Others will talk about gangs of criminals that terrorised stagecoaches and post offices, and hid in caves and secret valleys. Some will describe convicts or settlers taking to crime out of frustration with their poverty and the injustices of the colonial system. And someone else will tell a romantic story of heroes of the bush standing up to the cruel troopers and robbing to share the wealth with the poor – a sort of Mudgee version of Robin Hood.

The truth is that they would all be right, because our bushrangers were a mixed bag. History has a habit of applying universal terms and tags. That's why we need to remember that there is always more to the story.

EVERYONE IN THE mining camp at Tambaroora Creek near Hill End in New South Wales avoided 'Cranky Sam'. He was usually in bad humour and often threatened people. When he disappeared from his hut on the outskirts of town in January 1865, no-one was sorry. They assumed he had moved on. But on the morning of 3 February, Sam was to reappear in their lives.

Senior Constable John Ward was returning to his station at Coonabarabran after escorting a prisoner to Mudgee when he was stopped near Barney's Reef and told that a bushranger was robbing people on the road nearby. He was armed and had threatened violence. Witnesses gave Constable Ward a description.

At that time, police were on alert for Ben Hall, who was said to be in the area. But the description of this bushranger was unlike anyone in the Hall gang. Senior Constable Ward was absolutely certain the suspect was 'Cranky Sam'. He rode to the area where the witnesses said the most recent robberies had occurred and began a search of the bush. After some hours, he saw a camp and rode up. He was met by Sam, armed with a shotgun.

Senior Constable Ward drew his revolver and told Sam to put down the shotgun, but instead of surrendering, Sam pulled the trigger, wounding the trooper in the side. He escaped as the policeman fell to the ground in pain. Ward struggled to his horse and rode to Coonabarabran, but died the next day.

The district police inspector ordered a full-scale search for Sam, now a murderer. Mounted police from towns throughout the area joined the hunt. They combed the bushland and hills for more than two weeks before three constables and an Aboriginal tracker found Sam. He shot at them and ran into heavily timbered hill country. The next day they picked up his tracks and finally cornered him. In the shoot-out that followed, 'Cranky Sam' was wounded but kept firing until he ran out of ammunition. When the bullets were gone, he used the butt of his rifle to knock out a trooper trying to grapple with him.

Sam was tried for the murder of Senior Constable Ward and for the attempted murder of the three constables who eventually arrested him. He was convicted and hanged at Bathurst Gaol on 19 December 1865, although he was never charged with any bushranging offences. But, as usual, there's more to the story.

'Cranky Sam' was only a bushranger for a few days and he didn't steal much of value; probably because his patch along Slap Dash Creek Road wasn't exactly a main thoroughfare for the thousands of prospectors working the goldfields of Bathurst and Mudgee. All in all, he was a pretty amateurish highwayman. Had Sam not murdered a policeman and put up such a fight to avoid arrest, he may not have even rated a mention in bushranging history, except for one other thing – Sam was our first and only Chinese bushranger!

'Cranky Sam' Poo was an outcast at Tambaroora Creek. Even the other Chinese in the area would have nothing to do with him. He lived alone in a remote hut. When he took to bushranging, it was only a matter of time before he was caught, especially when surprised witnesses described their robber as a very angry Chinese man. That is why Senior Constable Ward knew exactly who he was looking for and where to find him.

Another bushranger who was easy for police to identify was our only woman bushranger, Mary Ann Bugg. Mary was the partner of Frederick Ward – also known as Captain Thunderbolt.

The daughter of a former convict, she was part Aboriginal and was educated at boarding school in Sydney. She was a very intelligent young woman and highly literate, yet she was given away in marriage at the age of 14 to a shepherd named Edmund Baker.

Mary became involved with Frederick Ward when they met on a property near Mudgee, where Edmund Baker was working. Soon after they met, Ward was imprisoned for four years for horse stealing. By the time he returned in 1860, Mary's husband had died, so they took up with each other and moved to Dungog, where they married. As Frederick Ward spent year after year in prison for horse stealing, Mary raised her two children in bush huts, stealing and begging for money in the streets; at one stage she was imprisoned for receiving stolen goods.

In 1863, Mary went to Sydney and helped Ward escape from the jail on Cockatoo Island in Sydney Harbour. They then took to the bush in the Hunter Valley, holding up coaches and gold shipments from southern Queensland to the Liverpool Plains near Sydney. Mary often disguised herself as a man and went into towns to gather information on coach schedules.

In 1870, Captain Thunderbolt was tracked down by police at Kentucky Creek, south of Uralla in the north of New South Wales, and shot dead.

There are several theories about what happened to Mary, who had three children by now, but it seems she married again and had up to ten more children while living in the Gloucester area of New South Wales. The most credible account is that she died in 1905 at the age of 70.

DAGWORTH

My 'Little Brother', John Williamson, writes the most wonderful songs about Australia and Australians. He is, without doubt, the finest balladeer in this country.

John's songs not only tell a story but also teach us about our language and culture. I suppose that's why the Australian Rugby Union ask him to lead the singing of 'Waltzing Matilda' at the big matches – John Williamson doesn't just sing words, he touches your soul with the spirit of the story that he understands completely.

If you have the chance, sit down and read some of John's lyrics without the music. The poetry is beautiful, but the emotional experience is quite amazing.

THE QUEENSLAND SHEARERS' strike was at its height in September 1894 when violence broke out between the strikers and armed soldiers and police protecting non-union shearers. After three months of fruitless protests against savage pay cuts and poor working conditions, some shearers went looking for revenge against property owners who had engaged non-union labour. They began burning down sheds where the non-unionists worked.

In August 1894 the paddle-steamer *Rodney* was boarded by union shearers who had heard she was carrying non-unionists down the Darling River to work on Tolarno station. There was a fight between the unionists and the crew before the vessel was burned to the waterline.

On 4 September, the three Macpherson brothers, who had just set up Dagworth station near Winton, got word that they were the next target of the union activists. The three brothers armed themselves and sent for the police.

Shortly after midnight, in heavy rain, the first shots were fired into the shearing shed from the darkness. The Macphersons and a local constable were ready and returned fire. The shooting continued until the shed was set alight and the brothers dropped their guns to try to save hundreds of young sheep trapped in the yards around the shed. The shed burned to the ground and 140 sheep were killed in the fire.

Those responsible for setting the shed alight disappeared into the night. But at dawn, the eldest of the Macpherson brothers, Bob, and the police constable found rifle and revolver cartridges in a gully behind the shed and gathered them for evidence, then rode 30 kilometres to Kynuna to get help from two other policeman stationed there.

Together, the four rode to a place called Four Mile Billabong near Kynuna, upstream from the Diamantina

River, where the unionists had set up their camp. They expected to find the arsonist there. However, when they arrived they were told that one of the most militant of the union organisers, Samuel 'Frenchy' Hoffmeister, was dead.

The police were told that he committed suicide when he realised he would be hunted down for the Dagworth attack. Rather than surrender, he had taken his own life. Others at the billabong suggested he may have been murdered by shearers angry at what he had done to damage their cause. Still others said he had been wounded in the shoot-out with police at the shed.

One thing was certain, the Dagworth incident was the turning point in the shearers' strike as they lost what public support they had previously enjoyed. All striking shearers went back to work in Queensland six days later.

But there's more to the story of Dagworth. Within a year of the Dagworth shoot-out, the family and their property would again feature prominently in Australia's unfolding history.

The Macpherson brothers had moved to Queensland from Victoria to take advantage of a land offer. They staked out a 100,000-hectare property for their sheep station and then sent for their father and two sisters.

On her way to Dagworth to join her brothers, Christina Macpherson stopped at Winton to prepare for the two-day carriage ride out to the station. While there, she met an old school friend named Sarah Riley, who was visiting Winton with her fiancé, a young Sydney solicitor.

Bob Macpherson invited the couple to stay at Dagworth for a few weeks. Bob showed the solicitor, named Andrew, around the property, including the Combo Waterhole. At the waterhole they found the skin of a sheep and Bob explained how swagmen often killed his sheep and took only enough meat to last them a few days.

After dinner one night, the Macphersons and their city guests gathered in the drawing room of the homestead to hear Bob, Jack and Gideon tell the yarns that had made them famous in the district. Among them was the story of the shoot-out with Frenchy Hoffmeister and his subsequent suicide at the Four Mile Billabong.

Andrew, the Sydney solicitor, borrowed a school exercise book from one of the Macpherson children and began making notes. Then Christina Macpherson entertained everyone with a tune on the zither (a small harp). She played a song she had heard at the Warrnambool races shortly before she left Victoria. It was an old English marching tune called 'The Craigilee March'.

That is how Sydney solicitor Andrew 'Banjo' Paterson came to write an anthem for a nation. He combined a story about sheep being stolen on Dagworth station, the suicide of a union organiser near a billabong, and some common terms used in the bush about swagmen carrying (or waltzing) their bedrolls (matildas).

With the help of Bob Macpherson, AB Paterson

turned a story into a poem. Then with the help of Bob's sister, Christina, he turned the poem into a song. It was Christina who wrote the first score of 'Waltzing Matilda' on Dagworth station in 1895.

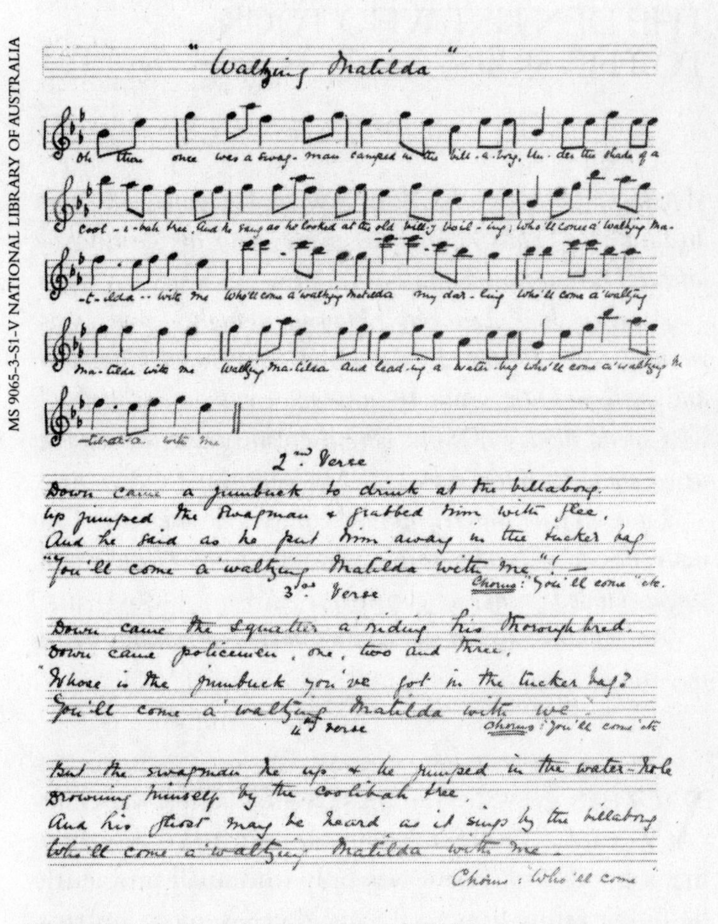

The original musical manuscript of 'Waltzing Matilda' penned for Banjo Paterson by Christina Macpherson at Dagworth Station in 1895.

THE DENTIST WHO TOOK TO THE SKIES

Where is Dick Smith? Why has he not done any more breathtaking flights around the world or to the South Pole lately? Dick, we need you!

America had Lindberg, Howard Hughes and, more recently, Steve Fossett; England had Sir Donald Campbell; and we have Dick Smith. We need more of the rich daredevils who spend money to make boyish dreams come true and let us go along for a free ride.

I much prefer the 'self-funded enjoyees' to the clowns our navy has to go and rescue every time a round-the-world, single-handed yacht race goes awry.

Australians have always had a soft spot for adventurers, as this story proves.

WHEN NEWCASTLE DENTIST William Ewart Hart paid £1300 for an aeroplane in 1911, it seemed like a good deal. There was only one small problem – he didn't know how to fly and there were no instructors in the country.

Hart fell in love with the Bristol Boxkite biplane

the moment he saw it being flown by New Zealander JJ Hammond and Briton Leslie MacDonald. They were the first aerial barnstormers seen in Australia and they had come here at considerable expense to try to sell Bristol aircraft to the Australian military. When the Australian Army showed no interest in aeroplanes, the Bristol company decided to sell the Boxkite to the highest bidder rather than ship it all the way back to England by sea.

William Hart quickly stepped forward and offered £1300, provided the sale included flying lessons from Leslie MacDonald. These were the early days of aviation and Bristol did not want their design to be copied, so they agreed to the deal on condition that Hart undertake not to build aeroplanes in Australia. The irony of this was that the Boxkite was based on the design of Australian inventor Lawrence Hargraves!

William Hart had no intention of building aeroplanes, but as a matter of principle he refused to sign the agreement. After a stand-off, Bristol sold Hart the aircraft without the condition and without the lessons. Orders were sent to MacDonald and Hammond that they were not, under any circumstances, to teach Hart to fly the aircraft.

Of course, they obeyed. But Bristol head office said nothing about teaching Mr Hart to *taxi* the aircraft. So William Hart spent several days taxiing his aeroplane around paddocks near Penrith under the watchful eye of Leslie MacDonald.

At first he wondered if he had made a horrible mistake buying an aeroplane he couldn't fly. But within a week, he was grateful he had not signed the Bristol undertaking. During a sudden windstorm, the Boxkite was overturned and wrecked. William Hart salvaged what he could from the wreck and, with the help of some friends, built another aeroplane of similar design. He then continued his on-the-ground training, to the amusement of all who knew him.

One day he told a friend that he would probably attempt a take-off the next morning. When he arrived at the field where his plane was hangared in a tent, more than 500 people were waiting anxiously. Not wanting to disappoint the crowd, William Hart climbed into the cockpit, warmed the engine then opened the throttle. Before long he was airborne and trying to work out how to land. To his surprise, and to the excitement of the watching throng, he set his aircraft down gently on the field, near to the fence where everyone sat cheering.

Before long Hart was flying beyond the perimeter of the field. One day he flew to Parramatta and landed in the national park before returning to Penrith. Next he flew to the Sydney Showground and landed on the arena; that stunt caused him some problems because he needed spectators to hold the wings while he increased the engine revolutions enough to clear the fence on take-off.

William Hart's regular flights around Sydney were attracting considerable public and media attention. He was also attracting the attention of the law. Once he crash-landed on a Chinese market garden and had to compensate the angry owners. Then he was ordered by the District Court to pay a dairy farmer £20 in damages after flying low over his farm and stampeding the milking cows, causing two to die and the rest to go dry. But, of course, there's always more to the story.

On 5 December 1911, William Hart became the first person issued with an Australian pilot's licence, despite not having had a single flying lesson. However, as well as holding the Aerial League of Australia's Certificate Number 1, William Hart had the dubious honour of being the first person to crash an aeroplane in Australia. In January 1912, he was demonstrating the benefits of aerial reconnaissance to the Australian Army when he suddenly began losing altitude at 600 feet (190 metres) and had to set down beside the railway line between Mount Druitt and Rooty Hill. As he came in low, he clipped a signal stanchion and the aircraft slewed then flipped on to its back. He and his passenger, an army major named Rosenthal, escaped injury and continued on to Parramatta by train after flagging down the Mountains Express as it came past a few minutes after the crash.

William Hart set up a flying school at Ham Common near Windsor, on the site of the present Richmond RAAF base, and began offering joy flights around Sydney.

One day an American stuntman and aerial barnstormer named Eugene 'Wizard' Stone challenged

The *Sydney Morning Herald* captured the scene as a curious crowd gathered around aviation pioneer W.E. Hart after he landed his plane on the Sydney Showground in 1911.

Hart to race him the 32 kilometres from Sydney to Parramatta for a purse of £250. After a few false starts because of bad weather, they finally raced on 29 June 1912. Hart arrived in Parramatta in 23 minutes and landed on the park. Stone got lost in clouds and ended up near Lakemba.

The celebrity status of 'the Flying Dentist' continued to build in Sydney, so it was front-page news when he was nearly killed on 5 September 1912. A new monoplane that he was testing crashed, leaving him with fractured legs and multiple fractures of the skull. Although he was not expected to survive, he recovered and continued flying.

When World War I broke out in 1914, William Hart joined the fledgling Australian Flying Corps, but his injuries from the near-fatal crash in Sydney caught up with him and he was sent to England as an instructor without seeing action.

William Hart died in Sydney on 29 July 1943. For the record, although he was granted the first Australian licence, Hart was not the first Australian to receive a pilot's licence. Navy Lieutenant AM Longmore was granted International Aviator's Certificate Number 72 on 25 April 1911.

DETERMINATION PERSONIFIED

In Australian country towns, the local doctor has always been one of the most respected members of the community. Along with the priest, the bank manager and the solicitor, the doctor was considered an educated and worldly person who could not only dispense medical treatment but also advice on matters from personal relationships to finances.

In the days before successive Federal and State Governments 'improved' our health system, almost every town had a doctor in residence or visiting on a regular basis, and country practices were prosperous. Many country doctors practised in the same community for their whole career, delivering and treating two or three generations of local families.

We could do worse than get back to those days.

CHARLES PAGE WAS a blacksmith and coachbuilder at Grafton in northern New South Wales in the 1880s. He and his wife, Annie, struggled to raise their eight boys and three girls.

One day, Annie was helping Charles in the workshop when a piece of metal struck her in the face, rupturing her eye. It was a painful injury, made all the more dangerous because there were no surgeons in Grafton. Annie was told she would have to get help in Sydney, so for months she travelled back and forth between Grafton and Sydney as doctors tried in vain to save the eye. At Annie's side, comforting and encouraging her during the long hours on the road, was the fifth of the Page children, Earle.

After one of the visits to Sydney, Earle declared to the family that he was going to be a doctor. He was only starting school when he made that decision, but still seemed determined to carry it through when he duxed his final year at Grafton Primary School then won a scholarship to Sydney High School, where he matriculated to Sydney University at the age of 15.

Unfortunately, Earle's parents could not afford the entry fee for medicine, so the young boy from the bush enrolled in Arts, determined to win a scholarship with a strong first-year performance. He did just that, topping the university and winning a funded place in medicine at the age of 16. He achieved the highest score in the class during his final year, and in 1902, when he was still only 21, Earle Grafton Christmas Page became house surgeon at Royal Prince Alfred Hospital in Sydney.

Earle Page was a country boy at heart, however, and two years later, he walked away from a potentially lucrative career in Sydney to return to Grafton – fulfilling a promise that he made to his mother that no-one else would suffer the way she had for lack of surgeons in the area. He set up an extensive practice and a private hospital, complete with state-of-the-art x-ray equipment and operating theatres. In order to cover such a wide district, he also bought one of the first cars seen in northern New South Wales.

His practice prospered and Dr Page invested his new wealth in other businesses, including a timber mill, dairy farms, the local newspaper and property development. He also helped his father to be elected Mayor of South Grafton in 1908.

In 1915 Earle Page became concerned at the lack of attention given to roads and other infrastructure in the north of the state by the Sydney-based State Government, so he started the push for a separate state to be established in the north-east of New South Wales. His campaign was gaining momentum when all attention was diverted from national politics by the heavy casualities being suffered by Australian troops in Gallipoli. Dr Page shelved his political agenda and enlisted in the Army Medical Corps, spending the next 15 months in Egypt and then France as a surgeon.

On his way back to Australia after Armistice in 1918, Dr Page diverted his journey to Canada and the United States of America to look at innovative hydroelectric power projects. Soon after he arrived home, he followed in his father's footsteps by becoming Mayor of South Grafton. Dr Page immediately put into effect the knowledge he had acquired in North America, establishing the Nymboida hydroelectric scheme.

The following year, he was elected to Federal Parliament as the independent member for the local seat of Cowper. He would hold the seat for 42 years, through 15 general elections and another world war. An incredible achievement, but there's always more to the story.

A year after he was elected to Canberra, Dr Earle Page joined with ten other MPs from rural electorates who were concerned about the lack of attention given to issues affecting farmers and settlers; they formed the Country Party and elected Earle Page their leader.

During his colourful years in politics, Earle Page served as a minister in several coalition governments, only retiring to the backbench in 1956 at the age of 76. Notoriously difficult to work with, he was ruthless in his politics. Page forced the sacking of Nationalist Prime Minister Billy Hughes in 1922 because Hughes didn't do enough for rural areas. He was a strong supporter of Prime Minister Joseph Lyons because of the protectionist policies of his conservative friend. It may have also helped that Lyons recommended a knighthood for Page in 1938.

When Joe Lyons died suddenly in 1939, Sir Earle Page stepped forward and advised the Governor-General to appoint him Prime Minister in a caretaker role. He did this to block the man he disliked most in the parliament – Robert Menzies. Page attacked Menzies, calling him a coward because he did not enlist in World War I and said that Menzies would not be strong enough to lead Australia through the war that was inevitably approaching.

But the United Australia Party elected Robert

AWM OO4146

Sir Earle Page pictured in London in 1941 while preparing his report for the War Cabinet in Canberra.

Menzies as leader and Sir Earle Page agreed to serve in the Menzies government. He was made a member of the Australian Advisory War Council during World War II by the Curtin Labor government. However, Sir Earle Page was never again the influential figure that he was before his attack on Menzies.

Even though he was 81 and dying of lung cancer when the 1961 election came around, he refused to give up his seat in parliament. He was unable to campaign and died 11 days after the election without knowing he had lost the seat he had held since 1919.

A DICKENS OF A COUNTRY

After William Shakespeare, Charles Dickens would probably be the most read author in Australia, thanks to our education system. If you went to school in this country, you almost certainly studied Oliver Twist, Pickwick Papers, A Christmas Carol, Great Expectations *or* David Copperfield *– whether you liked it or not. Even if you didn't read a Dickens novel, you would certainly have seen a play, a movie or a television series based on one.*

But did you know that the inspiration for many Dickens characters came from Australia? Read on for the story of a special connection between our country and one of the world's greatest authors.

TEN THOUSAND POUNDS was a lot of money in 1863 – it was much more than the head of the largest bank in the colony of New South Wales earned in a year. But it was not enough to entice Charles Dickens to visit Australia. He politely, but definitely, declined the offer from a Melbourne catering firm.

Now, if you've read any Dickens, you'll probably find his reluctance to visit Australia a little curious.

After all, Australia featured regularly in his writings. The earliest mention of the colonies of Australia was in 1843 with the novel *Martin Chuzzlewit*, in which Miss Pecksniff had a futile wait for Augustus Moddle, who had been sent to Van Diemen's Land (Tasmania).

Seven years later in London, Dickens met Caroline Chisholm. It seems as a result of the stories she told him and the letters she showed him – which he published in a series of articles – an Australian flavour was injected into the book he was writing at that time, *David Copperfield*. The Micawbers and the Peggottys in that book went to Australia, as did Mrs Gummidge. They travelled with the help of a loan from a woman named Betsy Trotwood, who was similar to Caroline Chisholm in that she lent money to emigrating English families.

A leading character in Dickens' 1861 novel, *Great Expectations*, is the returned convict, Abel Magwitch, who turns up again in *Oliver Twist*. Of course the leading characters in *Oliver Twist*, Fagin and the Artful Dodger, are said to have been based on London characters who, in real life, ended up in Port Arthur in Tasmania and in Western Australia.

The Australian connection comes out yet again in *Pickwick Papers* with Count Smorltork, who bears a strong resemblance to scientist and explorer Count Strzelecki, who opened up so much of Australia.

The Dickens novel that most features characters resembling flesh-and-blood Australian figures is probably *Great Expectations*. The character Miss Havisham was almost certainly based on a Miss Eliza Donnithorne of King Street, Newtown, in Sydney. Miss Donnithorne was the daughter of a judge in the East India Company's Bengal Service. The judge retired to Australia and lived with his daughter. After he died, she remained in the house, called Camperdown Lodge. The adventures of the eccentric Miss Donnithorne, including her distress at being jilted at the altar, featured frequently in colonial newspapers – newspapers that were regularly read by Charles Dickens in London.

Some commentators warn against reading too much into the Australian references in the Dickens writings. They say they were simply commentary on events of the time. But when you hear more about the story, you might choose to think otherwise.

You see, Charles Dickens had more than a passing interest in Australia – he was much more than a mere witness to events. Over time he gathered a wealth of knowledge about this country and its people. Although he chose not to visit our shores personally in 1863, it seems that this was not the snub it first seemed.

Within five years of turning down the £10,000 offer to visit Melbourne, Charles Dickens sent two of his beloved sons to Australia. First it was Alfred, who wanted to be a sheep farmer, then a younger son, Edward. Edward was just 16 and, naively, Dickens put him into agricultural college in England for eight months to prepare him for a career in the Australian outback. Charles Dickens wept openly on the railway platform in London when Edward (nicknamed

'Plorn') left, but he insisted that time in Australia would be his sons' making as men.

Alfred Dickens and Edward Dickens both settled in New South Wales. Alfred managed Conoble sheep station before moving closer to Sydney. In 1911, after Charles Dickens' death, Alfred toured the world, lecturing on his late father's work. He died during a visit to the United States in 1912.

Edward Dickens, also known as EBL Dickens, managed Momba station on the Darling River in New South Wales and later Mount Murchison station at Wilcannia. In 1880, he married Constance Desailly, the daughter of the owner of nearby Nettley station. He died in Moree in 1902, where he worked in the Lands Office following five years in the New South Wales Parliament as the Member for Wilcannia in the Legislative Assembly.

When Charles Dickens sent Edward to Australia, he packed for him a complete set of his novels and told him to go and find his fortune. Edward kept the books with him to the end. The Dickens Fellowship erected a memorial to Edward Dickens in the grounds of the Anglican church in Moree.

If there is any doubt remaining about Charles Dickens' fascination with Australia, let it be put to rest with one more 'coincidence'. Dickens named the seventh of his ten children – a boy – Sydney.

DID *HE* GO ALL THE WAY?

It is not easy to keep an open mind in the face of what appear to be indisputable facts. But we should remember that there is always more to the story.

Management gurus like to say, 'You know what you know, but that's all you know.' In other words, you can be right in so far as what you do know, but you might not have all the information.

When I first saw the material that gave rise to this story I could not see any other conclusion but the obvious. I hope that there is more to this story, because otherwise it is a disgraceful episode that discredits more than one famous name in world history.

WHEN VICE-PRESIDENT Lyndon Baines Johnson took the oath of office on board Air Force One in November 1963, hours after the assassination of President John F Kennedy in Dallas, Texas, he made a point of wearing a small red, white and blue ribbon on the left lapel of his suit coat.

At a time when his country was in shock and grieving the loss of a hero, Lyndon Johnson wanted

LBJ ARCHIVE

Lyndon Baines Johnson is sworn in as President of the United States of America aboard Air Force One just hours after the assassination of John F Kennedy in 1963.

everyone to remember that he, too, was a hero. That ribbon on his lapel signified that he had been awarded the Silver Star, the third highest award for gallantry in action with the enemy. The Supreme Commander of Allied Forces in the Southwest Pacific, General Douglas MacArthur, had personally recommended Johnson for his bravery during a bombing mission over New Guinea in June 1942 in an American aircraft with an Australian co-pilot.

When Lyndon Johnson became the 36th President of the United States of America, it was the culmination of a 25-year preparation to assume his nation's highest office, beginning when he was elected to the House of Representatives in 1937 at the age of 29.

On 7 December 1941, when Japanese planes bombed Pearl Harbor, Lyndon Baines Johnson was not only a congressman, but also a Lieutenant Commander in the United States Naval Reserve. Two days after the attack, he reported for active duty – the first member of Congress to do so. He was assigned to a Washington desk job then to a war production job in San Francisco. However, in May 1942, Lieutenant Commander Johnson was assigned to observe US operations in New Zealand and Australia. It was in that role that he convinced General MacArthur to allow him to fly on a bombing mission out of Townsville.

In the early hours of 9 June 1942, Lieutenant Commander Johnson flew from Townsville to Port Moresby in a B-17 Flying Fortress to join a flight of 11 B-26 Marauder bombers from the US 22nd Bomb Group. The Marauders had flown from Townsville the night before and were fuelled and armed for the mission. Each plane carried thirty 50-kilogram bombs to be dropped on the Japanese airfield at Lae, an hour from Port Moresby.

Four other military observers were going on the mission; each had been assigned an aircraft. Lieutenant Commander Johnson was to fly in *The Virginian*; however, he was delayed getting to the aircraft and another observer, Lieutenant Colonel Francis R Stevens, took his place. Lieutenant Commander Johnson boarded another bomber, *Heckling Hare*, for the mission. He carried with him his diary and a small movie camera.

The citation for the Silver Star describes the events that followed:

> As our planes neared the target area they were intercepted by eight hostile fighters. When, at this time, the plane in which Lieutenant Commander Johnson was an observer developed mechanical trouble and was forced to turn back alone, presenting a favourable target to the enemy fighters, he evidenced marked coolness in spite of the hazards involved. His gallant actions enabled him to obtain and return with valuable information.

As fate would have it, the aircraft that Lyndon Johnson was supposed to be aboard crashed during the mission, killing all crew, including the observer, Lieutenant Colonel Stevens. But there's always more to the story and this is no exception.

President Lyndon Baines Johnson made much of his time in the Pacific theatre of war and the bombing mission during which he was decorated for gallantry. When he visited Australia in 1966, he even visited Buchanan's Hotel in Townsville, where he had been billeted. He also used his Silver Star to advantage in political debates, often pointing to his lapel saying that he knew what it was like to be shot at by the enemy. This was a favourite line during the bitter administration debates over the Vietnam War. But there is another version of the Lyndon Johnson story – a version that involves more politics than gallantry.

President Johnson often said that he didn't ask to go to the Pacific or to be shot at by the Japanese. Yet official records indicate that Lieutenant Commander Johnson lobbied long and hard to be assigned to the South-west Pacific command. Latter-day critics have said this was because he knew that he had a better chance of getting ahead in politics if he served in a theatre of war. Given that his role in the Naval Reserve was in weapons production, it is not clear why it was necessary for him to observe operations in person.

It was after a private meeting with General Douglas MacArthur that permission was given for the observer flight with the Marauders out of Townsville. MacArthur had not long arrived in Australia after evacuation from the Philippines and was outraged when he found that no great rescue force had been assembled in Australia to push the Japanese back from their foothold. In fact, no additional military resources had been allocated to the Pacific command.

Diaries hint that Congressman Johnson may have suggested that he could better lobby President Roosevelt on his return to the US if he had a first-hand understanding of the situation on the battlefield. In any event, Lieutenant Commander Johnson was given permission to fly one mission over enemy territory, even though in later years he claimed to have flown several missions.

US Army records indicate that the bombing

mission involving Lieutenant Commander Johnson over Lae was delayed by more than an hour because the VIPs and observers arrived late from Townsville. They say that Lieutenant Commander Johnson was reassigned to the *Heckling Hare* after he forgot his camera and had to return to the briefing room. However, ground crew claimed that the commander was caught short and had to rush off to the toilet, thereby missing the ride on his assigned aircraft, *The Virginian*.

Squadron flight logs show that the aircraft in which Johnson eventually flew encountered mechanical problems 120 kilometres from the target, dropped its bombs at sea and returned to Port Moresby without further incident. According to at least two of the crew, in recent years, there was no contact with the enemy that day, either from the ground or in the air.

Then, what of Lyndon Johnson's diary entry for that date? It reads:

> Generator went out: crew begged to go on. For next 30 minutes we flew on one generator. Due to drop bombs at 10:10. At 9:55 we turned. At 9:58 Zeroes intercepted. Andy leader got 3 and probably another. B-25 got two more and fighters got four. Total 9 zeroes.

That account is completely at odds with the records and the recollection of crewmen. However, the diary does seem to record accurately what happened to the other aircraft that continued on with the mission.

Even more confusing is a 1960s book claiming to quote crewmen from the *Heckling Hare* who said that Lyndon Johnson's aircraft was shot to pieces by the Zeroes. The official post-mission maintenance records show that the *Heckling Hare* had no damage at all apart from the faulty generator.

Any doubt might have been cleared up quickly had the infamous movie camera carried by Lyndon Johnson captured anything. Unfortunately, it seems it did not provide any footage of the Japanese attack.

The citation for Johnson's Silver Star came directly from General MacArthur, who told the young congressman about the medal before he returned to Washington. Ten days later, all congressmen on active service were recalled and Lyndon Baines Johnson became a vocal advocate for more resources to be allocated to MacArthur in the Pacific.

The critics say that Lyndon Johnson exaggerated his war service, that he was, at best, in proximity to the enemy for just 13 minutes, was never shot at by Japanese aircraft, and did not display bravery greater than the rest of the *Marauder* crew, none of whom were decorated.

That criticism is fuelled by an unsigned letter in the Lyndon Baines Johnson official archives. It suggests that Johnson may have had some twinge of conscience about the commendation. The letter is addressed to the Adjutant General of the War Department, it is typed on Johnson's congressional letterhead and it is dated 15 July 1942.

The letter says, in part:

> I should not and could not accept a citation of recognition for the little part I played . . . for a short time in learning and facing with them the problems they encounter all the time. The coolness for which the General commends me was only the reflection of my utter confidence in the men with whom I was flying.
>
> Watching the fighting crew of my ship save their crippled plane despite interception by hostile fighters outnumbering us, burned into my mind knowledge of concrete conditions which you can make sure I shall use to the best of my ability in the service of my country.

The final sentence reads: 'I cannot in good conscience accept the decoration.'

So far as anyone can establish, the letter was never sent. Coincidentally, it was typed the day before all congressmen were recalled from service to resume their political careers.

A DISHONOURED HERO

It was not an easy decision to include this story, because it doesn't reflect well on the Australian Army and it doesn't end happily. But it is our history and we need to know the good and the bad.

There was an American movie made some years ago about the true story of a GI who went absent without leave (AWOL) from his unit after being refused permission to go to his sick wife. While he was absent, his unit was sent overseas. Despite the extenuating circumstances, the hierarchy demanded that he be made an example of. He was found guilty of desertion in time of war. Those who insisted on his conviction believed that the mandatory death sentence would be commuted. However, they discovered to their horror that there was no discretion – the young soldier died in front of a firing squad.

Justice is blind, especially when it is bound in red tape.

WHEN THE GUILTY verdict was read out by the officer in charge of the court martial, 25-year-old Private John Leak showed absolutely no emotion. He simply saluted, turned and marched out of the courtroom under escort to begin his life sentence in prison for desertion.

No-one expected anything less from the tough bullock driver from Rockhampton in Queensland, who was the son of an English coalminer. He had not denied that he left his post in the face of the enemy – the most despised crime a soldier could commit in France in 1917.

Pale and gaunt from three years in combat, including seven months at Gallipoli, John Leak had listened carefully as the charge was read out. Then he told the court martial his side of the story. He and a mate had been gassed, and Leak had asked permission from the company commander to seek medical treatment.

Not only was the request denied, the pair was accused of malingering. So John Leak did what he thought was right – he took his blinded mate by the arm and went to find the help they both so urgently needed. If that was desertion, then he was guilty.

Despite the mitigating circumstances and some concerns by the court about the failure of the senior officer to allow the medical treatment, Private Leak was found guilty. There could be no leniency shown to deserters in the thick of battle.

After a few days, the conviction was reviewed: the sentence was reduced and ultimately suspended. Within four weeks, John Leak was back in the trenches with his battalion. He fought on until March 1918, when he was so severely gassed again that he had to be shipped home.

But, as we have come to expect, there is always more to the story.

John Leak's conviction for desertion and the life sentence imposed on him was a travesty and the accusation that he was faking injury to avoid battle was a disgrace. He was a scapegoat.

Everyone in the court martial knew the truth about Private John Leak – he was no deserter. Sixteen months earlier he had been involved in the bloody Battle of the Somme that resulted in 12,000 Australian casualties and he played a key role in victory for the Allies during the first significant engagement of that campaign – the battle for the town of Pozieres.

Three times the Germans turned back British attacks at Pozieres, threatening to stall the advance of 13 British divisions and five French divisions across the Somme Valley, so the Australian First Division was ordered forward to try to break through. They made one unsuccessful charge. Then, under cover of an intense artillery barrage, they pushed forward just after midnight and forced their way into the German trenches.

At one point in the battle the Australians were pinned down by two German machine guns and a team hurling hand bombs into the Australian positions. John Leak jumped out of his trench and ran through withering machine-gun fire hurling bombs of his own, to silence single-handedly the machine guns and capture the enemy trench. In the process he bayonetted three German soldiers and wounded all the others in the machine-gun position.

AWM H06716

Private John Leak V.C.

John Leak was neither a deserter nor a coward – the proof was on his chest as he stood before the court martial. To the everlasting shame of this country, the young soldier we court-martialled and convicted as a deserter in France in 1917 wore our highest award for courage in the face of the enemy – the Victoria Cross. Leak was one of five Australians awarded the Victoria Cross in the battle on the Somme.

A month after that action he was again in the thick

of the fighting, a kilometre and a half from Pozieres at Mouquet Farm, where he was wounded. He was sent to England to recuperate and it was when he returned to his battalion that he was gassed and asked for medical attention.

John Leak returned to Rockhampton after the war in 1919, but left Queensland and lived for a while in New South Wales and South Australia before settling at Esperance in Western Australia. There he ran a motor garage and worked as a mechanic.

He died in October 1972, in South Australia, of a heart attack. He is buried in Stirling Cemetery in the Adelaide Hills.

The court-martial conviction was never removed from his record.

A DIVER'S STORY

It is during times of disaster or emergency that you see the best qualities in Australians emerge. It is not the usual mateship, because often in these exceptional circumstances people won't know those they are helping – it comes from a deeply ingrained ethic that in this country, we look after each other.

I wish those qualities came to the fore more often.

Here is a story that is one of the best illustrations I have ever seen of how far Australians will go to look after someone they might not even know, but who needs their help.

A CHEER WENT up from the crowd of 500 gathered near the entrance of the Westralia and East Extension mine at Bonnievale, near Coolgardie, when Modesto Varischetti emerged, covered in mud and shielding his eyes from the sunlight. It was March 1907, and for nine days Varischetti had been trapped 300 metres below ground in a flooded mine shaft – huddled on a ledge, kept alive by a pocket of air and given little chance of survival. The water level in the mine was 30 metres above where he sheltered.

Varischetti, a widower with five children from Gorno in the north of Italy, was one of hundreds of Italian miners brought to Australian goldfields to break a union stranglehold. He had been working alone a level below his colleagues on the afternoon of Tuesday 19 March when heavy rain suddenly flooded the shaft. As the other miners scrambled to the surface covered in mud, there was little hope that the man left behind could have survived the initial crush of mud and debris that washed through the shaft.

The next day, a team from the mining company went down to the level where the survivors had come from and immediately above where Modesto Varischetti was last seen. His best friend, Guiseppe Masingoni, insisted on going with them. Guiseppe had a hunch that his friend was still alive, and when he lay on the floor of the shaft and tapped on a metal pipe on the ground, he was not surprised to hear faint tapping come back in reply. Masingoni worked his way along the pipe until the response was loudest. He knew then that he was right above his friend. Maps showed they were standing above a small rise in level ten. Varischetti had scrambled into this small dead-end, where a pocket of air kept the floodwater at bay.

A rescue team started pumping out the shaft, but they soon worked out that it would take them two weeks to empty 30 metres of flooded shaft and that would be too long for a man to be able to survive.

There had to be another solution. The mine supervisor, Josiah Crabbe, came up with the idea of a deep-sea diver going into the flooded shaft to rescue the stranded miner. But there was no-one in Kalgoorlie or Coolgardie with those skills or equipment.

The call went out to Perth for urgent help. Two divers, 44-year-old Welshman Frank Hughes and Londoner Tom Hearn, volunteered to go. Hughes was a former miner, so he had the special knowledge needed to work in the dark, dangerous, flooded mine.

The Perth to Coolgardie rail line was cleared for 600 kilometres, as a locomotive with one carriage and a loaded coal truck left Perth to cheering crowds as it raced to the rescue scene. Watered and coaled locomotives were waiting in sidings at two stops along the way to take over the relay of the carriage so that no time was lost. The rescue train reached Kalgoorlie in a record time of 25 hours.

While Masingoni kept tapping on the pipe to let his friend know that he wasn't forgotten, Hughes and Hearn began the slow and dangerous descent into the pitch dark of the blocked and flooded mine. It was at about this time that miners realised air was escaping from Varischetti's chamber – that meant the water would begin rising. They had no time to lose.

Wearing more than 80 kilograms of diving gear and dragging 300 metres of breathing hose, Frank Hughes worked his way down ladders, through shafts and on his hands and knees up the rise to where the Italian miner crouched on a ledge. On 22 March, after three days alone in darkness and cold, Modesto Varischetti heard Frank Hughes surface in the air pocket with him. He could not see him in the dark, but knew he was there. Hughes could not remove his heavy helmet to speak, so he could only hope Varischetti would understand that he was part of the rescue effort. Without communicating further, Hughes returned to the surface to get a container with food, warm drinks, candles, a pencil and some paper.

The first thing that Modesto Varischetti did when he got the paper was write a note to his friend Giuseppe Masingoni and send it to the surface with Frank Hughes. In his note, Varischetti apologised for the trouble he had caused everyone. He thanked them all for everything they were doing to save his life and said he was more than satisfied with the food being provided. Then he bid everyone farewell and asked them to remember him.

For eight days, Frank Hughes and Tom Hearn went through the flooded mine shaft time and again to take Varischetti messages, food and drink. Several times the divers became tangled in debris and were nearly killed. But they were determined to continue the rescue mission for as long as it took.

Modesto's spirits were raised by the novelty of the meals brought to him each day in sealed containers – one day it was beef jelly and fruit; another it was roast beef, boiled ham and potato; on yet another it was minced meat and chocolate sponge. But the most welcome surprise was the container with chicken, ham, macaroni, bread and red wine along with some tobacco and matches. Even though he could not talk to the divers, he could show them his gratitude with handshakes and pats on the back.

On 27 March, eight days after he was first trapped, Modesto Varischetti heard a human voice for the first time when Frank Hughes was able to remove his face glass and speak with him for about five minutes. It was too dark for Varischetti to make out the face behind the voice, and unfortunately he spoke only a little English. But nonetheless it was a conversation.

Frank Hughes brought back another note written in Italian. When translated, it said that Modesto felt his strength was disappearing but that God was helping him to keep up his courage in the hope of seeing daylight and his beautiful country again.

By now, large crowds were camped at the entrance to the mine following each day's events with interest. Newspapers around Australia were carrying daily reports from the mine on progress with the rescue. A nation was watching and praying for the Italian miner. Another two divers arrived from Perth to help Hearn and Hughes clear rubble from a second passageway near where Varischetti was trapped. As the water level began to fall, the divers were able to wade through the mud without diving suits.

Finally, on Friday 29 March 1907, Frank Hughes reached Varischetti and told him to prepare to leave his tomb. It was the first time Modesto had seen Frank Hughes's face and tears flowed down his cheeks. Then, gently and slowly, the rescue team of divers carried

Modesto Varischetti through the mud, over the debris and up the shaft, into the daylight.

Three cheers went up for the Italian miner and his rescuers, who had endured and overcome a nine-day ordeal that no-one expected to end in success. But there's always more to the story, isn't there?

When Frank Hughes surfaced with Modesto Varischetti, he was surprised to find that he had become a national hero. Throughout the rescue he was unaware that so much attention had been focused on what he was doing in the flooded shaft. The story of his rescue of Modesto Varischetti had been published around the world.

Of the many telegrams of congratulations, there were two that Frank Hughes was most eager to read after he showered and had a hot meal; one was from his union expressing pride in what he had done to save a brother miner. The other telegram was from the Boulder Mines Philharmonic Society in Kalgoorlie, expressing their pride in the efforts of their second bass singer.

It was a story that made all Australians proud.

DOCTORS STONE

Germaine Greer has been a sparring partner of mine for years. We always find something to disagree about.

Thirty years ago Germaine made a name for herself with some confronting statements about the attitudes of men to women and women to themselves. At the time I didn't agree with her, and even now I don't think she was entirely correct.

Germaine and the other feminist crusaders of the 70s and 80s achieved some significant advances for women – mostly forced on us by law.

But surely their biggest achievement was to convince us to stop asking 'Why?' in relation to women, and start asking 'Why not?'

THERE ARE ALMOST 40,000 general medical practitioners registered in Australia – 16,000 of them are women. Thousands more work as specialist doctors and as staff medical officers in health clinics and hospitals. But there was a time when Australia had no women doctors and no women medical students. Indeed, women were discouraged from medicine because it was thought to be too demanding a profession.

That was certainly the opinion of the Dean of the Sydney University Medical School, Professor Anderson Stuart. He believed that women should be in the home, raising children and caring for their husbands. In the 1880s, Professor Stuart refused to accept female students in his medical school. His colleagues at Melbourne University shared his views and they also restricted entry to men.

However, when the world's first registered woman doctor, Dr Elizabeth Blackwell, returned to her birthplace in England from the United States and began breaking down the gender barriers in the British medical system, the two leading Australian medical schools came under intense pressure to change their policy. In 1884, Sydney University agreed to accept women transferring to medicine from other disciplines in the university.

One of the first women to take up the opportunity was Miss Dagmar Berne, a young Arts student. Dagmar was the daughter of a Danish migrant father and the eldest daughter of eight children. When she was a small child, her father drowned trying to save a man in the Bega River on the New South Wales south coast. Her mother remarried – to a local grazier – but her second husband also died, when Dagmar was just a teenager. Her mother took the eight children and moved to Sydney, where Dagmar and her sister, Florence, opened a small private school and began teaching.

Dagmar was accepted to Sydney University to study Arts but she intended to transfer to a science degree at the first opportunity. When she nominated for medicine, Professor Anderson Stuart tried to convince her to pursue another course. He told Dagmar that she could never gain the respect of male colleagues and would eventually find medicine too distressing.

In her first year, Dagmar passed all her subjects with honours. But in her second year she moved into classes taught by Professor Stuart. From that time she did not pass another exam at Sydney University. Later it was revealed that Professor Stuart had managed to frustrate the university decision to admit women by failing every female medical student before their final year.

After four years of frustration and disappointment, Dagmar Berne met a British doctor named Elizabeth Garrett Anderson. Dr Anderson was the world's second registered female doctor and she knew what discrimination was all about. Dr Anderson told Dagmar Berne that if she could not overcome Professor Stuart in Sydney, to move to London to study at London's All-Women Hospital.

Dagmar's sister, Florence, also wanted to study medicine, so the two girls left together for England in 1889 and began studies under Dr Anderson. On their small allowance, they had to live in cheap accommodation in London and the damp and cold conditions left Dagmar with pneumonia and regular bouts of pleurisy.

In 1890, during the Depression, all of Dagmar and Florence's savings were lost in the collapse of their bank in Sydney. With Dagmar in her final year, it looked as if both girls would have to withdraw from university and return to Australia. But at great personal sacrifice, and without first telling Dagmar, Florence pulled out of her studies and took a job as a governess to raise money to pay for her older sister's.

Dagmar qualified as a doctor in 1893 and, after two years of a residency in London, returned to Sydney. On 9 January 1895, Dr Dagmar Berne registered with the Medical Board of New South Wales and set up practice in Macquarie Street.

Unfortunately, as a result of the conditions that she had been forced to live in while studying in England, Dagmar developed a chronic chest complaint and died in August 1900 at the age of 35 – a victim of the discrimination that forced her overseas to study medicine.

But there is always more to the story.

When Dagmar Berne returned to Sydney to register as a doctor, she became Australia's second registered female medical practitioner. The first was Dr Constance Stone in February 1890.

Born in Hobart and schooled in Melbourne, Constance ran a small primary school until she was 28, when she applied to Melbourne University to study medicine. Because of the discriminatory policy there, she was rejected. So Constance wrote to the Dean of the Women's Medical College in Philadelphia in the United States and was accepted for medical studies. She left Melbourne without enough money for a return ticket.

In 1885, Constance Stone graduated in medicine and applied for registration in her home state of

Victoria. However, the authorities said they could not recognise the American medical qualification and that she would have to qualify in Britain. Constance had already enrolled in Canada for advanced studies, and she graduated with honours from Toronto University in 1888. But still the Victorian Medical Board would not register her.

So Dr Constance Stone went off to England to complete an internship at the New Hospital for Women and Children in London. A year later, she gained her British qualification and returned to Melbourne.

She opened a clinic for the poor in Melbourne and soon was joined by her sister, Clara, and cousin, Mary – who had both qualified as doctors in Australia after being among the first group of women to force open the doors of the Melbourne University Medical School. The three women worked tirelessly to treat the sick and injured in the inner-city suburbs of Melbourne, often travelling alone at night in a horse and buggy to reach their patients.

Constance, Clara and Mary Stone became the driving force behind the establishment of Melbourne's Queen Victoria Memorial Hospital. In 1896 their dream was realised – a hospital staffed *by* women, *for* women.

Tragically, Constance Stone died at just 46 years of age from tuberculosis contracted while working with the sick and poor. Her only daughter also became a doctor.

THE ELECTRIC RENEWER

A credit card company ran a television advertisement a little while ago with a message along the lines of 'Who remembers who came second?'

Every time I saw that ad I felt a little sad because it is true; we do tend to focus on the winner. We do it with sport, politics, entertainment and even science.

I have been number one in the radio ratings for more years than I care to remember, but there have been occasions when I have come in second, or even third; so what? I am the same person at number one as I am at number two. It doesn't make any difference to me.

However, some people have just one chance in their lifetime to be recognised for their contribution to humankind. Here is a story of someone who came first but no-one remembered.

IT'S NOT THAT people in the small Victorian town of Malmsbury didn't respect their town doctor, Edward Davy, it's just that whenever he told the story of how he invented the telegraph, they couldn't help but smile. After all, everyone in the 1850s knew that the telegraph was invented by British scientists Cooke and Wheatstone; all the science books said so.

Dr Davy was well liked in Malmsbury. He had farmed – not very successfully – for a while and he and his wife, who died in 1877, had raised a very large family. He had also been elected Mayor of Malmsbury three times.

Edward Davy came to Australia in 1839, when he was 33 years old. He had been trained as a surgeon but worked as a pharmacist and industrial chemist in London. When he arrived in Adelaide, he decided to try his hand at something different. He sold property, edited the Adelaide *Examiner* newspaper for three years, then managed the Yatala copper smelting works. Because of his background as an industrial chemist, Davy took a keen interest in the smelting process and he invented a more efficient way to process copper. He set up his own plant, but it failed and he lost his investment. For a year, he was the Assay Master in Melbourne – one of the highest-paid government officials during the Victorian gold rush – responsible for certification and processing of gold. In 1854 Edward Davy chose to return to medicine and he settled with his family in Malmsbury as a humble GP. It was only two years before his death that the townspeople finally learned the truth about their Dr Davy.

In 1883, John J Fahie, an old friend from England, came to visit the 77-year-old doctor. Fahie was writing the official history of electric telegraphy and wanted to talk to the man he believed was responsible for inventing the telegraph. To everyone's surprise, Fahie confirmed that the doctor had, indeed, been telling the truth for the past 30 years. But, of course, there's always more to the story.

When John Fahie published his 500-page history of the telegraph, he devoted almost a quarter of the book to Edward Davy's work. He then went on a personal crusade to have history corrected and Davy recognised for his achievement. Eventually, on the weight of evidence produced by Fahie, the Society of Telegraph Engineers in London and the Royal Society of Victoria conceded that Edward Davy was, in fact, the first to develop and patent the electrical relay system on which all subsequent telegraph systems relied.

Edward Davy began his work on the telegraph in 1835. By December 1837, he was demonstrating his invention in Regents Park in London, laying out a mile (1.6 kilometres) of copper wire around the park and using a small relay system that he called an 'electric renewer' to transmit a signal along the circuit. In late December 1837, he demonstrated his needle telegraph, using the relay, in Exeter Hall in Central London, and in July the following year, applied for, and was granted, a patent on the design. The British Solicitor-General received expert advice that Davy's invention was different from a telegraph system patented in December the previous year by competitors Cooke and Wheatstone.

Davy's relay was the crucial element that overcame the problem of transmitting a signal over long distance.

Two railway companies in England were ready to adopt Davy's telegraphic system when he suddenly abandoned the project and left England for Australia forever. Edward Davy's sudden departure was prompted by a marriage breakdown and a subsequent financial crisis as his angry wife went on a spending spree at the same time as some of his business investments failed. In the end his debts rose to such levels that he was near bankruptcy. Had his father not helped, Davy may well have ended up in jail.

In the face of mounting problems, he decided to emigrate, leaving his father to deal with the telegraph patent and the divorce from his wife. His father, a doctor, had always considered Edward's inventing a waste of time, money and talent. In 1847 he was approached by Cooke and Wheatstone, who convinced him that they had sewn up the most important aspects of the telegraph patents. So Dr Davy senior sold Edward's patent for the relay to Cooke and his partner for £600 to recoup some of the money he had lost bailing his son out of debt. The English pair now had the key to long-distance telegraphic transmission and Edward Davy had nothing.

When the Royal Society of Victoria and the Society of Telegraph Engineers voted to acknowledge Edward Davy's contribution to the invention of the telegraph, it seemed that justice would finally be done. However, there was one more disappointment in store for Edward. Not wishing to admit their mistake, the societies decided in the end simply to add Edward

Davy's name to the list of those credited with the invention.

When he died, Edward Davy left a large family and a small estate. Today you would be hard pressed to find a mention of him in the history books – not even for that invisible ceramic cement we all use for mending broken china and glass. Yes, Edward Davy invented that as well, and got nothing for it.

FIGHTING MAC

I have upset a few people over the years by criticising the holier-than-thou who think that they make a contribution to humanity by telling others how they should live their lives.

If you are going to quote the Bible, the Koran, or any holy book, at people, you should make sure you practise what you preach. I have a great deal of respect for people like Mother Teresa, our own Bill Crewes from the Sydney City Mission and Yusef Islam (Cat Stevens) because they actually live by the principles they espouse: they set examples for others, rather than rules.

I chose the story of 'Fighting Mac' not only because it is a remarkable and inspirational story of an Australian who practised what he preached, but also because I believe we must ensure that there is more to this story.

An injustice remains an injustice until it is put right. I am sure when you read this story you will understand that we must write the final chapter together.

WILLIAM LINDSAY MCKENZIE was born on a small farm in Lanarkshire, Scotland, five days before Christmas in 1869. His simple, honest village upbringing and schooling were to develop qualities in the boy that would become outstanding features in the man.

William was 15 and had not long finished school when his parents told him that he and his five brothers and two sisters were emigrating to Australia, where their uncle owned a large cattle station.

William worked hard to help his father establish the new family farm at South Kolan, near Bundaberg. They spent long days toiling together in the steamy Central Queensland heat. After the first year, young William McKenzie was sent to his uncle as a jackeroo to learn more about farming in this new country. When he had done his time, he returned to Bundaberg as an overseer on a sugar plantation. Eighteen-year-old William, who now answered to 'Bill', had grown into a tall, powerfully built young man with a reputation as a tireless worker and a fearless bare-knuckle fighter.

But one day in 1887, he met his match in the most unlikely place – a Salvation Army Kingdom Hall. Within days of attending the meeting, burly Bill McKenzie shocked family and friends by announcing that he was giving up farming and devoting his life to God. After two years of voluntary work, he entered the Salvation Army College in Melbourne. On graduation, he was commissioned and posted to Newcastle, then West Maitland, Hillgrove, Sydney, Brisbane, New Zealand, Tasmania and, eventually, Bendigo in 1914.

It was in Bendigo that Bill first heard the news war

had broken out in Europe and that Australia was raising an expeditionary force to support Mother England. He knew instinctively where he was most needed and was one of the first to apply for a chaplaincy in the Australian Infantry Force. Within weeks Chaplain McKenzie was in Egypt with the First Infantry Brigade, tending both to their spiritual and temporal wellbeing. He won the hearts of the troops by demanding for them, and getting, improved living conditions in the desert staging camps.

In April 1915, when the first Australian troops landed at Gallipoli, the padre was with them. In the midst of a military nightmare, big Bill McKenzie was a reassuring figure. He carried the wounded, comforted the sick, prayed with the scared, and buried the dead. In one three-week period, Chaplain McKenzie conducted 647 funeral services, mostly on his knees to avoid Turkish snipers. After one burial, he had three bullet holes in his hat.

During the bloody battle of Lone Pine, the unarmed Chaplain McKenzie crawled time and again through the battlefield under enemy fire to drag wounded Australians to safety. His unselfish devotion to troops on the frontline, combined with his prowess during impromptu boxing tournaments, earned him the nickname 'Fighting Mac'.

For his conspicuous bravery at Lone Pine, William McKenzie was awarded a rare military honour for a chaplain – the Military Cross. But, as we've learned by now, there's always more to the story.

'Fighting Mac' stayed with the Australian troops after evacuation from Gallipoli. He was alongside them through the bloodiest battles of the Western Front, including Pozieres, Bullecourt and Mouquet Farm. No-one knows how many Australian lives he saved; however, army records and witnesses suggest it was hundreds.

But eventually even the burly body of the Bundaberg sugar farmer reached its limits. Though he protested his fitness, army doctors could see the warning signs of complete physical breakdown towards the end of 1917, and so, just before his 48th birthday, Chaplain Bill McKenzie was ordered home. His war was over. He had done more than his share.

Padre McKenzie returned to Australia downcast at leaving his 'boys' behind. But there was a surprise awaiting him. Returned diggers he had saved, families of those for whom he had cared, and communities of grateful citizens had planned a hero's welcome with parades and ceremonies in all parts of the country. The deeds of 'Fighting Mac' had become legend. A man armed only with a Bible and a prayer had inspired a nation. Indeed, some described him as 'the most famous man in the AIF'.

After the war ended, McKenzie continued his Salvationist missionary work, including a stint as Commissioner in China in the 1920s. He was ultimately promoted to head of the Salvation Army in the southern and eastern states of Australia. In 1935, William McKenzie was awarded the Order of the

AWM G01347

Chaplain McKenzie on the front line at Gallipoli in 1915.

British Empire for his outstanding work for the community. It was a great honour, but it did nothing to correct a great wrong done to this Australian hero. A wrong perpetrated by his own government.

Although Bill McKenzie was too humble a man ever to discuss it, his 'boys' certainly did, and they found their own way to protest his treatment. Every

ANZAC Day, no matter where he marched, 'Fighting Mac' was ushered to the front rank. Without a word, he was shown the utmost respect and honour.

Why? Because the diggers knew that this man of God with the Military Cross on his chest was possibly our bravest soldier. They knew that in Gallipoli and France amid those ferocious battles, this humble chaplain performed acts so heroic he was three times recommended for our highest bravery award – the Victoria Cross. And they knew that three times the recommendation was denied.

It may be to our everlasting shame that Chaplain William McKenzie was denied the recognition he truly deserved because of an army regulation that said chaplains could have only one military award. Mac already had the Military Cross and so he was denied the VC and two bars.

THE FLYING PIEMAN

We need more characters about town because we are at real risk of becoming boring. Every one of our cities would benefit from an injection of eccentricity, colour and personality.

I blame the city councils, who have taken all the fun out of life. Paid parking, restricted access, busking licences, hoarding and display guidelines – these town halls have turned into red tape factories.

I like hearing the old Chinese man playing that stringed instrument that sounds like six cats in a fight and enjoy watching the Scottish guy in a kilt juggling burning torches while telling corny jokes, just as much as I like a student string quartet and South American guitarists.

If we don't get more colour in our lives, we may have to go back to black-and-white television.

HE WAS KNOWN affectionately in the streets of Sydney in the early 19th century as 'The Flying Pieman'. He wore a top hat, a waistcoat and knee-breeches with long white stockings, and carried a staff with coloured streamers flowing from both his hat and his staff. He whistled and sang as he walked along the streets of the colony.

The 'Pieman' was actually William Francis King, the son of the Paymaster of Petty Accounts at Whitehall, the headquarters of the English Civil Service. William was educated in London with the full expectation of his family that he would enter the church. But William didn't share the vision his parents had for him. Instead, he became a stockbroker, then a clerk in the treasury office at the Tower of London.

In 1829, William King migrated to Sydney looking for adventure and romance. His first job was as a schoolmaster at Sutton Forest near Moss Vale on the Southern Tablelands of New South Wales. It was arranged for him by an old family friend who was Bishop of the region. The Bishop also arranged for William to give private tutoring to some of the wealthy children of the district.

But 23-year-old William King wanted some excitement in his life, and he wasn't going to get it in Sutton Forest. So he packed his bags and walked to Sydney, where he took a job as a barman in the Hope and Anchor Hotel in Sussex Street and then as a wandering pieman. He didn't really care how much he earned because all the while he was receiving an allowance from his father in England.

William's mischievous sense of humour soon earned him a title as one of the clowns of the colony. However, as well as being a comedian and extremely intelligent and well-educated, William King was a naturally gifted athlete, and he took the fullest advantage of his ability.

Often for a dare, but more often for wagers, he performed extraordinary feats that filled the front pages of the colonial newspapers and drew crowds of clamouring fans. Once, for a bet, he carried a 30-kilogram dog the 50 kilometres from Campbelltown to Sydney in eight hours and ten minutes. Another day it was a 42-kilogram goat *and* a 6-kilogram dead weight that he carried from Brickfield Hill, near the current Surry Hills, to a pub in Parramatta, 29 kilometres away, in seven hours.

In October 1848, he visited Queensland and, while he was there, walked from Brisbane to Ipswich carrying a 45-kilogram pole. Just for good measure, he beat the mail coach on the same route by an hour.

'The Flying Pieman' was up for any dare if there was a bet involved. It must have been a considerable wager that persuaded him to pick up 100 live cats, 100 live rats and 100 live mice placed a metre apart from each other. But he did it.

In December 1847, he also accepted a challenge to run a mile (1.6 kilometres), walk a mile, wheel a barrow half a mile, pull a carriage with a lady in it for half a mile, walk half a mile backwards, pick up 50 large rocks and then perform 50 leaps – all in one hour and 30 minutes. King gave himself a short rest break of about five minutes and finished inside the time by 45 seconds.

For all William King's bravado, showmanship and clowning, there was a serious aspect to his feats – his amazing stamina and fitness. On 28 September 1847, he set out to walk 192 miles – that's more than 300 kilometres – around Maitland Racecourse, non-stop, in 48 hours. He had failed once before, but he was convinced it could be done. This time he not only finished an hour-and-a-half short of the deadline, but did a lap of honour with the town's brass band and a cheering crowd in breathless pursuit.

A few weeks later he took a bet at the Fitzroy Hotel in Maitland that he couldn't walk a thousand quarter miles (400 metres) in a thousand quarter hours. He did it. King once walked more than 2600 kilometres in five weeks and four days for no other reason than he felt like doing it and wanted to see how long it would take him.

Twice he beat the stagecoach from Windsor to Sydney – a distance of 55 kilometres. Of course it had to make stops along the way, but they followed the same route. He walked the 48 kilometres from Sydney to Parramatta and back twice a day, for six consecutive days, to win one bet. And on three consecutive days, he walked the 70 kilometres from St John's Church in Parramatta to St Matthew's Church in Windsor and back, each day taking half an hour off the previous day's time.

But there's always more to the story. William Francis King was dubbed 'The Flying Pieman' because of one of his favourite stunts. He would set up his stand at Circular Quay, selling pies to passengers boarding the steam ferry to Parramatta. As the ferry pulled away from the wharf, he would wave them farewell. While the ferry was making its way up the Parramatta River, picking up and dropping off passengers, William King would walk briskly along Parramatta Road, arriving at the Parramatta wharf in plenty of time to set up his stand and welcome the passengers that he farewelled at Circular Quay earlier. The performance earned him plenty of applause and quite a considerable amount in gratuities from the amused passengers.

William King was a happy and colourful character in public. But his private life was marked by loneliness and disappointment. A long love affair ended unhappily and William chose never to marry. And although he continued for many years with his entertaining feats, he eventually died lonely and ill in a men's home in Liverpool, west of Sydney, at the age of 67.

FOR THE LEISURED MULTITUDES

Australia is a wonderful country blessed with a wealth of resources and a stable democracy. That puts us well ahead of more than half the countries of the world. But where are we going?

The Europeans spent 30 years talking about a common market before they finally got the European Community up and running, but they had a plan that all political parties were committed to follow in principle.

What is our ten-year or 20-year goal? The only sign of foresight is the talk of us having a single economy with New Zealand. Good start, but what's the rest of the plan?

To many outsiders, we look like we just live for today.

JOURNALISTS ATTENDING A Melbourne press conference in 1891 were stunned when the 26-year-old British author launched into his attack. 'You don't know what work is in this part of the world,' he said. 'You don't suppose that this eight hours' work, eight hours' rest and eight hours' recreation is going to last forever, do you?'

But the young man didn't stop there. He told them that there was too much politics in Australia for such an immature country.

Most of the crusty old journalists were amused. After all, this upstart had been in Australia only a matter of days, yet he had already made up his mind that we were unworthy of his respect. But then you only have to read *Gunga Din*, *Mandalay*, *Captains Courageous* or *The Light That Failed* to know that it was perfectly in character for Joseph Rudyard Kipling. He didn't mince his words and he didn't waste them either. It was a product of his upbringing and the deep psychological scars he carried through life.

Kipling was born in Bombay (now Mumbai), India, in 1865, the son of an architectural sculptor and designer who was principal of an art school. When Rudyard was six, his mother and father sent him and his three-year-old sister to live with a family in England. For five years, little Rudyard was bullied and physically mistreated in the foster home. Then, when he began boarding school at the United Services College in Devon, he was teased and bullied because of his near-sightedness and frail physique. He found he could survive by taking refuge in literature; he also found others just as unhappy and formed strong friendships.

After school, he trained as a journalist and editor and in 1882 he returned to India, where he worked in newspapers and wrote his first works. Several of these, including 'The Light That Failed' and the poem 'The Broken Link Handicap', carried reference to Australia, even though he had never been here.

In 1891, he embarked on what was to be a world tour. But he made it only to South Africa, Australia,

New Zealand and India before falling in love and marrying an American woman, Caroline Balestier. Kipling spent ten days in Melbourne during November 1891. He also had one day each in Sydney, Hobart and Adelaide.

Fiercely loyal to the British Empire, and an advocate of strenuous personal effort, Kipling found a lot to dislike in what he saw during that whirlwind visit to Australia. He wrote of Sydney being 'populated by leisured multitudes all in their shirt sleeves, picnicking all day'.

When our own great author AB 'Banjo' Paterson stayed with Kipling in his home in England years later, he was still lamenting our attitude to life. 'You people in Australia haven't grown up yet. You think the Melbourne Cup is the most important thing in the world,' he told Paterson. Of course, there's always more to the story.

Banjo Paterson liked Rudyard Kipling very much. He described him as 'a hard-working, commonsense, level-headed man without any redeeming vices', who liked nothing more than to take his two small children out for a walk. 'He wrote of things as he saw them. Bearing in his own way the white man's burden and expecting no fee or reward,' Banjo recalled.

Kipling was devastated by the death of his eldest child, six-year-old Josephine, in 1899. He was still struggling with his emotions when, in 1907, he was awarded the Nobel Prize for Literature. Then, in 1915, he suffered a further crippling blow when his son,

John, was killed in action in World War I. He told Banjo Paterson – himself a former soldier – that he was asked to write an epitaph for his son's gravestone in the middle of the war cemetery. Kipling, in his inimitable style, wrote: 'Had our fathers not lied to us, so many of us would not be here.' The inscription was rejected.

But perhaps Rudyard Kipling did not always call it exactly as he saw it. For instance, it was only when his autobiography was published after his death in 1936 that Australia learned a secret about that short visit here 45 years earlier.

Kipling's brief reference to Australia ends: 'They volunteered that they were new and young, but would do wonderful things some day, which promise they more than kept.'

That might explain why Kipling told Banjo Paterson during his visit:

> I must buy a house in Australia some day . . . I'd like to live in Australia for a while. I've been there, but I only went through it like the devil went through Athlone, in standing jumps. You can't learn anything about a country that way. You have to live there and then you can get things right.

It seems that for more than 40 years, Rudyard Kipling watched Australia develop the character he thought at first it lacked, mature as he thought it should, and deserve what he thought he could never give us – his respect and admiration.

GENEROUS TO A FAULT

We all go through good and bad times in our lives. Usually we experience the pleasure or the pain with family or friends.

We seem to have more of both during the good times, and distinctly fewer when things are not going so well. However, it is the friends and family who gather around you in the bad times you should remember when things eventually get better.

It is amazing how much a hug, a kiss, a phone call or a short note can mean when you are feeling blue. It is as if that contact transfers energy into you.

I hope when my time comes to shuffle off this earth that my good friends and my family know how much I appreciated them.

IN THE 1820S John Piper was the best-known man in the colony of New South Wales. They called him the 'Prince of Australia', 'The Gay Cavalier' and 'The Prince of Hosts'. He lived in the biggest house, held the most lavish parties, owned the best racehorses and gave more than anyone else to the less fortunate. John Piper was a rich fellow, but a good bloke.

He first came to Sydney as an 18-year-old ensign in

the New South Wales Corps in 1791. He hailed from Maybole in Ayrshire and was a lovable rogue of a young man who made lots of firm friends, including the influential John Macarthur.

After a short time in Sydney, Ensign Piper volunteered for duty in the remote penal colony of Norfolk Island. In 1795 he was promoted to Lieutenant and returned to Sydney, where he got into trouble for being involved as a second for his commanding officer in a duel. He was court-martialled for insubordination after writing a rude letter to the Governor telling him he shouldn't have interfered in a dispute between gentlemen. He was acquitted of the charge.

In 1804, Piper was sent back to Norfolk Island as Acting Governor and stayed there for six years. He was considered by all on Norfolk at that time to be the most compassionate commandant ever to serve in the settlement. While on Norfolk Island, John Piper met a young woman named Mary Ann Shears, the daughter of a convict. According to the laws of the time, they could not marry because he was an officer, so they lived together and had two sons.

In 1811, John and Mary went to England and Piper resigned his commission. They returned to Sydney in 1814 and two years later married.

When John Piper returned to Sydney at the age of 41, and with a family to support, he had little idea what he would do. He had been promoted to Captain before his resignation, but there was no prospect of work for him. Unexpectedly, and clearly through intervention by someone influential, he was appointed Senior Naval Officer in the Port of Sydney, a civilian position carrying a base salary of about £375 but with extra salaries for also being Chairman of the Harbour Trust, Chief of the Water Police and Master of Lighthouses.

But the real benefit of the job was the 5 per cent commission he made on all customs duties collected in the Port of Sydney as Comptroller of Customs. Of course, that commission turned into a fortune as Sydney Harbour became one of the busiest ports in the Pacific. Before long, John Piper was one of the highest paid men in the colony. He was also Chairman of the Board of Directors of the Bank of New South Wales, Chief Steward of the Sydney Jockey Club, a magistrate and a wealthy landowner.

His employment contract included, on top of salaries and commissions, grants of land at places such as Neutral Bay, Vaucluse and Woollahra. Eventually, he held more than 10,000 hectares of land around Sydney.

As John and Mary's family expanded to 13 children, Piper built a mansion on a plot of his land at Point Eliza, later to be renamed Point Piper. He called his luxurious palace Henrietta Villa. It employed more than 100 staff and included a banquet room, enclosed gardens, stables and a ballroom.

Even though he had become rich, John Piper remained the same kind-hearted person he had always been, and he spent money on people regardless of their social status or wealth. Many people took advantage of his generosity over the next ten years.

At 52, John Piper had lots of money, lots of property, more friends than he knew what to do with and a large family around him. Then, in 1825, things began to unravel. First, the Piper's 12-year-old son Hugh was killed when he fell from a horse. Then Sir Ralph Darling arrived in New South Wales as the new Governor; one of his first targets was John Piper. Jealous at Piper's handsome income, Darling ordered an inquiry into the customs accounts and found that they were short by more than £100,000. The inquiry found that, although John Piper had not defrauded the accounts, he had been negligent in administering payments from them.

Darling then ordered a second inquiry into the Bank of New South Wales, where it was found that he had influenced lending to a group of businessmen who were his acquaintances. Many had not repaid their loans. John Piper was forced to resign from all his appointments and ordered to pay large sums of compensation to the Government for his negligence.

Facing bankruptcy and the sale of his family home, John Piper ordered his boatmen to row him out into the middle of Sydney Harbour. With a piper playing a lament, he stood in full-dress uniform on the bow with sword raised and jumped into the water. His staff dragged him back into the boat and took him to shore. But there's always more to the story. Even though John Piper had to sell some of his property for a pittance, he paid all of his debts in full.

With what money Piper had left over after paying

his debts, he took Mary and the children to Bathurst, west of Sydney, where they bought a small property that John called Alloway. He raised cattle and sheep, and worked as a magistrate in the town. Unfortunately, John Piper didn't change his lifestyle to suit his modest country income and soon he had given away, spent or lent all his money, and when the Depression of 1844 hit, he lost the property as well.

John Piper died in 1851 at the age of 78, poor but living comfortably with Mary on a small property at Westbourne near Bathurst.

Despite losing so much over the years at the hands of spongers and so-called friends, it was his true friends from Sydney who finally came to his aid. When he lost his fortune the first time in Sydney, they secretly put away some money for him, knowing that it was only a matter of time before he would be in trouble again. When he lost everything a second time, they used that nest egg to buy John Piper the farm that became his final home and resting place.

THE GOLDEN ARCH

A standard joke in broadcasting is about the journalist who asks, 'What do you think of Australia?' of a visiting celebrity who has just stepped off the plane.

'I love it so far, but I just got here,' is the usual response.

How anyone would know what Longreach is like by visiting Adelaide, or what Launceston is like by visiting Perth is beyond me. But people often form opinions of Australia based on very limited experience.

That is how some of Australia's history was written.

BEFORE CHARLES DARWIN became an evolutionist, he attended medical school and theological college. But he didn't want to be a doctor or a minister of religion; his passion was for zoology and geography.

In 1831, Charles learned that a 26-year-old naval officer named Robert FitzRoy was about to leave on a voyage of world exploration. He was looking for a young, well-educated gentleman to be the naturalist and scientist on the trip and to provide companionship – sharing the Captain's table and relieving the loneliness of command with intellectual conversation.

Charles presented his credentials and was signed on to the crew of HMS *Beagle* for a five-year journey to South America and Australia.

Charles Darwin was not overly complimentary after his three-month visit to Australia in 1836, although in his own words, 'Of course, after so very short a visit, one's opinion is worth scarcely anything . . .'

The then 27-year-old visited Sydney, Bathurst, Hobart and Albany, in Western Australia. He made several excursions into the bush to study flora and fauna as well as the geography and geology of the areas near the settlements of the colonies. But by the time he reached Albany, he had seen enough and was ready to leave.

'Farewell, Australia!' Darwin wrote in his diary on 14 March 1836:

> You are a rising child, and doubtless some day will reign a great princess of the South: but you are too great and ambitious for affection, yet not great enough for respect. I leave your shores without sorrow or regret.

Even though he was required to be everything on the *Beagle* except a sociologist, Charles Darwin declared that the three things he was most interested in observing in Australia were the state of society among the higher classes, the condition of the convicts and the degree of attraction sufficient to induce persons to emigrate. There appeared little scientific rigour in his examination of our society.

'On the whole, from what I heard, more than from what I saw, I was disappointed in the state of society,' Charles wrote in his diary. 'The whole population, poor and rich, are bent on acquiring wealth . . .' He went on to note:

> On the whole I do not like New South Wales. It is no doubt an admirable place to accumulate pounds and shillings; but heaven forbid that I should live where every man is sure be somewhere between a petty rogue and a bloodthirsty villain.

In Darwin's view, Sydney had too many alehouses, Bathurst was too hot and dusty, Hobart was pretty but primitive, and Albany was the most boring place he had ever visited.

Charles Darwin did have some kind things to say about Australia as well: he thought the climate was 'splendid and perfectly healthy'; that some of the countryside was 'picturesque'; and that the views in the Blue Mountains were, in places, 'stupendous'. Nevertheless, the final image he took with him back to England was of a desolate and untidy place where he would only live if forced by extreme circumstances. He was unlikely to be a promoter of migration to Australia.

Charles Darwin's words would have had his paternal grandfather, Erasmus Darwin – himself a doctor, writer and philosopher – turning in his grave. Erasmus Darwin had written a glowing poem about Australia called 'Visit of Hope to Sydney Cove, near Botany Bay' for the preface of a book entitled *The Voyage of*

Governor Phillip to Botany Bay, which was published in London in 1789, 47 years before his grandson's visit to our shores. Erasmus was asked to write the poem by his good friend and business partner, Josiah Wedgwood, who was also a grandfather to Charles Darwin. Josiah's daughter had married Erasmus's son, and Charles was among their offspring.

Josiah Wedgwood had been commissioned by Sir Joseph Banks – botanist on Cook's *Endeavour* and, by 1790, President of the Royal Society – to take some white clay brought from Sydney Cove by Arthur Phillip and see if it was suitable for pottery. Wedgwood produced a medallion designed by his leading artist, Henry Webber. It represented the figure of Hope encouraging Art and Labour under the influence of Peace. The date, 1789, was inscribed with the word 'Etruria', the location of the Wedgwood factory.

Josiah asked Erasmus to write a short verse to accompany the medallion in its box. Darwin senior found his inspiration in Arthur Phillip's diary and Wedgwood's design. But there's always more to the story, isn't there?

Charles Darwin's paternal grandfather, Erasmus, was an inventor and scientist. He was often described as 'a man of great vision'. Who would argue with that statement after reading the poem about Sydney that he wrote more than 200 years ago, especially the lines:

There the proud arch, colossus-like, bestride
Yon glittering streams, and bound the chaffing tide

A proud and colossal arch? There is only one proud and colossal arch in Sydney – the Sydney Harbour Bridge. But surely that could not be what Erasmus Darwin envisaged; he had never been to Sydney, and the Sydney Harbour Bridge was not built for another 140 years!

HAIL TO THE CHIEF

Sometimes our lives are inextricably linked, but it takes history to reveal it and then to explain it.

This is the story of one of the most influential figures of the early 20th century and his links with Australia; connections that would cement his reputation and probably save his life.

It is one of my favourite stories because it came as such a surprise when I first discovered it a few years ago, and also because it is a reminder we shouldn't underestimate the impact this young country of ours has had on world events and world figures.

HE CALLED HIMSELF 'Bert'. But the tough gold-miners who came and went from Coolgardie and Kalgoorlie in 1897 called him 'The Chief' or 'Hail Columbia'. The brash 23-year-old American was something of a curiosity in outback Australia in the late 19th century. But the miners teased him with a mixture of amusement and respect.

Bert had come to Australia representing leading London mining firm Bewick, Moreing and Company.

With little more than a geology degree from Stanford University and a job shovelling ore in a California mine, he had answered a newspaper advertisement for an experienced geologist of at least 35 years and with a 'lifetime of experience' for an assignment in Australia. He bought a tweed dress suit and a top hat to make himself look older, and forged an impressive resumé. It fooled the principals of the London firm, and Bert soon found himself in one of the world's most remote goldfields carrying great expectations of success.

The tough prospectors didn't understand much of what Bert said, but they liked the way he handled adversity: no spare water, so he bathed in beer; little fresh food, so he got by on tins of sardines and cocoa; no transport, so Bert rode a camel. His ingenuity would have come as no surprise to people who knew of Bert's strict Quaker upbringing. His father was a blacksmith and a disciplinarian. Once, when little Bert stood on a white-hot branding iron, his father told him it would remind him for life where he came from. His father died when Bert was six, his mother when he was 11. The orphaned Bert went to live with a doctor uncle in Oregon, where he was educated and trained in book-keeping and business.

It was in Oregon that young Bert first discovered Australia – in the stories of Charles Dickens. Most Dickens books had some reference to Australia, especially Bert's favourite, *David Copperfield*, which featured the Micawbers, the Peggottys and Mrs Gummidge, who all emigrated to Australia. Bert began to fantasise about adventures on the other side of the world. When he saw the advertisement from Bewick's, he could hardly contain his surprise.

While Bert may have connived his way to Australia, he soon justified the faith shown by Bewick's in his skill as a mining geologist. Within a year, he had discovered what he predicted would be one of the richest gold veins in the world and convinced his company to pay the then extraordinary sum of $1 million for the unproven lease. That lease became known as the Sons of Gwalia mine and to date it has returned the original investment hundreds of times over.

There's always more to the story. After his Gwalia success, Bert's grateful employers doubled his salary to $10,000 a year, paid for his wedding to his university sweetheart, Lou Henry, and sent him off to China for a new challenge. Bert and his bride arrived just in time to become involved in the Boxer Rebellion and the siege of Tientsin. But once again, fate played a hand. Bert and Lou, along with hundreds of other foreigners in Tientsin, were rescued and then protected by sailors from New South Wales and Victoria – part of a contingent sent to help the English put down the rebellion. Australia had once again played a key role in Bert's life.

After China he went to Burma before returning to Australia in 1905 to manage Bewick's interests for another two years. Then he established his own mining company and became the world's most famous mining consultant, with 175,000 employees on three continents. He was now also a multi-millionaire.

But Bert had some more surprises in store. As Europe was torn apart by war in 1914, he launched a personal humanitarian campaign to feed the homeless and displaced on both sides. He continued his work after the Armistice in 1918 and is credited with feeding billions of people in 57 countries, including during the aftermath of World War II.

Bert's simple philosophy was that business had to be balanced with responsibility for the welfare of others. He carried that philosophy into politics and into the White House as the 31st President of the United States of America.

Herbert (Bert) Clark Hoover won office in a 1928 landslide but became the scapegoat for the Great Depression of the 1930s. Ironically, he was blamed for putting millions of his countrymen out of work.

He died in 1964 with much of his reputation restored, thanks to his stubborn determination to keep going despite adversity.

Through it all, Bert Hoover never forgot the part that Australia played in his remarkable life. Especially his nicknames – 'The Chief' and 'Hail Columbia'. Coincidentally, these were two names that would resurface 32 years later whenever he walked into a room and the band would strike up the presidential tune 'Hail to the Chief'.

Herbert Hoover pictured in 1898 after his success in Australia.

HELENA TITUS

I am married to the most beautiful woman in the world and I fall in love with her all over again every time she does something different with her hair or wears a dress or a scarf in a slightly different way. I just adore the way women are able to transform themselves time and again.

We're no different from any other family – we drag out the old photograph albums occasionally and give each other a ribbing about the flares and body shirts or the miniskirts and beehive hairstyles. But, for all the laughing, every time I look at those old photos of the Princess, I feel the same flutter in my chest that I felt when the photograph was originally taken.

We might grow older, but hopefully we grow old graciously as well as gracefully. I know in the case of my darling wife, it is also beautifully.

HELENA DIDN'T WANT to be a doctor. Chemicals and laboratories made her physically ill, and the university medical school that she attended was in Switzerland, far from her family in Krakow, Poland. But her wealthy merchant father, Horace, insisted that, as the eldest of eight daughters, Helena had to set the example for the others.

A headstrong young woman, when Helena returned home in 1901 during university holidays, she told her father she was not going back. He was furious. Without her knowledge, he arranged her marriage to a widower friend in the Jewish community. But 18-year-old Helena had no intention of getting married, and certainly not to her father's friend, who was in his thirties. So Horace's plans came to nothing.

As a beautiful young woman, she was besieged by handsome Polish army officers, so her family decided to send her as far away as possible while she cleared her head and considered her priorities. Helena left Poland in 1902 for Coleraine, in country Victoria, to live with an uncle and cousins and to work in their family grocery store. It was a long way from Poland and Switzerland – in more ways than one.

Helena's mother, Augusta, had heard from her relatives that the Australian sun was savage, so she packed some jars of face cream for Helena – it was a special-formula moisturiser developed by Augusta's pharmacist for a friend who was a famous Polish actress.

When Helena heard so many women coming into the shop at Coleraine complaining about sun-damaged skin, she remembered her mother's cream and hit on the idea of selling some of it. Soon Helena was sending telegrams to her mother requesting more jars of the cream, and it became a thriving business. She even opened a store in Melbourne selling just one thing – her 'Crème Valaze'. Helena added value for customers by giving personal advice on skin care and treatment.

At first she imported the creams and lotions from Poland with the help of her father's trading company, but eventually she set up a manufacturing plant in Melbourne and arranged for the industrial chemist who developed the first secret formula for her mother to migrate to Australia to work with her in the business.

Ceska, one of Helena's seven sisters, joined her in 1908 and took over management of the shop in Melbourne while another sister, Regena, went to Sydney and set up operations in Pitt Street above what is now the Soul Pattinson pharmacy.

With the Australian business in the hands of her sisters, Helena went back to Europe to study dermatology with some of the world's leading medical specialists. Then she went to London to try to break into the European market. With the profit she had made from her Australian operations she opened a beauty salon in London in 1908. Shortly afterwards, she met an American journalist named Edward Titus, whom she married that same year. Edward and Helena moved to Paris, where she set up another exclusive salon in 1912 and started a family with two sons.

When World War I broke out, Edward moved Helena and the boys to the United States. It turned out to be an opportunity for even greater success, as she opened a chain of salons in 1914 in Chicago, Boston, Los Angeles and, eventually, New York. In 1917, Helena began wholesale distribution of her face creams, lotions and skin care products.

By the time she died in 1965, aged 92, she was a billionaire and one of the most influential women in the world, with stores on five continents selling her products. Always proudly retaining her maiden name, Helena Rubinstein became one of the most famous names in cosmetics, fragrance and skin care, and survives today as part of the L'Oréal empire. But there's always more to the story, as you'll see.

Helena Rubinstein divorced Edward Titus in 1937 and the following year married Prince Artchil Gourielli-Tchkonia, a Russian prince from Georgia, who was 20 years younger than her. She developed a line of male cosmetics in his name, and they remained happily married until he died in 1956.

Even when it was by accident, Helena Rubinstein was a success story. Once, feeling disillusioned, she sold her business for $7.3 million dollars, only to buy it back for $1.5 million within a year when the 1929 stock-market crash ruined the company that bought her out.

There were tragedies in her personal life, however, for which money could not compensate her – the bitter breakdown of her first marriage to Edward Titus; the death of her second husband, Artchil; and the death, two years later, in 1958, of her younger son, Horace.

But Helena Rubinstein took some consolation from her pain by giving. She established a foundation to promote high achievement in the arts and became one of the most generous philanthropists in the United States, particularly for Jewish causes.

Interestingly, Helena was always frugal in her own life, carrying a packed lunch with her every day of her working life. She lived alone in her final years. In 1963, at the age of 90, she was robbed at gunpoint in her New York apartment.

Although she lived in the United States, Helena Rubinstein always considered herself an Aussie. She regularly visited the country that gave her a start in what became a global business.

To the end, Helena Rubinstein remained as headstrong and opinionated as when she stood up to her father about medical studies. Her most famous quote remains 'There is no such thing as an ugly woman, only a lazy one.'

'HUGE DEAL' McINTOSH

There aren't too many of the big promoters of sport and entertainment who haven't had flops and financial disasters. I have known many who have made bad business decisions. I guess they accept that their business comes with risk.

But the good ones always seem to bounce back – some because they are battlers, others because they have the gift of the gab.

I think our Australian entrepreneurs and promoters are all terrific. Without them we wouldn't have big-scale entertainment and concert tours, the international circuses and the sporting spectaculars. I don't mind one bit that they make a dollar for the risks they take.

I just think it's a shame they have to share the industry with that American boxing promoter Don King.

NEXT TIME YOU see a meat pie, think of Hugh McIntosh. He didn't invent them, but he did make a lot of money out of them.

Hugh was born in Sydney in 1876 and educated at the Marist Brothers' College. After he left school, he worked at various jobs, including a stint as a miner in

Broken Hill, before becoming a chorus boy. But the theatre didn't pay enough for Hugh, so he turned to bread-carting then pie-vending in Sydney in the 1890s. Before long there were white-coated piemen at racecourses, beaches and parks all over Sydney – and all of them were working for Hugh Donald McIntosh.

His pie business grew into a catering business, which, in turn, grew into a chain of restaurants, and that developed into a promotions business. Hugh McIntosh became known as 'Huge Deal' McIntosh.

McIntosh filled the Sydney Cricket Ground when he offered a thousand-sovereign purse for a one-mile (1.6 kilometre) world championship bicycle sprint. The best in the world turned up to race, including a black American named Taylor, who was considered the fastest cyclist in the world on the day.

Then, in 1908, he staged a boxing match in Sydney between the world champion, Tommy Burns from America, and Australian Bill Squires. It was fought in a ring constructed on a leased market garden in Rush-cutters Bay. After a sell-out, McIntosh set about arranging an even bigger fight, this time between Tommy Burns and black American boxer Jack Johnson. It was the first time in a major professional bout that anyone had matched a black man against a white. McIntosh himself refereed the fight to ensure fair play. It drew a huge crowd and international media attention. The gate receipts were a world record £26,000. McIntosh was so encouraged by his success and his new fortune that he built a permanent boxing venue on the Rushcutters site and called it Sydney Stadium.

Within a few years he had made more than a quarter of a million pounds from his boxing promotions. Then, in 1913 he sold the stadium to concentrate on the Tivoli Theatre, which he had bought a few years earlier; he was still a chorus boy at heart. His stage productions, like his boxing matches, were hugely successful. McIntosh used the profits from his stage shows to buy newspapers – first the Sydney *Sunday Times*, then the *Referee*.

In 1917, Hugh McIntosh was so influential in Sydney that he was appointed to the New South Wales Legislative Council. It was at this time that he became involved in one of the most shameful stories of Australian sporting history. In the midst of a war of words between the Catholic Archbishop of Melbourne, Daniel Mannix, and Australian Prime Minister Billy Hughes over the war in Europe and conscription, Hugh McIntosh was convinced by a political powerbroker named John Wren to blackball brilliant young New South Wales middleweight boxer Les Darcy.

Darcy had resisted volunteering to fight in World War I. He was underage and could not convince his mother to sign the recruitment papers. But that didn't stop him being blackballed by Hughes and those supporting the war and conscription, who labelled him a 'traitor'.

Hugh McIntosh used his newspapers to run a campaign against Darcy. He also used his strong connections in American boxing to stop Darcy getting any fights until he signed up for military service. In the end, Darcy relinquished and volunteered for the American Army. Sadly, he developed blood poisoning from a dental procedure carried out on teeth damaged in an earlier fight and died before donning a uniform.

Whether it was because of the backlash over Darcy's death or not is unclear, but at about this time, Hugh McIntosh decided to pursue his real dream of fame and fortune in England. He set himself up in luxurious surroundings at Broome Park, the former residence of the famous general Lord Kitchener. One of his first actions was to replace the cricket pitch on the estate with soil shipped from Sydney.

McIntosh lived an extravagant lifestyle in England, entertaining and bankrolling major boxing tournaments and harebrained ideas such as breeding Angora rabbits on Broome Park. Instead of the success he found in Australia, he ended up in bankruptcy.

But there is always more to the story. Hugh McIntosh might have been broke, but he still had ideas. He returned to Sydney and built up a chain of cake shops. In 1935, he took his profits and went back to England, determined to succeed, this time with a string of 500 milk bars to be called 'Black and White' – no doubt capitalising on his fame as the promoter of the world's first professional boxing match between black and white men. But again, he lost everything and died in 1942 without achieving his dream.

In Australia, Hugh McIntosh could not put a foot

wrong. He made pie-vending a respectable business. He brought world-class sport to Australia. He was the father of professional boxing and the Sydney Stadium. He even pioneered big-stage productions in Australia. Yet, for all his success, he was consumed by his failures in England. He had never failed like he failed in England.

The irony of the story is that when Hugh McIntosh died in 1942, he was penniless. His friends paid for his funeral – in England, the country that refused to let him succeed.

AN IMPOSSIBLE POSITION

The human mind is an extraordinary instrument – extremely powerful and versatile, yet very delicate and easily broken.

Those comments you hear almost every day such as 'Oh, she's paranoid,' or 'He doesn't handle pressure well,' or 'He's very highly strung,' illustrate just how many of us need to take better care of ourselves.

Even the most brilliant and steely mind can falter. During wartime this is called battle fatigue, afterwards it is known as post-traumatic stress disorder, and in peacetime it is usually referred to as a mental breakdown. Sometimes there is no apparent warning of what is coming.

Suffering anxiety or mental fatigue is nothing to be ashamed about, but it is something to take seriously and to treat. Otherwise the consequences can be disastrous, as this story shows.

WHEN 16-YEAR-OLD Charles Yelverton O'Connor decided that he wanted to be an engineer, he could not have imagined how far from his native County Meath in Ireland he would confront his greatest challenge, and what a price he would pay for success.

After completing his studies at Dublin University, Charles worked on the Irish railways. One day he saw a newspaper report about gold being discovered in New Zealand and within days he had applied to emigrate. He was 21. During the next 26 years, Charles O'Connor built a reputation as New Zealand's most dynamic and innovative public works and marine engineer. He was involved in major construction projects in both the North and South Islands, including development of new ports and harbours. But in 1891, amid financial crisis for the New Zealand Government, his works programs were cut drastically and his salary was reduced.

At the same time, the West Australian Government of Sir John Forrest stepped in to offer Charles a five-year contract worth 25 per cent more than his New Zealand salary if he would move across the Tasman and continue his work. He eventually accepted the WA offer when it was increased a further 20 per cent.

When Charles O'Connor arrived in Perth, he was told that his priorities were an all-weather port for the state capital and improvements to the primitive railway network. Perth had been using Albany, 400 kilometres away, as its port and relying on rail to carry freight to and from the ships. Charles soon discovered that the port that had been chosen for him to develop faced west into the Indian Ocean and the prevailing wind, had a dangerously shallow entrance and was some distance from Perth. He also learned that the WA Government owned just 300 kilometres of railway line

– all of which was poorly constructed and of varying gauge – and totally inadequate rolling stock and locomotives. It was going to take time and money as well as skill to deliver the results on these projects.

The experience that Charles O'Connor had gained building harbours on the west coast of New Zealand's North Island would come in handy. He soon drew up a plan to dredge the entrance to the Swan River and build two long breakwaters out to sea to give safe entrance to Fremantle Harbour. Within two years, he had cleared the way for large ships to berth at the new wharves.

His next objective was the railways. In five years, he trebled the rail line in Western Australia and designed and built the Midland Junction rail workshops. He had extended the railways into the new, booming goldfields near Kalgoorlie and Coolgardie and was looking at plans for a transcontinental rail link.

But an unexpected problem had arisen – a problem that would challenge even Charles O'Connor's engineering skills. By 1896 there were more than 4000 people living in Coolgardie, with thousands more settling in Kalgoorlie. The goldrush had brought people from all over the world. There was only one problem – there was no water for them.

Hundreds of prospectors died in Coolgardie during a drought when they drank stagnant water from the Coolgardie Gorge in desperation. Typhoid, dysentry and cholera were claiming victims every day in the gold cities. Drinking water was being sold for the equivalent of a dollar a litre.

Charles O'Connor pictured in the 1890s soon after he arrived in Western Australia.

But the news got worse. The new rail services into the region were grinding to a halt without water for the steam locomotives' boilers. Even with specially converted tanker carriages, they could not carry enough to get to the goldfields and back to Perth. Attempts to build giant reservoirs at key points along the track failed as drought stole the supplies.

Charles O'Connor was Chief Public Works Engineer and it was up to him to devise a plan to get almost a million litres of water a day to Coolgardie and Kalgoorlie and meet demand.

He came up with a daring plan to build a new dam in the Darling Range, east of Perth. Water would then be moved hundreds of metres uphill through eight steam-powered pumping stations and along a 600-kilometre pipeline to the gold cities.

The project was so unlike anything attempted anywhere in the world that it drew the inevitable doubters. Critics soon surfaced in the Parliament and the media. They condemned the plan as ludicrous and unworkable.

Approval for money for the dams and pumping stations was slow as the political in-fighting began. Equipment was slow in coming from the USA, UK and Europe. And, just to add to the headaches, the new Federal Government decided to impose customs tariff on all the equipment, adding £100,000 to the final bill.

As the years wore on and the project encountered problem after problem, Charles O'Connor was accused of wasting money, risking lives, ruining farms and failing to compensate landowners properly for resumed property.

In the end the criticism turned to accusations of corruption. This was the last straw for a man committed to efficiency and honesty. O'Connor went to England to consult the most prestigious college of engineers in the world. They gave his project their approval and confirmed his budget estimates. While in London, the Prince of Wales invested Charles with the Order of St Michael and St George on behalf of Queen Victoria as recognition of his outstanding work on Fremantle Harbour. But none of this stopped the critics in Perth.

So, on 10 March 1902, Charles O'Connor rose early and went to his study. He took a pen and paper and wrote a note that began: 'The position has become impossible.' He finished the note, saddled his favourite horse and rode to South Beach, Fremantle, within sight of the harbour he had built. He rode the horse into the shallows of the beach and shot himself.

But there's always more to the story.

Charles O'Connor was buried in the cemetery in Palmyra, overlooking Fremantle Harbour. He left a wife and seven children, an estate worth only little more than £10,000, and a suicide note. In typical fashion, in that note he gave detailed instructions for the completion of the Coolgardie pipeline, including the Mundaring Weir.

Within a year of his suicide, the goldfield pipeline was finished. Water flowed in Coolgardie three days before Christmas in 1902 and in Kalgoorlie a month later.

Despite all the critics and all the doubters, it was completed on time and only slightly over O'Connor's original estimate. The sole blowout in the budget was caused by the federal customs tariff, added after the project started.

The Coolgardie pipeline remains one of Australia's – and the world's – greatest engineering feats.

INDIAN RUBBER BRACES

If I were asked what the most popular breed of animal is in Australia today, I would have to say scapegoats. We must have one of the world's biggest breeding programs because we don't have any trouble finding one when the need arises.

I'm not sure when it started, but Australians today just seem to love finding someone to blame – whether they are at fault or not.

One of the many lessons I have learned after 50 years on radio is that it is often the innocent who get the blame while the uninvolved take the credit.

The most dangerous by-product of scapegoating is a tendency to punish to the extent necessary to placate those who have been offended or wronged, rather than to the extent warranted by the circumstances. Here is a story of such a situation.

QUEEN VICTORIA'S SECOND son, Prince Alfred, Duke of Edinburgh, was 23 years old when he visited Australia for six months in the summer of 1867–68 as Captain of the Royal Navy frigate HMS *Galatea* on a world tour that included Adelaide, Melbourne and Brisbane and two visits to Sydney.

Prince Alfred, Duke of Edinburgh, in the uniform of Admiral of the Royal Navy (possibly with braces) circa 1887.

He arrived in Australia from South Africa, dropping anchor at Glenelg, near Adelaide, on 31 October 1867. This was the first visit to Australia by a member of the royal family and cause for great ceremony and celebration in the colonies.

From Adelaide, Alfred sailed to Sydney and Brisbane, then back to Melbourne. In March 1868, he charmed Melbournians by taking part in a parade through the city then attending a cricket match at the MCG. From Melbourne, he returned to Sydney for a more formal second visit. On 12 March 1868, Prince Alfred was invited to a Masonic Lodge picnic at Clontarf Beach to the south of the colony to help raise funds for the Sydney Sailors' Home. After finishing his lunch, the prince rose from the table to make a presentation of cash to the President of the Home, Sir William Montague Manning. As he walked towards Manning, a man rushed forward and shot him at close range in the back.

As the prince fell, the gunman, Henry James O'Farrell, raised his pistol for a second shot at point-blank range, but the gun misfired. The Grand Master of the Lodge, William Vial, rushed to shield the prince as Sir William Manning and some bystanders wrestled the would-be assassin to the ground. As they struggled, another shot rang out and William Vial also fell wounded.

Prince Alfred was rushed to a nearby tent, where Royal Navy surgeons who were accompanying him on the world tour were able to assess his injury quickly. Meanwhile, the crowd began beating O'Farrell, even trying to lynch him. Police intervened and dragged him away, bloodied and unconscious.

Prince Alfred was taken back to HMS *Galatea*, where a bullet was removed from his back. He was then returned to shore and into the care of three of Florence Nightingale's most experienced nurses, who had just arrived in Sydney to set up the first training school for nursing.

The Lady Superintendent of the Sydney Infirmary, Miss Lucy Osburn, led the team looking after the prince. She was a protégé of Florence Nightingale and had been trained in the techniques for treatment of gunshot wounds developed by Nightingale on the battlefields of the Crimea.

Word spread quickly of the shooting and that it had been carried out by an Irish Catholic linked to the Fenian rebel movement. Alfred was not only Duke of Edinburgh but also Earl of Ulster and a leader in the Protestant Church of England. More than 20,000 people attended an 'Indignation Meeting' in Sydney the next day. Colonial Secretary, Sir Henry Parkes, fuelled the Fenian theory and promised to conduct a personal investigation to get to the bottom of the conspiracy theories.

When it emerged that O'Farrell was from Melbourne, some newspapers claimed that Victoria was to blame for the embarrassment caused to New South Wales. The *Sydney Morning Herald* pleaded for calm and respect for the process of law amid increasing calls for O'Farrell to be hanged immediately.

Three weeks after the incident, Henry James O'Farrell confessed to the shooting and said that he acted alone out of resentment at the treatment of the Irish at the hands of the British. He denied any involvement with the Fenians.

Prince Alfred recovered fully within a month and resumed command of his ship for the return voyage to England.

In spite of strong evidence that O'Farrell was insane, he was convicted of attempted murder and hanged at Darlinghurst Gaol on 21 April 1868.

William Vial, the man who was shot while shielding

the prince, survived his wounds and was presented with a claret jug and some money in gratitude for his bravery. He donated the money to a fund for a large and permanent monument expressing the gratitude of the people of New South Wales for the recovery of Prince Alfred. That was the beginning of Royal Prince Alfred Hospital. A similar fund was launched in Melbourne at the same time and that launched the Alfred Hospital in the southern capital.

But that is not the entire story – there's always more. Some say Prince Alfred was saved by William Vial, who shielded him. Others say it was the misfiring pistol that prevented a second, fatal shot. Still others credit Sir William Montague Manning, who tackled O'Farrell to the ground. But the Royal Navy surgeons who treated the Duke of Edinburgh immediately after the shooting had a very different theory.

They found that O'Farrell's bullet had entered the prince's back just centimetres from his spine, travelled around his rib, and then lodged in his right abdomen. Amazingly, no vital organs had been damaged and his spine was intact. It was a miraculous escape.

The official report of the surgeons reveals the reason for the miracle. It says that the prince was saved from serious and possibly fatal injury by . . . his royal braces. O'Farrell's bullet struck the prince's Indian rubber braces at their thickest point, deflecting its path from the spine and heart.

KABBARLI

I don't understand why we still have not solved the problems in Aboriginal health and welfare.

I have been talking about these issues on my radio program for at least 30 years, maybe longer, with people like Pat Dodson and Aboriginal advocate Noel Pearson, whom I respect.

Is it because we haven't devoted enough resources to them? Or is it because we still don't understand the issues underlying the problems? I don't know. If I did, you can bet I would be telling the governments who have grappled with these issues for more than two centuries how to fix them.

Unfortunately, it is not just this generation that has struggled with this issue. Some remarkable Australians have devoted their entire lives to trying to solve Aboriginal health and welfare problems. This is the story of one woman's amazing battle to try to make a difference.

THE ABORIGINES OF Western Australia and remote South Australia called her 'Kabbarli', meaning 'Grandmother'. Stockmen on her 90,000 hectare cattle station called her 'Boss'. But to friends and admirers, she was just plain Daisy Bates. She was born Daisy May O'Dwyer in Tipperary, Ireland, in 1859. Her mother died when she was five and her father died when she was in her early teens.

At 24, Daisy was diagnosed with tuberculosis and sent to Australia, where doctors hoped a warmer climate would help clear her diseased lungs. Townsville and Charters Towers, in North Queensland, came as quite a shock to a beautiful young woman used to the nightlife of Dublin and London. But Daisy was determined to beat her illness and she persevered in the north, working as a governess for almost a year.

No sooner was she given a clean bill of health by doctors than she headed south to Berry, near Nowra, on the New South Wales south coast. There she worked as governess to the children of the Bates family. Daisy fell in love with the eldest son of the family, John (Jack) Bates, and they married in 1885. Daisy and John had a son within a year, but the marriage fell apart when Jack refused to give up droving to settle with his wife and child.

Following a bitter split with Jack, Daisy was determined to reclaim her life. In 1894 she left her seven-year-old son, Arnold, with the Bates family and went to England, where she blazed a trail through the exclusively male profession of journalism.

It was five years before Daisy Bates returned to Australia to reunite with her son and re-establish contact with Jack Bates. Soon after arriving from

London, she was commissioned by *The Times* newspaper to write a series of articles about allegations of settlers' cruelty to Aborigines in the north of Western Australia. Daisy reported to *The Times* readers that the stories of cruelty were untrue. But in conducting her investigation, she was shocked to see the poor health and welfare of remote Aborigines.

After finishing her reports for *The Times*, Daisy stayed on in the outback, living and working with Aboriginal tribes. She lived on missions near Broome, compiled dictionaries of Aboriginal languages and wrote reports for the West Australian Government, all the time dressed neatly in an Edwardian skirt with high-collared blouse and a hat.

Jack Bates bought a property called Ethel Creek station in the Ophthalmia Ranges near Peak Downs on the Murchison River in the hope that it would give him and Daisy a chance to form a family again with young Arnold.

But Jack was drinking heavily and by 1902, 39-year-old Daisy realised that her marriage was doomed. She was determined that when the inevitable happened she would be able to survive alone in the bush. She convinced Jack, who was one of the best drovers in Western Australia, that they could make a small fortune by buying cattle from properties at Roebuck Plains near Broome, where she had been working, and bringing them overland more than 1000 kilometres to Ethel Creek.

Jack, Daisy and 15-year-old Arnold left their homestead in April 1902 for what would be a 4800 kilometre, six-month round trip to bring 770 Hereford cattle south through the Kimberleys. Daisy rode the whole way side-saddle.

They made a profit of a thousand pounds on the venture, but lost 200 head on the way. Daisy blamed Jack for taking inexperienced drovers, insufficient horses and no dogs. Because of his poor planning, they worked 18 hours a day and lost weeks trying to find water when wells were dry along the route. It was the final straw for the marriage. Jack and Daisy went their own ways and legally separated in 1912.

When Daisy Bates died in Adelaide in 1951, at the age of 92, she left behind an extraordinary legacy in the form of her library of writings about Aboriginal people and their customs. Wherever she camped in the bush, Aborigines would come from miles around to sit down with the woman in the big dress. She was trusted and loved because she respected Aboriginal custom and tradition. She was particularly committed to the young, the elderly and the sick. That's why they called her 'Grandmother'. When she died, Aboriginal leaders from throughout Australia stood at her grave and celebrated her passing into the next life. But you haven't heard all of this story yet.

There was no doubt that Daisy Bates had a gift for dealing with people – well, most people. She was the first to admit that she failed dismally with her two husbands. Yes, two husbands. Jack Bates, the cattleman, was her second husband. Daisy had an earlier, and even unhappier, marriage. Her first husband was an Englishman named Edwin Murrunt. They met in Charters Towers when she first arrived to recuperate from TB. They fell madly in love and married on a whim. But the marriage lasted just weeks because Daisy found she could not live with Edwin's unpredictable ways. A month after the wedding he was arrested and charged with stealing a saddle and some pigs. He was acquitted a week later, but Daisy had left him. Edwin later died in the Boer War. He was executed on order of a court martial for killing Boer prisoners of war.

You probably know the story of Daisy's first husband, although you probably wouldn't know him as Edwin Murrunt. He used a different name in Queensland, where he worked as a horse breaker. He called himself Harry 'Breaker' Morant. Yes, Daisy Bates, 'Grandmother' to the Aboriginal people of Western and South Australia, was also Mrs Edwin Henry Morant.

KING OF THE DUFFERS

Australians often draw a fine line between larrikinism and vandalism, and between opportunism and crime.

Someone climbing the roof of the Opera House for a school break-up-day dare is probably going to invite a shake of the head and pity for their stupidity, whereas a person who climbs up there to write slogans in paint on the expensive ceramic tiles will be viewed as a criminal.

It's the same with the tax office and the banks – we love to see someone get one back on the biggest bushrangers in the country, but we wouldn't condone people defrauding them.

We have the law, and we have what is right and wrong. It's a shame the two aren't one and the same.

THERE WAS LITTLE love lost between the 'haves' and the 'have-nots' in Australia's early years. That's why settlers – many of them ex-convicts – often protected and even encouraged bushrangers. It's also why the crime of cattle stealing – called 'duffing' – was so widely tolerated. Some said it dated back to the days of the first settlement, when food was in short supply and desperate families drove cattle off government grazing areas and slaughtered them for the meat. Even when the case was strong, juries in the bush were unlikely to convict duffers. There's no better example of this phenomenon than the case of Harry Redford, the man they called 'King of the Cattle Duffers'.

Henry Arthur Readford was born in the Hawkesbury area north of Sydney in 1842. His father was an ex-convict and his mother a poor young local girl. In 1869, and now known as 'Redford', the 17-year-old Harry and four mates left New South Wales for Queensland, where they worked hauling produce from Tambo to Bowen Downs, one of the largest cattle stations in Australia. It was north of Longreach and stretched 200 kilometres across, covered 3 million hectares and carried more than 60,000 head of prime cattle.

In March 1870, Redford hatched a plan to steal a thousand head of mixed cattle from Bowen Downs and drive them 1300 kilometres to South Australia, where he could sell them without the brand being recognised. Harry and his men took the cattle along the Thompson, Barcoo, Cooper and Strzelecki rivers – a previously unknown route that provided the cattle with water all the way. It was a route that would later be known as the Strzelecki Track. Attempting the Queensland-to-South-Australia trip was either very foolish or very daring because it was the same trip that took the lives of Burke and Wills.

But Redford and his small gang made it to Blanche Water station in South Australia and sold the cattle for

£5000 before heading for Adelaide to celebrate. It was there that they were eventually arrested and transported back to Queensland to stand trial in Roma.

The trial drew a large crowd, who were entertained by a spectacle to rival any ever seen in Queensland. Forty-eight potential jurors were called, and one after another 41 of them were discharged on the basis of likely prejudice in favour of Redford. When the trial finally began, the evidence against the cattle duffers was overwhelming and not a single witness was called by the defence. Yet, after just one hour of deliberation, the jury returned a finding of 'Not guilty – but he should return the stock'.

The crowd outside the courthouse cheered, the judge chastised the jury, and Harry Redford and his gang walked free. But you haven't heard all of this story yet; there's more.

Harry Redford thought he had pulled off the perfect crime when he sold the stolen cattle from Bowen Downs in the north of South Australia. Surely no-one would think of looking for them so far away from Central Queensland. But he had made two mistakes. The first was to steal the cattle from the Bowen Downs yards; an overseer spotted the tracks around the yards and was suspicious because the wet season had just finished and the yards had not yet been used. The station manager and the overseer then followed the tracks all the way to Hill Hill station in north-eastern South Australia, where Harry Redford's second mistake was all too visible. There in the paddocks of

Hill Hill, the overseer spotted the very large and very distinctive pure white stud bull that Bowen Downs had recently imported from England. Redford had sold the bull to buy provisions for the rest of the trip.

If this duffing story sounds familiar, it's probably because you've read something very similar in Rolf Boldrewood's classic novel *Robbery Under Arms*. In that novel, a Redford-like character was called Captain Starlight. But what you won't read in the book is the bizarre but true story of the white bull's role in Harry Redford's trial. The bull was penned outside the court-house for the duration of the trial and at one stage was even involved in a line-up with 20 other bulls.

By the way, Harry Redford continued cattle and horse stealing after his acquittal. He was arrested and charged several times but, as with the Roma trial, he was found not guilty by a jury each time. His luck finally ran out in Toowoomba in 1877, when he was convicted and sent to prison. After his release, he went on to become a respectable and highly successful cattleman in Far North Queensland and the Gulf Country before moving into the Northern Territory, where he was the first manager of Brunette Downs station.

In an incredible twist, the man who used water to such advantage in 'The Great Cattle Duff of 1870', drowned in the Northern Territory in 1901.

LAST FAREWELL TO MELBOURNE

I don't know exactly how many people I have interviewed during 50 years in radio and television but it would have to be more than 30,000.

People often ask me who I most enjoyed interviewing. Apart from the fact that I can't remember all of them, I usually end up saying that each one was so different from the others that it would be unfair to compare them.

However, I do tell people that there is a handful of interviews I have done that made a lasting impression on me, and they did not always involve people I liked. Each one of those interviews involved someone with a larger-than-life personality – a persona that not only matched their reputation, but exceeded it to the point where I was totally absorbed by it.

This is the story of such a character from our early colonial days.

THE HISTORY OF the Australian theatre has many famous names, but not all of them are familiar. Take, for example, Gustavus Vaughan Brooke. Hardly a household name today, but in the 1850s a ticket to one of Brooke's performances of Shakespeare was worth gold – literally.

Gustav Brooke was the first internationally recognised actor to perform on the Australian stage. In fact, in 1855, he was the *only* internationally recognised actor to perform on the Australian stage.

That made it all the more unusual that a genuinely famous Shakespearean actor would want to travel to the colonies. And Brooke *was* famous. He had been on the Irish stage since the age of 14, when he performed the role of William Tell. He was still only 17 when he made his London debut in 1834 at the Royal Victoria Theatre.

It was on 3 January 1848 when he appeared in the role of Othello at the Olympic Theatre that he made his name in English theatre. He was a triumph; comparisons were made between him and the great Edmund Kean. Brooke later toured the United States of America in that same role.

By now Brooke was one of England's leading Shakespearean actors, playing leads in *Romeo and Juliet*, *Hamlet*, *Othello* and *Macbeth*. But he was also drinking heavily and living the high life. His voice began to fail, and doctors limited his performance and told him that his failing health would considerably shorten his career. Brooke shrugged them off and went on to even greater success in England, Ireland and the USA.

In 1854, at the height of the gold rush in Victoria, Melbourne promoter George Coppin visited Brooke in London and convinced him to tour Australia. Brooke

A 19th century lithograph of Gustavus Vaughan Brooke in his most popular role of Othello.

agreed to 200 Australian performances of *Othello*, beginning at the Queen's Theatre in Melbourne on 26 February 1855.

The Irishman arrived four days before his first performance was scheduled and immediately fell in love with Melbourne and its people. The infatuation was mutual. His performances were sell-outs and his 200-night booking turned into a six-year tour that took Shakespeare to every established theatre in the country and even to the goldfields, where stages were built specially for him.

The purpose-built venues were not limited to the goldfields. George Coppin shipped a pre-fabricated cast-iron, corrugated iron, timber and glass building from London and constructed it in 30 days, just to show off Brooke's talent. The theatre was called the Olympic.

Critics who saw Brooke perform in Australia said that it was his best work – better even than his triumphant performances in London.

Gustav Brooke made a small fortune, with which he bought the Olympic Theatre, the Theatre Royal and Cremorne Gardens. The Theatre Royal had a stage as large as any in London's West End. But his business partnership with George Coppin fell apart and Brooke was left in the unfamiliar role of managing the Theatre Royal. Within a short time he was penniless and drinking heavily once again.

He went back to England in 1861 to try to revive his European career and regain financial security. But in the English theatre he was a forgotten man. He managed to secure a season at Drury Lane, but was struggling to survive. Without his knowledge, Brooke's wife contacted George Coppin to ask for help. Coppin offered his former partner a two-year season in Australia if he cleaned himself up. Brooke did just that and launched a farewell Irish season in Belfast to large and appreciative audiences.

But there's always more to the story. Gustavus Brooke sailed from Plymouth for Melbourne on the steamship *London* on 1 January 1866, to begin his two-year season in Melbourne. But he never arrived. On 11 January the ship foundered in the Bay of Biscay during a gale, smashing most of the lifeboats and taking heavy seas.

Brooke was one of the first to man the pumps to keep the ship afloat. He continued to pump and lift spirits as women and children were loaded into the only remaining lifeboat. As passengers and crew begged him to join them, Brooke waved them away and continued pumping. A Shakespearean actor to the last, his final words to the survivors were: 'Goodbye. Should you survive, give my last farewell to the people of Melbourne.'

Brooke's wife, Australian actress Avonia Jones, died nine months later of consumption and what her family and doctors described as a 'broken heart'.

Melbourne also mourned Brooke's death. As a tribute to his art and the gift he gave to a young country, the press corps of Melbourne commissioned a bust of Gustavus Brooke and placed it in the Art Gallery of Victoria.

THE LINCOLN CONNECTION

I am going to do a program one day on the difference between a cold and the 'flu'. I don't know how many times people tell me they have a dose of the 'flu'. Sorry, folks, you've almost certainly got a cold; if you had a 'flu' you would be down and out for a couple of weeks.

It's the same with 'fate'. Most of what is described to me as 'fate' is mere coincidence – luck. Fate is to do with destiny.

However, when we were putting this story together I was forced to agree that while one coincidence might be luck, two or three simultaneously could well indicate the hand of fate.

ONE OF THE unexpected benefits that flowed from the Australian gold rushes of the 1850s was the steady stream of famous actors who came from the United Kingdom and the United States of America to perform in our theatres. There was everything from vaudeville to Shakespeare being presented almost every night, not only in Sydney and Melbourne, but on temporary stages in the goldfields. The attraction was the big purses being offered by promoters confident the nouveau riche would snap up the tickets as soon as they went on sale. Grand new theatres such as the Olympic and the Theatre Royal in Melbourne drew some of the biggest names and the biggest crowds of the time.

Two of the stars to arrive in Australia in 1854 were Americans Laura Keene and 20-year-old sensation Edwin Booth. They arrived in Sydney fresh from performances together in San Francisco.

Laura Keene was actually English – her real name was Mary Frances Moss and she took to the stage at 25 without any training after her husband of seven years disappeared, leaving her with two small children. Coincidentally, her estranged husband, the Duke of Wellington's godson, Henry Wellington Taylor, ended up in Australia and with considerable wealth; he came to see her in Sydney to try to win her back. She declined the offer.

Edwin Booth was the second son of famous Shakespearean actor Junius Brutus Booth and had been on stage with his father since the age of 16. After his father died, Edwin stepped into the limelight with roles in *Hamlet*, *Richard III*, *Othello* and *King Lear*. He was destined for stardom when he grabbed the chance to go to Australia.

Laura Keene and Edwin Booth started their Australian tour in Sydney on 23 October 1854. They performed nine plays in 11 nights, including the play that launched Laura Keene in New York, *The Lady of Lyons*, as well as *Hamlet*, *The Stranger* and *Richard III*. Unfortunately, after a full year of performances by big-name artists, the audiences were not as large as expected. So the troupe moved on to Melbourne, where they opened on 20 November. But the problem was the same as in Sydney and so they performed for only five nights before moving out to the goldfields for a couple of performances.

Keene and Booth were very different actors – Booth the Shakespearean lead, Keene the all-round dramatic actress. However, when they returned to San Francisco from Australia in 1855, they continued to work together as Laura moved into production. In San Francisco they starred in *Camille*, with Booth playing Armand. The following year, Laura moved to New York and refurbished the Metropolitan Theatre as Laura Keene's Varieties Theatre, becoming the American theatre's first female producer. Within a few years she built her own new theatre, called simply the Laura Keene Theatre. Her all-star company at that theatre included Edwin Booth.

But there's always more to the story and so it is in this case. When Laura Keene and Edwin Booth toured Australia in 1854, it was the beginning of a link between the two actors that would continue for many years. On Good Friday, 14 April 1865, the connection would become a nightmare for them both.

For seven years from 1858, Laura Keene had starred in a New York hit production called *Our American Cousin*. In 1865, she was invited to reprise her role in a special performance at the Ford Theatre in Washington. In the middle of her performance, a man walked into a private box at the side of the stage and shot dead one of her admiring audience – the President of the United States of America, Abraham Lincoln. As Lincoln fell to the ground with a bullet in his head, the assassin jumped onto the stage in front of Laura Keene. She recognised him immediately as Edwin Booth's brother, John Wilkes Booth. As Booth limped from the theatre with a broken leg, Laura Keene rushed to the President and cradled his head in her arms until he was taken away to hospital, where he died. Both Laura and Edwin Booth were so traumatised by the assassination that they both retired from the theatre. Laura Keene did not perform or produce again in the years before her death in 1873.

Edwin Booth stayed out of the public eye. By chance, his connection with Australia arose again in 1867 when his younger brother Junius Brutus Booth junior married Marian Agnes Land Rookes from Sydney. Agnes had migrated to the United States in 1858 to pursue her acting career. She ended up appearing at Maguire's Opera House in San Francisco, where Junius was the manager of the company. Agnes Booth went on to become a star of American stage and continued performing until she was 53.

Meanwhile, Edwin Booth was lured back onto the stage, where he went from success to success, eventually opening his theatre, the Booth Theatre, in New York in 1868. It seemed the loyal crowds bore him no animosity for his brother's actions.

It is said that until the day he died, Edwin Booth

carried a piece of paper in his pocket; it was a letter from the office of General Ulysses S Grant. Reading that letter seemed to give him comfort as he wrestled daily with the shame of his brother's action in killing President Lincoln.

General Grant's official secretary had written to Edwin Booth on behalf of the White House a year before the Lincoln assassination to thank him for saving the President's son's life. Robert Todd Lincoln had been standing on a New Jersey railway platform late at night waiting for the New-York-to-Washington train. As passengers surged forward to try to buy limited sleeper car tickets from the conductor, Robert was pushed into the gap between the train and the platform. The train began to move and he was about to be crushed, when a hand reached down and grabbed the collar of his coat, dragging him to safety.

Robert Lincoln immediately recognised his rescuer as the famous actor, Edwin Booth, and thanked him. Edwin had no idea of the identity of the young man he had saved until he received the letter of thanks. Now, in his grieving, he took some consolation from the fact that, while his brother had taken the life of a Lincoln, he had saved one.

LIVERPOOL MUTINY

The ANZAC tradition is a cornerstone of our national culture, and we expect everyone who wears an Australian military uniform to uphold and respect it. Having created that expectation, we are always disappointed when we discover that someone in our armed forces falls short of the standard.

However, our army, navy and air force are made up of humans who have the same flaws and frailties as the general population. While the overwhelming majority are outstanding Australians, some drink too much, some use drugs, some are bullies, and some are thieves and rapists.

We should never excuse or ignore inappropriate behaviour to protect the ANZAC tradition; in fact, we reinforce the tradition by being open and honest. However, we should also acknowledge that some of the standards we set for the new ANZACs are higher than those displayed by some of the originals.

St Valentine's Day 1916 is a day that Australia, and Sydney in particular, would rather forget. What started on 14 February ended in a three-day riot involving 15,000 people across several suburbs. The violence came to a head at Central station in the city, where police shot dead one of the troublemakers and wounded another six. Several policemen were also hospitalised.

The trouble began near Liverpool with a protest march by 5000 men. They were joined by another 10,000 as feelings boiled over. Angry mobs broke away from the main protest and stormed hotels and shops in Liverpool's George Street, looting and smashing as they went. Several hundred of the rioters then hijacked trains and headed for Sydney, where armed police – warned of what was coming – waited for them on the railway platforms. It was in the violent battles that followed that a young man was shot in the eye and killed by a police bullet and six others received gunshot wounds.

After the riots were put down, the New South Wales Premier and the Federal Defence Minister blamed the trouble on a combination of alcohol and a small group of agitators who were on the payroll of German agents trying to disrupt the war effort. Few were willing to accept the German conspiracy theory, but most agreed that something had to be done to curtail heavy drinking. Police recommended to the New South Wales Government a change to the opening hours of hotels. As a result, a referendum endorsed a new law introducing six o'clock closing for pubs across the State; that law remained in force until November 1954.

But there's more to the story, as always. The three-day riot that began in Liverpool and ended in Sydney's eastern suburbs shocked Sydney and the nation. It was difficult for a country sacrificing so much to support a war in Europe to understand what possible reason there could be for 15,000 people to wreak havoc on Sydney.

It was even harder to accept that all those involved wore the uniform of the Australian Army!

Australians struggled to reconcile what amounted to a mutiny at home with the stories in the newspapers on the same day of courage and sacrifice in Gallipoli. To make matters worse, this was the second ugly incident involving drunken Australian soldiers in a matter of weeks. In January, near Perth, soldiers ransacked shops and cafes trying to get alcohol late at night. But perhaps the hardest pill to swallow was yet to come, with newspaper reports that the Sydney riots were sparked simply by an order for an extra hour and a half of training each day.

Amid disbelief and calls for urgent political action, the story began to unfold. For weeks, new recruits – all volunteers – had been gathering at Liverpool, Casula, Holdsworthy and the Warwick Farm Racecourse for basic training before embarkation to Gallipoli and France. In the sweltering January and February heat, they had been marched for hours on end around dusty parade grounds, wearing winter uniforms and carrying broomsticks. Most were tough bushmen who signed up for the Light Horse in the hope of getting into battle after reading newspaper reports of the heroic ANZACs. They didn't see much glory in drills and more drills in camps and racecourses in urban New South Wales. In the face of simmering resentment, the army commanders responded by imposing even tighter discipline and extending training programs.

The final straw for the diggers was that the New South Wales Government had imposed six o'clock closing in hotels near to training camps to try to curb the problems. When the order for extra training came down on 14 February 1916, thousands of cavalry troopers stormed into Liverpool and invaded the Commercial and Golden Fleece Hotels, consuming all the alcohol on the premises. They then moved on to Rafferty's Hotel, where they broke down the doors and occupied the bar.

The twist in the story of the Liverpool mutiny was that peace was restored to Sydney by 250 ANZACs, recently returned from Gallipoli, who worked with police to calm the rioters and convince them to return to their camps.

In a striking coincidence, the Liverpool riots happened almost exactly a year after riots involving 5000 Australian troops in Cairo. Those riots also ran for three days and also resulted in one Australian soldier being shot dead.

The soldier killed by police at Sydney's Central station was Private EW Keefe, a reinforcement for the 6th Light Horse, which was suffering heavy casualties at Gallipoli. That regiment, and the soldiers who caused so much trouble in Sydney, would go on to fight some of the most famous mounted battles of

World War I, including the Charge at Beersheba and the Battle for Gaza.

During five years in action, the 6th Light Horse lost 134 killed and 461 wounded, and had 16 taken as prisoners of war. The regiment won 29 bravery decorations. Private Keefe was the only soldier the regiment lost before it sailed from Australia.

MOLLIE'S BOOK

I often say to people with a dream that they should never give up on it coming true, because we never know what is around the corner.

For instance, let's say you had a dream of being a famous author but there was little chance of it happening because you lived in a small, remote country town and knew no-one in the publishing industry. Who is to say that one day a famous author wouldn't come to your town and offer to write a book with you?

You think that that scenario is too far-fetched? You might change your mind after you read this story.

MARY SKINNER RAN a guesthouse with her friend Nellie Beakbane in Lukin Avenue in Darlington, about 22 kilometres east of Perth, in the early 1900s. Mary was born in Perth, the daughter of the last British officer commanding imperial troops in Western Australia. She was educated in England and Ireland before returning to Perth in her early twenties to take up nursing.

She made her way to London and worked with the poor in slum areas, and during World War I she served in India as an army nurse. After the war in Europe ended, Mary returned to Western Australia and worked in a number of hospitals as a relieving matron.

Yet, as much as she loved helping the underprivileged, Mary Louisa Skinner had a dream that didn't involve nursing. She wanted to write. The guesthouse at Darlington was her chance to fulfil her dream and she spent all of her spare time at the typewriter working.

One day in May 1922, fate delivered two visitors to Mary's guesthouse. They were introduced simply as David and his wife, Frieda. Mary quickly realised that 'David' was famous British author DH Lawrence.

Lawrence and his German wife had come to Perth from Ceylon on the recommendation of some Australians they met on a ship travelling from Italy to the subcontinent. Because their travels had extended well beyond what they'd planned, the Lawrences were running short of money and decided to stay at a guesthouse a little way out of Perth until more funds were cabled from London. It was by chance that they chose Mary and Nellie's establishment.

After a couple of days, Mary summoned all her courage and asked Lawrence to read one of her manuscripts. To her dismay, he said it lacked structure and needed a considerable amount of work on its characters. But he said it would make a good story with a bit of rewriting and he offered to work through it if Mary, or Mollie as she was better known, would share the credit and royalites for the book, should it ever be published.

Well, Mollie Skinner's book *was* published, two years later in London, and it became an Australian classic – it was called *The Boy in the Bush*. It was the only book that DH Lawrence ever wrote with a co-author. In fact, when the book was first published in London in 1924, a reviewer said he doubted if ML Skinner existed.

But there is always more to the story. Mollie Skinner's novel was published a year after DH Lawrence's own book about Australia, called *Kangaroo*, which he wrote at Thirroul, near Wollongong. Now, it may seem a little curious that a famous author like DH Lawrence would spend 1922 in out-of-the-way places like Darlington and Thirroul. But they were exactly the sort of places he wanted to hide away. They were where the British press could not find him.

Lawrence had been hounded after his novel *The Rainbow* was banned for obscenity. Thousands of copies were destroyed on order of the courts. This had left Lawrence struggling financially and searching for a new publisher.

For six years, but particularly between 1914 and 1918, during World War I, Lawrence had also endured endless accusations of disloyalty, and even treason, because he married a German woman while British soldiers were dying by the thousands across the Channel at the hands of the Kaiser's forces.

The Lawrences were 'expelled' from the English coastal town of Cornwall because they were often heard singing German folksongs and seen strolling the cliffs overlooking the shipping channels. Both Frieda and Lawrence were accused by locals of being spies. Anger in the township grew when the Nottingham air ace Captain Albert Ball was shot down and killed by Lothar von Richthofen, brother of the Red Baron, Manfred von Richthofen, and the cousin of Frieda. England could not accept that its favourite author had spent much of the war in the arms of the Red Baron's cousin. By the time the Lawrences arrived in Australia in 1922, they were looking for new attitudes and landscapes – and they found them.

There is little doubt that Darlington in Western Australia made an immediate impression on Lawrence. He wrote in his diary:

> We are here about 16 miles out of Perth – bush all around – marvellous air, marvellous sun and sky . . . It is so democratic, it feels to me infradig. In so free a land, it is humiliating to keep house and cook still another mutton chop.

Mollie Skinner went on to write a number of books and short stories, including *Black Swans* in 1925, *Men Are We* in 1927 and *Where Skies are Blue* in 1946. She died in May 1955 at York in Western Australia.

MONORAIL MAN

In the 1990s there was a push from Canberra to promote Australia as the centre of research and discovery in the Asia-Pacific region. We went to Japan looking for investment partners to build cities of the future here called multi-function poleis, we published countless books about Australian discoveries and inventions, and we ran television advertisements throughout East and South-east Asia showcasing our innovative technology.

It all came to very little – probably because it was organised and managed by government departments.

However, it occurred to me at the time that we really should get more mileage than we do out of the numerous discoveries Australians have made. Here is the story of an Australian inventor who is internationally renowned, but barely acknowledged in this country.

LOUIS BRENNAN WAS just 22 years old in 1874 and still living at home with his parents in Melbourne when he invented one of the most deadly weapons of war the world had seen – the guided and self-propelled torpedo.

The British Empire spanned most of the oceans of the world, and paranoia was rife about the emerging naval forces of Russia and Germany and the threat they posed of sudden invasion of unprotected harbours. When the young Irish-born engineer successfully tested his invention at Hobsons Bay near Melbourne, the Victorian Government quickly granted him funds to develop the idea for protection of Port Phillip Bay. Louis worked with Professor William Kernot, a lecturer in engineering at Melbourne University, to improve the original design to patent stage.

In 1880, Louis was invited by the British Government to bring his design to England for further trials. The Ministry of Defence was so impressed by what they saw that they granted him a lump sum of £5000 and a further £1000 a year for as long it took to develop a production model. After five years, Louis was finished and he called the Admiralty experts to his workshop in Kent to see the final model.

It was a cylindrical shape about half a metre wide and three-quarters of a metre high, weighed 3.5 tonnes and was packed with 90 kilograms of explosive. It could travel 2.5 kilometres at a speed of 55 kilometres an hour while 3 metres below the surface. Two thin steel wires wound tightly on drums inside the torpedo were connected to steam-powered winches on the shore. As the wires were drawn out of the torpedo, the drums spun and the attached propellors pushed the torpedo forwards. By varying the tension on the two wires, the torpedo could be steered to its target by a controller on shore. If it missed its target, the wires were used to retrieve the missile for reloading and reuse.

The British Government accepted the design on the spot and paid Louis £110,000 – a fortune in 1885 – and gave him the job of supervisor at the factory manufacturing the Brennan Torpedo. Hundreds of Brennan Torpedoes were manufactured from 1887 until 1907. For those 20 years it was the principal defensive weapon for all British ports, including Gibraltar.

Inexplicably, the British Government refused a request from the Victorian Government to purchase a Brennan Torpedo on the grounds that the design was too secret. This was despite the Victorian Government having been the first to fund the idea!

As the range and accuracy of artillery and naval guns improved, the Brennan Torpedo became obsolete and the Kent factory was closed.

But, as we know, there's always more to the story.

The Brennan family migrated from Ireland to Australia when Louis was aged nine. His father was also an engineer and inventor, and he always encouraged young Louis to persevere with the ideas running round in his head. With his father's words ringing in his ears, Louis hounded the War Office and the Ministry of Defence with a string of ideas from the moment he arrived in London. But no-one was interested in anything but the torpedo.

When it became obvious in 1902 that his torpedo was coming to the end of its life, Louis Brennan decided to spend some of his considerable fortune earned from the British Government to develop one of his other ideas. On 10 November 1903 at Gillingham in Kent, he rolled out for the media and the War Office the first operational prototype of a train that ran on a single rail. It was kept upright by two gyroscopes. Brennan loaded dozens of military observers onto flat cars and urged them all to stand on one side to demonstrate the stability of his invention. Brennan argued that a basic single track could be laid out quickly and cheaply in the battlefield to allow fast troop movements.

Although the War Office granted him £6000 to develop the idea further, it was eventually scrapped in about 1913 because of fears that the gyroscopes might fail and the train would fall on its side. Nevertheless, Brennan's idea was the catalyst for other inventors to develop today's monorail.

The War Office asked Louis to use his considerable skill and knowledge to develop munitions during World War I. But he did so on one condition – when the war finished, he was to be allowed to work on yet another of his pet projects. In 1919, the War Office was held to its arrangement and Louis set up base at Farnborough, where he worked with the Royal Air Force for the next three years to build a prototype of a strange new aircraft with large horizontal rotors and no wings. His invention was the helicopter.

There was plenty of competition in the race to fly successfully a vertical take-off aircraft – Frenchman

Paul Cornu, Russian-born American Igor Sikorsky, German Heinrich Focke and another Frenchman named Oehmichen were all working on similar ideas.

But Louis Brennan was way ahead. By 1921 he had built a 1.3-tonne machine with an 18-metre rotor, powered by a 230-horsepower Bentley motor. It was tethered inside a hangar in its early testing, but it lifted four people. The following year, Louis's aircraft flew without restriction, making 80 take-offs and flying distances of up to 180 metres. He believed that with time he could make it a potent fighting machine. However, on 2 October 1925, the Brennan helicopter was on the seventh of a series of test flights when it tilted and the rotor struck the ground. The aircraft crashed and was destroyed.

In 1926, the British Air Ministry cancelled the project, saying there was little future for such an aircraft in military operations. Ten years later, in 1936, Heinrich Focke took to the air in a design very similar to Brennan's, and a further three years on, Igor Sikorsky flew his first successful design. The aviation world was to become infatuated with the helicopter that the British Air Ministry didn't want.

Look in the history books and you won't see Louis Brennan's name mentioned as inventor of the helicopter. Focke and Sikorsky got the credit. He doesn't get a mention for the monorail, either.

The most likely reason that Louis Brennan missed out on much of the credit due to him was because he wasn't around to protect his interests. In December

1931, five years after his helicopter project was scrapped, he was hit by a car in Switzerland, where he had moved on doctor's orders. He died of his injuries a month later.

MR PRESIDENT

It's interesting how quiet the republic issue has gone in recent times. Two years ago it was difficult to get through a radio program without someone wanting to argue one side or the other; and it was always passionate argument. Now, it seems, other things are more important and we have put the republic aside for another day.

Maybe we will debate the whole issue again in five or ten years from now. Or maybe a republic will be demanded spontaneously when someone comes along who is so good, so charismatic and so universally supported that we change our Constitution to ensure they become our head of state.

This is the story of a man who thought he fitted that description.

ONE OF THE first champions of an Australian republic was an American named George Train. In fact, about 150 years ago he almost became our first President.

George Train was born in Boston, Massachusetts, in 1829. His parents died in a yellow fever epidemic in New Orleans when he was four years of age and he was raised by his grandparents. When he was old enough to leave home, he was sent to work with his father's cousin in a shipping company that ran steam packets to Liverpool Docks in England.

At 21, George Train went to Liverpool to manage the English end of his uncle's business. He later formed his own trading company and followed the trail of fortune hunters to the Victorian gold rush. Train set himself up as a shipping agent, merchant, insurance broker and developer. He was one of the founders of the Cobb & Co. stagecoach company that provided the first long-distance land transport in the Australian colonies, and he was involved in developing port facilities at Geelong. While in Australia, Train also reported as a correspondent for the *Boston Post* and the *New York Herald*. He was scathing of the British colonialists – a line that was well received in Irish Boston.

But George Train found another way to get under the skin of the colonial authorities. He expressed public sympathy with the Irish convicts, and urged Victorians to break away from England and set up a republic in the American mould. He rocked the Melbourne establishment by forming the 'Order of the Lone Star' and later the 'Independent Californian Rangers' Revolver Brigade' at Ballarat amid the Eureka uprising.

Train even publicly made the claim that he had been offered the presidency of a Victorian republic by the miners at Eureka. But nothing came of the push for a republic and, in 1855, George Train left Victoria discouraged and claiming that the people were apathetic in raising their own flag.

However, as he left, he predicted an Australian republic would come, 'sooner or later'.

But, of course, there's always more to the story. In 1855, George Train returned to the United States, where he became involved in the development of railways. In 1860 he went to London and Liverpool to set up the first light rail networks, but failed after strong opposition to his plans frustrated the approval process. In 1862 he returned to the United States and played a key role in the expansion of the Union Pacific Railroad through Iowa and Nebraska. During that time he took advantage of a federal government buyback of land along the railway lines and bought some of the excess land for re-sale. He made a small fortune.

Train additionally became involved in the women's suffrage movement, travelling the country urging the vote for women. He was also a strong supporter of the temperance movement and often spoke against alcohol and smoking. He travelled around the world in 80 days, and is generally thought to have been the inspiration for the character Phileas Fogg in the book *Around the World in 80 Days* by Jules Verne.

But George Train was not finished with politics and social justice campaigning. In 1868 he visited Ireland and was arrested for inciting rebellion. Then he went to France and joined the communists, resulting in his arrest and jailing for 13 days for making inflammatory speeches. In all, he was jailed 15 times in three countries.

In 1872 he stood unsuccessfully for the American presidency as the sole candidate for the Greenback Party. The following year he was certified insane. Among the evidence were his claims that he had invented the coal chute, the eraser on the end of pencils, perforated postage stamps, the fold-down steps on railway carriages and canned salmon. Interestingly, while in Australia, George Train claimed to have invented the prefabricated buildings used in the goldfields.

Despite his certification, George Train was released from the psychiatric hospital after a short time when an appeal court ruled that he was not insane – just eccentric. Train immediately signed all of his assets over to his wife then separated from her.

In 1890 he repeated his round-the-world trip, this time in just over 67 days. Two years later he did it in 60 days. After his travelling, he returned to New York, where he lived in a hotel. He spent most of his days in Central Park, where he handed out coins to people at random and spoke only to children and animals.

He died peacefully in 1904 in his hotel room with family by his side. Before his death he dictated his autobiography, in which he reflected on an extraordinary life – including the day he turned down the offer to become Australia's first President.

NATURAL TASTES BETTER

I don't know how much longer it will be there, but up on the Gold Coast along the old Pacific Highway at Miami there is an ice works still operating and selling block and cubed ice.

It looks like a heritage site in the middle of all the modern development. You can pull up at the lights outside that old timber building on a boiling hot day, look across and almost feel the cool breeze blowing off the wet loading dock.

It always brings back memories for me of when I was a small boy, before we had kerosene or electric refrigerators, and ice was delivered to the house by a man in a horse-drawn wagon. You could have a full or half block that he cut with a saw. The block was dropped into the ice chest in the kitchen, where it kept the milk, butter and meats cold for days.

IF ASKED TO name the inventor of refrigeration, few people, if any, would answer James Harrison. Even fewer would know that he was a Scottish journalist, and probably none would know that he was the editor of the Geelong *Advertiser* in Victoria when he discovered the secret of refrigeration.

It was common for printers in the 1800s to use

ether to clean the ink from the rollers of their presses. Harrison noticed that as the ether his workers were using evaporated, it quickly and dramatically cooled the metal of the printing machines until they were icy to touch. He engaged the services of a French engineer named Eugene Nicolle to help him explore this phenomenon and in 1852 they began to conduct experiments with both ether and ammonia to see if they could reproduce the same cooling effect on water to produce ice.

In 1856, armed with the results of the experiments, Harrison patented a design for the world's first refrigerator. His ether liquid-vapour compression fridge worked by exerting pressure on a refrigerant gas, forcing it to pass through a condenser, where it cooled down and liquefied. The liquid then circulated through the refrigeration coils and vaporised again, cooling down the surrounding air. The following year Harrison opened Australia's first refrigeration plant on the Barwon River, turning out 3 tonnes of ice a day.

James Harrison tried desperately, but unsuccessfully, to interest Australian and European scientists and businessmen in his invention. It seemed no-one here or in the cold northern hemisphere cared much for a refrigeration process. In an attempt to put his idea in front of potential investors, Harrison built a commercial ice-making plant in Franklin Street, Melbourne, producing 10 tonnes of ice a day. However, despite being the only provider of ice in the country, Harrison went bankrupt in 1861.

Disillusioned, James Harrison returned to editing newspapers. But he didn't give up on his invention and in 1873 he took his refrigeration idea another step forward, perfecting a process for snap-freezing carcasses of meat. He thought that at last he could demonstrate the immense potential of this invention in the export of meat to Europe.

He was given £2500 by the colonial authorities to ship 25 tonnes of beef and mutton to London. But the shipment was not handled correctly and the meat arrived in England spoiled. Harrison went bankrupt again. In frustration, he returned yet again to journalism. He died in Melbourne in September 1893.

James Harrison had frozen water, using ether and ammonia. But the French engineer who worked with him on his early experiments, Eugene Nicolle, had long contended that it was the ammonia that held the key to the puzzle. He was fascinated to receive news of an emerging French technique using pure ammonia to freeze water. In 1861, working alone in New South Wales, Nicolle perfected then patented the world's first liquefied ammonia ice-making machine.

His invention attracted immediate attention from two eager investors, in leading colonial merchant Thomas Mort and a pastoralist named Augustus Morris. Together, Mort, Morris and Nicolle formed the Sydney Ice Company, and opened the first commercial iceworks in New South Wales – appropriately, at the back of a pub, the Royal Hotel in George Street.

The George Street operation was later moved to

Darlinghurst, where the first large coolrooms were built for general storage of fresh food in the colony. Sydney Ice Company also opened commercial ice-making plants at Lithgow and Darling Harbour. All these plants were working towards one ultimate goal – frozen meat exports to Europe.

Mort and Morris bought Nicolle out of the business in 1875, and proceeded to spend a small fortune modifying the ammonia refrigeration machines to suit the meat export role; this included the fitting out of the holds of a chartered ship as giant coolrooms. But when they attempted their first full-scale shipment, on the *Northam* in 1877, Mort and Morris's modified refrigeration equipment malfunctioned, and the project was cancelled with heavy financial losses.

Thomas Mort was not used to failure; he had been involved in a string of successful ventures in wool broking, goldmining, kerosene shale extraction, shipbuilding, dairy farming and railways. Bitterly disappointed, Mort fell into depression and bad health, and eventually died in 1878. Paradoxically, within a year of his death, the same equipment that caused him so much grief was used to make the first successful delivery of frozen beef to Europe.

Augustus Morris was nowhere near as devastated by early setbacks as his partner, Thomas Mort. Morris was a battler and grafter. As a schoolboy, he was involved in the exploration of the Port Phillip district, and later explored and settled the Yanko area. He was the mastermind behind the establishment of the infamous native police force in 1848 and the architect of a peace settlement between Aborigines and the squatters of New South Wales in 1850. Morris went on from the London beef shipments to become a key player in the development of Australian exports of primary produce to the United States of America.

However, there's more to this story. The commercial ice-making plants developed by Harrison in Victoria, and Mort, Morris and Nicolle in New South Wales, were of little interest to thousands of people in the colonies trying to preserve precious food supplies through the sweltering heat of summer or to survive the shortages that followed drought, fire and flood. While the race to send frozen beef to London continued, families in Sydney and Port Phillip continued to use the trusty iceboxes that had served them so well since 1839.

Iceboxes in 1839? But that was 18 years before the first ice-making patent was even lodged by James Harrison in Geelong!

You see, the colonies got along quite well on imported, *natural* ice for almost 20 years until synthetic ice was produced, using ether and ammonia. Iceboxes in the colony of New South Wales were filled with ice from glaciers and frozen lakes as far away as the United States of America. The ice was brought to Sydney and Port Phillip in the hold of cargo ships.

At the height of the international ice trade in 1890, the USA exported 25 million tonnes of frozen water a year from its northern lakes. The first American ice arrived in Sydney in January 1839 aboard a vessel called the *Tartar*. Of the 400 tonnes loaded in Boston, Massachusetts, only 250 tonnes remained when the ship arrived in Port Jackson.

NEW WORLD – OLD WORLD

I love watching the Discovery and History channels on Foxtel. Some of the documentaries about the pharaohs and the pyramids are just terrific, and they make ancient history far more interesting than I remember it being when I was at school.

There is no doubt that the Egyptians and Greeks were the most innovative, creative and intellectual people among our early civilisations. I wonder why they did not stay ahead of everyone else as the centuries went on.

This is the story of two explorers – one from the new world and one from the old – who each opened our eyes to exciting discoveries.

MATTHEW FLINDERS IS credited with giving this country its name and its shape. The young Royal Navy officer and mapmaker was the first person to circumnavigate our shores, which he did in 1802. He overcame adversity and tragedy and made great personal sacrifice to open the way for the early development of our nation.

When he eventually published his charts and reports

A portrait of a young Matthew Flinders.

from the voyage in 1814, he gave the world its first look at the shape of a new continent, and he suggested it be called 'Australia' rather than New Holland or Terra Australis. That name was adopted formally in 1824.

Matthew Flinders first arrived in Sydney Cove in 1795, when he was just 21. He had been in the navy since the age of 16, learning most of his navigation and seamanship skills from the famous Captain William Bligh, who had been his commander for more than two years.

After sailing into the colony on HMS *Reliance*, Flinders and a young naval surgeon named George Bass spent as much time as they could charting the east coast of the landmass known then as Terra Australis. The young pair, both from Lincolnshire, risked their lives time and again to explore the coast north and south from Sydney. An outstanding achievement was their circumnavigation of Van Diemen's Land, now Tasmania, which proved it was separate from the mainland. All the information they gleaned opened the way for new settlement and development of the colonies.

Yet, when Matthew Flinders died in 1814 at the age of 40, the country that he named had still not said, 'Thank you,' despite there being many reasons for which to do so.

For instance, when Flinders returned to England in 1800, after his first journey to Australia, he married his sweetheart, Ann Chappelle. However, three months after the wedding, he left England to attempt the circumnavigation of our continent. He would not see his wife again for more than nine years and would spend only four years with her in total.

On his way back to England in 1803, after successfully charting our coastline, Flinders was arrested and imprisoned by the French Governor of Mauritius as a spy. He spent six-and-a-half years in captivity before being released.

He devoted that time – and another four years once back in England – to drawing up his maps and writing the detail of his exploration of this country in the form of a book called *A Voyage to Terra Australis*, which was finally published in London on 18 July 1814. Matthew Flinders died the next day.

Unlike most explorers, Flinders named not one thing after himself. He was far more interested in the challenge of the survey and the adventure of discovery. After his death others put his name to a mountain range, an island and a reef. Even a few streets, a ship and a naval station carry the name 'Flinders'.

Sadly, when Matthew Flinders died in England, after years of poor health, he was living in very modest rented accommodation with few assets. It was not until 38 years after his death that those who benefited most from his courage and skill – the people of Australia – took stock of what had happened to one of their pioneering heroes.

By 1853, it had become known that Flinders had died in near-poverty and that his widow and daughter had been left destitute; the British Government and the Royal Navy had treated them shabbily, providing only the standard pension of a former ship's captain. The parliaments of Victoria and New South Wales voted each to provide a pension of £100 a year to the widow of Matthew Flinders, with the money to revert on her death to her daughter, Anne. It might have been tardy, but at least it was a way of repaying a great debt of gratitude.

But there's more to this story of Matthew Flinders. Much more.

The two pensions granted by Victoria and New South Wales would have substantially improved the life of Mrs Matthew Flinders. Unfortunately, by the time they were granted, Mrs Flinders had been dead a year.

She was 80 years old and had outlived her husband by 40 years.

Their daughter, Anne Petrie, who was born after Flinders was freed by the French, promised to make sure the money and the gesture from Australia was not wasted. She used the income to educate her frail and sickly son, William – the grandson that Matthew Flinders never knew. Anne Petrie was delighted to be able to teach William at home, instructing him in Hebrew, Latin and Greek as well as mathematics and chemistry. The child had an insatiable appetite for knowledge and a quick mind.

At 22, William published his first book, an analysis of the recovery of ancient measurements from monuments such as Stonehenge. In 1867, he was inspired by a book written by a family friend about the pyramids of Egypt. It was to launch him into a lifelong obsession and take him to his own place in history, rivalling his grandfather's achievements in exploration and science.

Sir William Matthew Flinders Petrie would not only do much to unlock the secrets of Stonehenge, but also those of the pyramids of Egypt, and the ancient cities of Sinai and Palestine. He became the foremost Egyptologist of his time, opening the world's eyes to a past civilisation in the same way his grandfather had opened them to a new one.

Through him, Australia had given the world a wonderful gift – and finally ensured a fittingly impressive legacy for Matthew Flinders.

NURSES

When I was younger I spent a bit of time in hospital. I remember the nurses who looked after me more than I remember the doctors. Most of them were young and pretty and very caring, but they were all scared to death of the matron.

Matrons were a cross between a sergeant major and a mother superior. They told young doctors how to dress and how to conduct themselves, they inspected their nursing staff before changes of shift and they accepted no sloppiness on the wards. Yet, they were usually gentle and caring with the patients.

Many a nurse will tell the story of being sprung by Matron as they tried to sneak into the nurses' home after curfew; Matron, of course, was also responsible for morals among the nursing staff.

There is no doubt who was the boss of the hospital in those days.

THERE WERE EIGHT surgeons and two male surgical assistants among the hundreds of passengers, convicts and soldiers who arrived in Sydney on the First Fleet in 1788. The first trained nurses arrived

50 years later; yet, even then, no-one was interested in using their skills.

It was 1838 when five Irish nuns stepped onto the docks of Sydney Town. Two of them were trained nurses and they offered their services in any way the colonial authorities wished to use them. Rather than assign them to Sydney Hospital, however, the authorities sent them to Parramatta Women's prison. Another 19 years passed before the nuns raised enough money to establish St Vincent's Hospital at Darlinghurst.

The immediate success of St Vincent's convinced many community leaders, including Sir Henry Parkes, that the colony needed more trained nurses. So Parkes wrote to London asking for help. On 5 March 1868, Sister Lucy Osburn and five trained nursing sisters arrived on the *Dunbar Castle*. To their surprise and embarrassment, crowds lined Circular Quay and Macquarie Street to cheer them as they walked to the Sydney Infirmary and Dispensary – also known as the 'Rum Hospital' because it was built with taxes raised on the sale of rum. Miss Osburn and her staff were dressed in starched uniforms and white caps.

Lucy Osburn had been recruited to Sydney as Lady Superintendent of the hospital – a remarkable achievement for her because, even though she was in her early 30s, she had only finished her training the year before. She accepted the Sydney appointment because in cold and wet England she was suffering badly from chest conditions and bronchitis and hoped the warm climate would help. She was also keen to get away from

Lady Superintendant of Sydney Hospital,
Miss Lucy Osburn.

England because of a strained relationship with her family. Her father was a prominent archaeologist and Egyptologist and he had expected his educated and widely travelled daughter to follow him into an academic or scientific career. When Lucy decided to become a nurse, her father disowned her.

Lucy Osburn's welcome at the Sydney Infirmary and Dispensary, later known as Sydney Hospital, was probably no warmer than her farewell from England.

The male Superintendent of the hospital and the doctors resented a woman being appointed to the senior position, and they set about making life as difficult as possible for the five nursing sisters. Miss Osburn and her team also had to contend with wards swarming with rats, cockroaches and lice; patients and staff with no hygiene; and food that killed more patients than it satisfied.

But Sister Lucy Osburn had been hand-picked for this job because she was not the type to bow to discrimination or to a challenge. She persevered, and soon began recruiting and training local women to supplement the qualified staff from England and to replace the part-time prostitutes and vagrants who had worked in the wards before she arrived.

More trouble was to come, in the form of Dr Alfred Roberts, a visiting surgeon who saw the women nurses as a threat to his authority and a potential challenge to his skills as a doctor. Roberts even used a trip to London in 1871 to try to convince authorities there to recall Miss Osburn. He claimed she was causing division among the nursing staff. Having failed to have her recalled, he returned to Sydney determined to force Lucy to resign. When she ordered the destruction of mouldy, germ-ridden and cockroach-infested books in the wards, Dr Roberts encouraged the spreading of a story that a page of the Bible was burned. Before long the story had been exaggerated to the burning of Bibles in the hospital. Sister Osburn was subjected to a six-week investigation before being cleared.

Sir Henry Parkes realised what was happening and he weighed into the debate, sending to London a strongly worded letter of support and appreciation for Sister Osburn and her outstanding contribution to reforming health care in the colony. Soon afterwards, a colonial inquiry found that Sister Osburn had been correct to criticise the hospital, the standard of care provided to patients, and the conduct of the alcoholic male Superintendent. He was sacked and Lucy Osburn was given a free hand to rebuild the hospital and its services.

In 1884, after 16 years in Sydney, Lucy Osburn returned to England for a short visit to consult doctors about her emerging diabetes. She intended to return to live permanently in Australia, but her diabetes worsened and she was advised to stay near to medical care. In December 1891, at the age of 56, Lucy Osburn collapsed and died. But there's more to the story, as always.

The letter that Sir Henry Parkes sent to London in 1867 was the turning point for nursing, and health care, in early Australia. He had never been to the London School and Home for Nurses, and he had never met its Head, but he had heard a great deal about her – everybody knew of Florence Nightingale. Sir Henry had read the many newspaper reports of the courageous work done by Sister Nightingale during the Crimean War and when he searched for someone to ask for help, her name was the first to come into his head.

When the impassioned plea arrived from Sydney, Miss Nightingale personally selected her best graduate,

Lucy Osburn, who had been working in London's famous St Thomas's Hospital and the King's College Hospital training in surgical, medical and midwifery skills. The first Matron of Sydney Hospital was one of the best nurses in England.

Florence Nightingale continued to take a keen interest in her five nurses after they left for New South Wales. She corresponded with Lucy Osburn throughout her difficult years, giving her advice and encouragement to continue. When the doctors ganged up on Sister Osburn, it was Florence Nightingale herself who put them in their place with a very pointed open letter: 'No good has ever come of a Medical Officer doing a Matron's duty. And, anyway, a man could never govern a woman,' she wrote.

Sadly, Florence Nightingale and Lucy Osburn had a falling out over the discipline of some of the other Nightingale nurses sent to Sydney; two of the nurses complained that Lucy had gone too far in trying to assert her authority. Florence Nightingale died 20 years after Lucy Osburn, believing that her protégé had been a complete failure in Australia.

OLD FATHER WINE

I love my wines and am very proud of the fact that they come from the Hunter Valley, an area with which I am closely affiliated. There are also other fine Australian wines from Western Australia and South Australia – even some from Victoria, Tasmania and the ACT.

It's no accident that we ended up producing some of the world's best wine. It was the result of some good fortune to start with, followed by good planning, good skills and, finally, good marketing.

The result is an industry that brings millions in export earnings and provides us with the perfect complement to some of the best food in the world. If I sound like an advertisement for Australian food and wine, then I am delighted.

JAMES BUSBY IS referred to as the 'father' of the Australian wine industry even though he never made a drinkable wine himself. He earned the title because he did more than anyone else in the early years of colonial settlement to promote the potential benefits of grape growing in the Sydney and Hunter Valley regions and to encourage planting of vineyards.

Born in Edinburgh, Scotland, in 1801, James Busby was educated in England and France, where he studied viticulture. He arrived with his family in New South Wales in 1824 aboard HMS *Triton*. The first thing that impressed him about the terrain and the climate was that it was very similar to the Burgundy area of France, where he had studied winemaking. He was convinced that he could successfully grow grapes in this climate.

He quickly published a book combining translated passages from a number of French pamphlets he had brought with him on grape growing. The Governor of New South Wales, Governor Brisbane, was so impressed by the paper that he commissioned the 23-year-old James Busby to begin growing grapes in the colony immediately.

Busby negotiated a deal where he would plant a vineyard on the farm of the Cabramatta Male Orphans School. He would also teach the boys at the school viticulture in return for a third of the produce of the farm.

The arrangement ended in disaster and Busby left the school after just a year; he was given the job of Collector of Internal Revenue by Governor Darling, who had recently assumed control of the colony. That arrangement, too, ended in dispute.

James Busby left Sydney for London in 1830, angry and disillusioned. He said that he would take a sabbatical and draw up his claim for compensation over his removal from the two jobs.

After a few months in London, he went to Europe

in September 1831 and began travelling around Spain and France.

Over 18 months, Busby collected cuttings of 437 varieties of grapevine from the Botanic Gardens in Montpellier in France; 133 from the Royal Nursery at Luxembourg; and 44 varieties from Sion House, near Kew Gardens, in England. He brought all of these samples back to Sydney in 1832 and presented them to the Botanic Gardens in Sydney. Within six months, 362 varieties of grape were growing successfully in the Sydney gardens, including varieties suitable for raisins, dessert and wine. A condition of the gifting of the vines was that cuttings should be freely available to anyone interested in planting grapes. More than 20,000 cuttings were given away from the Botanic Garden plantings.

To ensure there was good food to go with good wine, James Busby also gave to the Sydney Botanic Gardens seeds for dates, pumpkins, tomatoes, cucumbers, onions, melons and sweet peppers – all foods that had not previously been grown in Australia.

Busby arrived back in Sydney not only with cuttings but with new enthusiasm for grape growing in the Hunter Valley, and he convinced the colonial authorities to grant him land in the valley for development of a commercial vineyard.

By now his sister Catherine had married William Kelman, a fellow passenger on the *Triton* when they migrated from England in 1824. In 1832 James Busby planted almost 10 acres (4 hectares) with cuttings from his European collection and left William Kelman in charge of the vineyard. William named the property Kirkton, after a town in Scotland. Over time, William Kelman expanded the vineyards at Kirkton to become the largest in New South Wales. Wines were produced from the vines there for a hundred years under the Kelman family, then under the Lindeman family, before it was sold in the 1930s.

The cuttings that James Busby brought back to Sydney allowed the wine industry to burgeon in the Hunter Valley and on the outskirts of Sydney. In 1836, George Wyndham produced his first vintage at Dalwood, near Branxton; then came James King's Raymond Terrace vineyard; and Sir John Jamison's vines near Penrith. In 1837, the Macarthurs settled six German families at Camden Park, west of Sydney, where they had a vineyard and began producing brandy. The following year the Macarthurs imported the first white Riesling grapevines for planting.

As for James Busby, he was lost to Australia in 1832, not long after planting Kirkton, when he was appointed First British Resident of New Zealand. He went to the Bay of Islands and took with him some of the grapevines that he had collected in Europe; with these cuttings, he also launched a New Zealand wine industry. During his time in New Zealand, James Busby was involved in several controversies – most relating to his claims of title over land there. He was a co-author of the Treaty of Waitangi, which established British rule over New Zealand after years of bloody conflict.

James Busby died in London in 1871 while still trying to sort out his land titles in New Zealand and compensation for his lost jobs in Australia.

But there's always more to the story, and this one is no exception.

James Busby, the father of the wine industry, came to Australia not because of wine, but because of water. His father, Major John Busby, a Scottish civil engineer and mineral surveyor, was contracted by the colonial authorities to develop coalmining in the colony and to find a means of supplying clean drinking water to the town of Sydney. Coincidentally, like his son James, John Busby spent a lot of time in the Hunter Valley – not growing grapes, but developing the Newcastle coalmines.

In 1837, John Busby finished a ten-year project using convict labour to tunnel through rock to create a fresh water supply from swamps near the present Centennial Park to Hyde Park. The tunnel came to be known as Busby's Bore.

John Busby retired to a farm on the Hunter River near Newcastle, where he died in 1857 at the age of 92.

ON THE RIGHT TRACK

Can someone please tell me which part of the government is responsible for our electrical plugs and our voltage? The free trade agreements and commerce treaties are all well and good, but I want to know why we have a different plug from everyone else and twice the voltage of most other countries. It means that our things don't work there and theirs don't work here.

Maybe logic and mathematics are not my strengths, but wouldn't it be cheaper if we could all use the same range of products and equipment? Or is this some form of protection barrier?

I am only a broadcaster, but it seems to me that the problem is getting worse by the day because of the increasing investment everyone is making in different equipment and infrastructure. So, the longer we leave it, the more it will cost!

This is the story of a man who tried to tackle another example of bureaucratic and political pigheadedness – our railways.

IN 1920, WHEN the Victorian Government wanted to electrify the Melbourne suburban rail system, there was only one man it wanted for the job – Harold

Winthrop Clapp. Clapp was the best in America; he had worked with the General Electric Company on electrification of the New York underground system in 1901, and later the Oakland and Berkeley rail network in California. He had also held senior executive positions with the famous Southern Pacific Railroad, the East Saint Louis and Suburban Railroad Company and the Columbus Railway Light and Power Company. No-one knew more about electric rail systems than HW Clapp.

Although the Victorian Government realised they could never match the salary he commanded in the United States of America, they had a hunch he would come if they asked. After all, Harold W Clapp might have been the golden-haired boy of American rail, but he was also a Melbourne boy through and through.

As a 20-year-old, his American-born father, Francis Boardman Clapp, arrived in the midst of the Victorian gold rush to set up a stagecoach company called FB Clapp that competed with Cobb & Co. He later established the Melbourne Omnibus Company with horse-drawn buses, and, in 1877, he launched the Melbourne Tramway and Omnibus Company to run the most advanced cable tram system in the world; it was a vast improvement on the San Francisco system on which it was based. The last of Francis Clapp's cable trams were still running in 1940, 63 years after they were introduced.

Harold Clapp was born in Melbourne in 1875 and educated at Brighton Grammar School, then the

Melbourne Church of England Grammar School, but he wasn't much of a scholar. When he was 18, he was apprenticed to the Austral Otis Engineering Works in South Melbourne. Two years later he joined Brisbane Tramways Company as a supervisor in the conversion of the Queensland capital's tram network from horse power to electric power. The fact that his father was a major shareholder of the company may have helped his selection for the job, but that didn't detract from young Harold's extraordinary skill and vision in installing the new system in Brisbane and training the staff. It was on the back of his success in Brisbane that the General Electric Company poached young Harold to work on the New York underground conversion.

All things considered, Victorian authorities were confident that an offer to Harold Clapp to give Melbourne a modern rail system would appeal to the local-boy-made-good. And it did; he started work as Chairman of Commissioners of Victorian Railways on 17 September 1920.

Although the electrification of the Melbourne suburban trains had already started when Harold Clapp returned to Australia, he extended the plans and accelerated the implementation. He went about the task methodically, introducing smoother, welded tracks; upgraded locomotives; new weekend services; and services to resort areas. He emphasised reliability and safety, bringing in automatic couplings on carriages to reduce death and injury in the shunting yards.

He paid attention to the salaries and conditions of employees to make sure he had a happy and loyal workforce.

Harold Clapp didn't just head the railways in Victoria – he ran them. Often he rode in the cab of the trains to talk with drivers and firemen about how the business was going. Frequently he inspected remote country stations for cleanliness and the quality of food in the tea-rooms and to ask the employees if there were things that could be done better. And Harold Clapp also looked for ways to support his customers. As a gesture to valuable rural customers, he introduced stalls on city railway platforms to sell fresh fruit, vegetables, cheese and juice.

However, all the time, his eye was on the bigger issues – particularly the need for luxury, high-speed passenger transport between Australia's capital cities. In 1937 he began to answer that challenge with the *Spirit of Progress* – the first all-steel, air-conditioned train in Australia. The *Spirit* was super-fast for its day, with a recorded top speed of 128 kilometres per hour; soft riding on bogeys fitted with shock absorbers; and it was fitted out with luxury first-class carriages, a dining car and a parlour car with all-round glass viewing window.

The *Spirit of Progress* had one serious limitation – it could run only as far as Albury, on the New South Wales border. There, passengers had to change trains in the middle of the night to go on to Sydney because the rail gauges were different from Victorian ones. Harold

W Clapp may have been able to work wonders with Victorian Railways, but even he couldn't solve the problem of Australia's three different gauges. But wait – there's more to the story.

By the late 1930s there were signs that Harold Clapp and others might break through in their quest for a standard rail gauge in Australia. However, the investment required to change all locomotives and rolling stock proved to be too great for some States to contemplate and all suggestions were dismissed.

In 1939, the Australian Government asked Harold Clapp to move from railways to chair the new Department of Aircraft Production in the hope that he would carry his management and project management expertise into wartime aircraft manufacturing. He was so successful that in 1941 he was knighted for his service, and the following year he was appointed Director-General of Land Transport to tackle the problem of moving troops and supplies around the country to defend against possible Japanese invasion.

Once again the different rail gauges presented a headache. It took more than a month to move an infantry division from Sydney to Perth, where it would have taken eight days had a single-gauge system been in place. But Sir Harold came up with the solution of a specially modified series of wide-gauge locomotives that could also run on the narrow gauges of Queensland, Tasmania, the Northern Territory and Western Australia.

Three years after the war, in 1948, at the invitation of the Federal Government, Sir Harold Clapp presented a comprehensive plan for a single national gauge for railways. To his disbelief, the plan was rejected by Parliament because of the cost involved. However, the momentum continued in Victoria and in July 1952, one of Sir Harold's dreams came true when the first diesel–electric locomotives rolled onto Victorian tracks.

It was the diesel era that ultimately opened the way for standardisation to begin – in 1957 – because only the bogeys had to be changed for different gauges, not the whole locomotive. Finally trains began running all the way between Sydney and Melbourne in 1962.

Sir Harold Clapp died in 1952, just three months after the first of his diesels was presented to the public at Spencer Street station in Melbourne.

Even though he was 77 years old, retired and very ill, he still insisted on riding in the cabin as acting assistant engineer when locomotive B60 took its first trip. After all, he always referred to himself as a 'railwayman'.

Given his exceptional contribution to rail in Australia, it was more than appropriate that the first diesel locomotive that he rode that day was named the Harold W Clapp.

ON A WING AND A PRAYER

There was a school headmaster in Queensland who enjoyed stumping young pupils by asking them to explain how it could be that the town's old stone police station was built in New South Wales.

He would get all sorts of answers about how it was taken apart, moved across the border on wagons and reassembled. Then he would take great delight in ruining those theories by telling his students that it had always been where it now stood.

The riddle was all part of a history lesson, because the answer was to be found in the story of Queensland being part of the colony of New South Wales before it was established as a separate colony.

I'm telling you this story because I want you to keep an open mind as you read on.

CAPTAIN THOMAS WALTER WHITE was 27 and already one of the veterans of the fledgling Australian Flying Corps when he left his base in October 1915 for a routine reconnaissance mission over enemy Turkish positions south of Baghdad. It was always dangerous duty in the unarmed, hand-me-down

Maurice-Farman biplanes that the AFC flew in those early days. With their tiny 70-horsepower Renault engines, they dawdled along at only 4500 feet – easy targets for machine gunners on the ground and fast German Fokker fighter planes.

Thomas White was something of a legend, even among fellow Australian pilots. On photographic missions over enemy artillery positions, he would regularly cut the engine of his aircraft at 7000 feet and feign a death dive. When he was just 1000 feet from the ground, he would open the throttle and level off, giving his observer the opportunity to take close-up photographs of the enemy gun positions. By the time the startled enemy gunners reacted, White was already turning for home.

On this October reconnaissance mission, Captain White was flying with his favourite observer, a British Captain named Yeats-Brown, of the 17th Cavalry. When they were deep over enemy territory near Ctesiphon, the engine of the Maurice-Farman spluttered and misfired. Both men thought immediately of two colleagues murdered by Arab tribesmen just weeks earlier when they crash-landed in similar terrain. This was no place to be stranded. But the engine trouble continued and Captain White had no choice but to land, right in front of the enemy positions at Zeur.

He knew he was not going to have time to investigate the fault fully, so whatever strategy he could come up with would have to take into account a sick engine. The daring young pilot decided to risk all and make a run for home. They would be even more vulnerable than usual on this trip, so he asked Yeats-Brown to stand in his cockpit and face the rear to guard against surprise attack. Their only defence if an attack did come was a bolt-action rifle. White nursed the aircraft 15 miles (24 kilometres) through enemy territory to the Australian airfield in Aziziyah.

It was not the last adventure for Captain White. Two weeks later, a seaplane carrying Major-General GV Kemball, Chief of the General Staff in Mesopotamia, was forced by engine failure to land between Kut and Aziziyah. The Australian unit was asked to send out a search plane. White went alone in his MF2.

After some time searching, he caught sight of the seaplane against the bank of a river and close to an Arab camp. He flew low over the plane and saw that the pilot and the General were alive. But just then the Arabs opened fire on White's plane, hitting his wing and propeller. He landed on a road about a kilometre from the river. He then tricked the Arabs into thinking he was not alone by barking orders to non-existent troops and pointing at the Arab camp.

As the Arabs hesitated, thinking they were under attack themselves, White ran to the seaplane, gave the General a rifle then helped him to his waiting plane, in which they flew to safety. An Indian cavalry unit saw White's aircraft land and came to investigate – they rescued the seaplane's pilot.

Then, on 13 November, needing to isolate Baghdad before they could begin the battle for Ctesiphon, the

Allies conceived a plan to cut the communication wires running north and west from Baghdad to Constantinople and Kifri. Captains White and Yeats-Brown volunteered to land behind enemy lines and cut the wires. They set off at dawn for the 120-mile (200 kilometre) round trip that would take them to the limit of their aircraft's range. Although they carried cans of extra fuel, if they encountered headwinds they would not make it back to their airfield.

Captain White flew low into enemy territory and eventually located telegraph wires running parallel to the main road out of Baghdad. He was now just 8 miles (12 kilometres) from the enemy city. He picked a spot where he would be hidden from the road and came in to land. However, canals nearby restricted his landing space and he clipped a telegraph pole, damaging a wing. Stranded, they were soon under attack from both Arab and Turkish forces. While Yeats-Brown blew up the telegraph line, White filled the fuel tank of his damaged plane and kept the attackers at bay with a rifle.

But it was in vain. They were overpowered by the Arabs and beaten badly before Turkish troops arrived and intervened. White and Yeats-Brown were taken to Baghdad and then to Mosul, where they were imprisoned for two-and-a-half years.

White was being shipped to Constantinople in July 1918 when he escaped amid the confusion of a railway accident. Disguised as a Turk, he stowed away on a ship with another English officer. The pair made their way to Odessa on fake Russian passports and joined the Bolshevik army. They then sailed to Bulgaria on a Ukrainian hospital ship and arrived back in Allied territory just a week before the Armistice ended the war. It's a tale to rival any Indiana Jones novel but, amazingly, there's more to the story.

Captain Thomas Walter White, Distinguished Flying Cross and Bar, went on to further fame in World War II and later, as Sir Thomas White, was appointed as Australia's Minister for Civil Aviation. But pilots would always revere him for that daring mission behind enemy lines in October 1915 when he nursed a sick engine home. They would shake their heads in amazement at the thought of him taxiing an aeroplane 24 kilometres through enemy territory. Yes, taxiing!

When Thomas White set his crippled plane down in the desert, he found the engine was running well enough only to move it along the ground – and only then because the wind was behind him. So he decided to head for home through sand hills and enemy lines. He finally crossed into friendly territory by travelling along a road and crossing right in front of Turkish troops, who were too startled to fire a shot. As he entered friendly territory the engine spluttered back to life and he took off for the short flight to his home base.

When he was captured a month later near Baghdad, he was filling the fuel tank of his damaged plane with every intention of trying a repeat of that daring escape.

OUR FIRST GP

When I was at school there were booklets for boys on gentlemanly behaviour, including taking off your hat indoors, standing for ladies on the tram or bus, opening the door for a lady and offering assistance to anyone in distress.

We were taught to do these things because they were the right things to do, not because there was a medal or other reward involved. It would be a sad day when the time came we expected something whenever we did the right thing.

Not so long ago we talked to a fellow working at a rubbish tip, who found a bag full of cash and handed it in so it could be returned to the businesspeople who had accidentally thrown it out. This action was apparently such a rare event it made front-page news nationally. To his credit, the finder said he would not have dreamed of doing anything else – the money wasn't his.

This is the story of someone else with a simple philosophy of doing the right thing.

'No man has ever served a country in a finer spirit of patriotism, no man more deeply deserved the gratitude of a generous people, than he has.'

THIS EXTRAORDINARY PRAISE was uttered in 1868 by Australian elder statesman WC Wentworth – one of the architects of self-rule for the colony of New South Wales. What made it even more extraordinary was that he spoke not about a Premier, a Prime Minister, a sportsman or even a war hero, but about a humble medical doctor named William Bland. The name Bland doesn't appear very often in material about early pioneers and heroes of the colony of New South Wales. It should, though.

William Bland was born in London in November 1789, the son of a prominent physician. When he completed his medical studies, he accepted an appointment as a surgeon in the Royal Navy and went to sea. He left the navy and travelled to Sydney in 1814. He eventually set up practice and became the first registered private medical practitioner in Australia.

As well as working in general practice, William Bland spent a great deal of time agitating for improvements in health and education for the poor and disadvantaged. His name is probably on a plaque somewhere as the founder of the Free Grammar School in Sydney or as patron of the Benevolent Society. He helped found the Sydney Benevolent Asylum – a home for the poor – and gave his services free of charge at institutions throughout Sydney.

But William Wentworth had even greater achievements in mind when he eulogised Bland so generously at his funeral. Dr William Bland was a kind and unselfish man with indefatigable energy. But when pushed to the limit, he also had a fiery temper. That temper was tested many times as he battled long and hard with William Wentworth to win independent government for the colony of New South Wales, taking on and overcoming the British House of Commons.

As a member of the first New South Wales Legislative Council, he fought fearlessly for the rights of convicts, demanding their humane treatment. This campaign brought him into frequent conflict with leading businessmen of the colony, including John Macarthur. William Bland pursued wrongs wherever and whenever he saw them. In 1818, he challenged in the press the personal excesses of Governor Lachlan Macquarie – his criticism earned him a year in jail for libel.

Dr Bland was a true defender of the common people. He campaigned for political freedom and trial by jury, and made time to serve on the Sydney Council and in the colonial Parliament to represent the views of the less wealthy and influential. And all the time, he continued to run his medical practice and free clinics. Through it all, William Bland expected and asked for nothing in return.

However, he had one self-indulgence – his inventions. He designed all manner of devices and machines that were far ahead of their time. In 1851, he designed an Atmotic Ship (atmotic from the Greek word for vapour) that he predicted could carry one-and-a-half tonnes of cargo or passengers from Sydney to London in five days, even against prevailing winds. His design involved a large hydrogen-filled balloon fitted with sails and suspending a car fitted with a steam engine and two propellers.

He was too late getting the plans of his Atmotic Ship to England for the Great Exhibition of 1851, but he demonstrated a model at Crystal Palace, in London, in 1852. He was still trying to promote the idea 14 years later, without success. Inexplicably, an almost identical design was used later in Europe for successful airships.

An inspiring biography? But there's more to the story. Dr William Bland was, of course, a fierce champion for the rights of convicts, who at that time were prevented from ever rising to official office or position, even after emancipation. However, he had good reason to fight that battle because Dr William Bland, medical practitioner, emancipist and patriot, was himself an ex-convict.

While serving as surgeon on HMS *Hesper* in the East Indies in 1813, 24-year-old Dr Bland was involved in a quarrel with another of the ship's officers, Robert Case. Case challenged Bland to a duel and the young doctor shot and killed his opponent. Bland and his second for the duel, Lieutenant Randall, were tried for murder, convicted and sentenced to transportation to New South Wales – William Bland for seven years, and Lieutenant Randall for eight.

When William Bland arrived in Sydney in 1814, it was as a prisoner. Colonial authorities soon realised his education and medical skills were invaluable to the community and two years after his arrival, he was pardoned. However, William Bland would forever carry the stigma of having been a convict. Thirty-six years after his conviction, it prevented him becoming a member of the first senate of Sydney University.

Dr William Bland died in Sydney on 21 July 1868. He was 79 years old.

PARLIAMENT CRASH

Parliament House in Canberra is a very impressive piece of architecture and apparently very functional, but it leaves me colder than the outside temperature of our national capital in July.

If you visit Canberra, make sure you stop at Old Parliament House, as it is now known, and take the guided tour through the building that was intended as a temporary home for our national houses of parliament. You can almost feel the ghosts of prime ministers past and hear the bells ringing for a division as you walk along the polished timber floors and sit on the leather benches in the Senate chamber.

There are lots of stories to be told about our first national Parliament House. Some are better known than others.

On 9 May 1927, the Duke and Duchess of York, later to become King George VI and Queen Elizabeth, opened Australia's new Parliament House in Canberra. For the 30,000 people who gathered in the open fields of the new national capital on that chilly but sunny autumn day, and for those who read the newspaper reports of events and saw the photographs in the weeks that followed, it was a day to remember – royal visitors, 2000 troops on parade, Dame Nellie Melba singing the national anthem, and full-scale pomp and ceremony.

What most of Australia and the world didn't know at the time, and perhaps still may not know today, is that a plane crashed only hundreds of metres from the new parliament building in full view of the large crowd and the official party just as the ceremonies were beginning.

As Dame Nellie Melba sang the national anthem, she was drowned out by the sound of five Royal Australian Air Force SE-5 fighters passing low overhead in formation in salute to the royal couple. When the aircraft were about 600 metres from Parliament House, one suddenly fell into a steep dive and crashed into the ground heavily, critically injuring the pilot, Flying Officer Francis Ewen. He was dragged from the wreckage alive, but died later in hospital from his injuries.

Air crashes were not uncommon in those early days because the fledgling RAAF was flying antiquated aircraft left over from World War I. But the incident at Parliament House on 9 May 1927 caused extra grief for all who witnessed it because it was the second such tragedy in three weeks. On 21 April, as Melbourne welcomed the duke and duchess on their arrival aboard HMS *Renown*, an inexplicable accident had caused more RAAF deaths.

The royal couple was to drive from St Kilda Pier through the streets of Melbourne to Government

House, where they would take the salute from seven RAAF DH-9 bombers flying past in formation. The aircraft had been in the air for about two-and-a-half hours, circling over the parade, waiting for the signal to fly past the dais. At the arranged time, the formation flew forward and dived from 1000 feet (300 metres) before pulling up – that was the salute. But as they did so, two of the bombers collided in mid-air and crashed to the ground, killing all four crew.

The commander of the welcoming parade, Australian World War I flying ace Squadron Leader Harry Cobby, stood in disbelief beside the Duke of York as the crippled aircraft fell from the sky and into the streets of Melbourne. The duke turned to Cobby and said sympathetically, 'Two of your buggers gone.'

But there's always more to the story. The loss of three RAAF aircraft in three weeks was not the only regrettable aspect of the visit to Australia by the Duke and Duchess of York in 1927.

As the crowd gathered for the opening ceremony of Parliament House in Canberra, an elderly man dressed in an old suit, but without shoes and accompanied by his two dogs, stood waiting patiently to see the duke and duchess. A policeman quickly approached and told him to move away because he was not appropriately dressed for the royal occasion. Jimmy Clements, a Wiradjuri elder from Queanbeyan, also known as 'King Billy' and 'Marvellous', silently stood his ground. He was there with another Wiradjuri man, John Noble, to represent the traditional owners of the land

NATIONAL ARCHIVES OF AUSTRALIA A3560,3049

The RAAF fly-past continued despite the crash of Flying Officer Ewen's aircraft.

on which the new Parliament House was built. As an Aboriginal elder, Jimmy had come to pay his respects to the duke and duchess.

The crowd nearby in the temporary stands called out their support for him and urged the policeman to let him be. Some shouted that an Aboriginal man had as much right as anyone to be present. Eventually, Jimmy was allowed to stay and in a place from where he could see proceedings. But he was not allowed to move within sight of the royal party. Although Jimmy Clements carried himself with dignity on the day, the insult was obvious. He should have been on the dais, not in the crowd.

The following day, when the good citizens of Canberra and Queanbeyan were invited to parade past the royal couple and offer their greetings, Jimmy Clements insisted on joining the procession, much to the alarm of organisers. When his turn came, he walked slowly forward, and as he passed the duke and duchess, he saluted them. They returned his greeting with a smile and a wave. 'King Billy' had made his point. He died 11 weeks later at the age of 80.

There is one more extraordinary twist to this story. After the opening ceremony at Parliament House in Canberra on 9 May 1927, another of the RAAF's Canberra-based SE-5 fighters was given the job of flying official photographs and film of the event to Melbourne. En route, Pilot Sergeant Orm Denny encountered engine trouble and crashed on Mount Buffalo in Victoria. He survived, but the aircraft was destroyed.

When he was found, Sergeant Denny told rescuers that he hid the film and photographs of the Canberra opening in a tree stump for security in case he did not survive. But despite exhaustive searches over the years, the stump and the film have never been found.

Of course, some suggest that the 1927 royal visit was plagued with disaster because it was cursed. That as the royal couple was coming to a ceremony on traditional Aboriginal land without permission from or involvement of the owners, their journey was troubled. And the official film and photographs that disappeared on Mount Buffalo were proof of the final insult – the absence of any Aboriginal person in the official party.

PAST CARIN'

If you ever feel life is tough, read a book about women in the Australian bush at any time since the First Fleeters moved out of Sydney Cove.

Working the farm, giving birth to 13 or 14 children, burying some of them as infants and more as teenagers, washing and cooking in primitive conditions (including dirt floors), living with no heating or cooling and no running water, and being days away from medical assistance were all part of life in the bush for a woman. Some women were bullied, beaten or raped, some were deserted or widowed in their early 20s, and most died before they reached 50.

There should be a monument in every city and town in Australia to the women who have kept this country going.

AUSTRALIA'S FIRST HIGH-PROFILE feminist, Louisa Larsen, was also one of our best-known authors and journalists at the turn of the century. She was born Louisa Albury on Guntawang station near Mudgee in New South Wales in 1848, the daughter of a shearer and the eldest girl of nine surviving children.

At 13, she was forced to give up school to help raise

her siblings. It ended any chance of her fulfilling a dream to be a schoolteacher. Louisa tried to satisfy her passion for writing and poetry with a small collection of books under her bed, but her mother – resentful of her own misfortune – burned Louisa's poems and her books.

In 1866, at the age of 18, Louisa ran away from home and married a Norwegian sailor named Peter Niels Hertzberg Larsen, who had jumped ship in Australia in search of his fortune in the gold rush. The couple went to live on the diggings near Mudgee, but didn't find a fortune. On the contrary, they lived in poverty in tents and later in a shanty hut on a small block of land that they bought. While Peter was away trying to make money doing contract work or gold panning, Louisa raised cattle and a family, maintained the house and farm, and ran a shop and post office at Eurunderee.

A drought forced them to sell up everything they owned in 1882. That was the final straw for Louisa. Traumatised by the death of one of her five children, without money or prospects, and with her husband away most of the time and beating her when he did return, she lapsed into depression and poor physical health.

Leaving Peter behind, Louisa bundled up her four surviving children and went to Sydney. Without education or training, 35-year-old Louisa did the only thing she could think of to make money – she took in boarders. After some success running a small boarding house in Phillip Street, near Circular Quay, she bought a larger house and increased the number of boarders. But she found it difficult to keep up with the cost of running the house.

By 1887, Louisa had bought a monthly newsletter called *The Republic* and was training her 20-year-old son to edit it. She was worried because he had started drinking heavily since the traumatic split in the family and was showing signs of alcoholism. Working side-by-side allowed her to keep an eye on him during the day. Together, they printed their journal on an old press set up in Louisa's cottage in Clarence Street. *The Republic* called for all Australians to unite under the flag of a federated Australia.

A year later, Louisa launched another journal called *The Dawn*. It was a monthly magazine for women, dealing with the issues that were most important to them. Over 17 years, Louisa Larsen wrote articles on everything from how a woman should ride a bicycle to how she should assert herself in the home. Through *The Dawn,* Louisa supported controversial proposed laws – allowing divorce for women on grounds of cruelty; and granting women custody of their children in marriage breakdowns.

The Dawn was a women's magazine in every respect, right down to the printers being women. They were Australian, but all trained overseas. Unionists from the Typographical Association tried to put the journal out of business by threatening advertisers and harassing the female staff – their tactics included using mirrors to flash light in the women's eyes while they were working on the presses. No sooner had Louisa put an end to that, than the New South Wales Postmaster General ruled that *The Dawn* was not suitable to be carried through the mail. Again, Louisa won the battle, using all of her contacts and support in the community and the legal profession.

On the back of growing success for *The Dawn*, in 1889 Louisa formed the Dawn Club to give women a venue to debate important issues. It became the centre of intellectual activity for women's suffrage in Australia. It was at about this time, too, that she became interested in spiritualism and began attending regular meetings where spiritualists helped her to communicate with 'the other side'.

In 1891, Louisa Larsen decided that the women's cause needed to be better organised, so she convened a meeting in Sydney to officially launch the women's suffrage movement. At an early meeting she declared that the greatest discovery of the century was the discovery of women. 'Men govern the world and the schemes upon which all our institutions are founded show men's thoughts only,' she wrote. To ensure that women's thoughts were seen and heard, Louisa granted the suffrage movement free access to her printing presses.

When women were given the vote in 1902, Louisa Larsen was cheered onto the stage. When the Women's Suffrage Bill was introduced to the new Federal Parliament, she was referred to as 'The Mother of Suffrage in New South Wales'.

Peter Larsen died in 1896 without ever reuniting with Louisa. However, he left her more than a thousand pounds; she used it to buy new printing equipment.

All was going well until a freak accident in 1900 changed Louisa Larsen's life forever. She was thrown from a tram and suffered serious leg and spinal injuries. Bedridden and depressed, she retired to a small cottage in Marrickville, from where she wrote occasional pieces for *The Bulletin* and other influential journals and newspapers. But there's more to the story.

Louisa Larsen never remarried. In fact, the longer she worked for women's suffrage, the more she developed a strong dislike of men. Except, of course, for her two sons.

All of Louisa's children suffered psychologically from the angry family break-up and the move from country Mudgee to bustling Sydney, particularly her eldest son, who had a hearing disability as well as a drinking problem. He had loved listening intently to his father reciting poetry in the quiet of the bush night in the goldfields at Grenfell and in front of the fire at their tiny home in Mudgee. Years later, memories of his mother's courageous battle to survive alone in the bush, the unhappy split between father and mother, and the recollections of a happier life in the bush would resurface in Louisa's son – or, at least, in his poetry – when he earned his own place in history as our greatest bush poet – Henry Lawson.

Lawson was the name written on the Larsens' wedding certificate by the minister who married them. Louisa decided to continue using it when Henry was christened, and from there on, the family became Lawson.

Henry Lawson was torn between his mother and father, and although he went to Sydney with Louisa, he returned often to spend time living with Peter at Mudgee. Later in life, Henry suffered his own marriage breakdown.

But there is no doubt that Louisa Lawson was a tremendous influence on her son. You only have to look at some of Henry's poems to see the extraordinary empathy he had with the woman's perspective – something few Australian male poets had thought important at that time. His 1899 poem, 'Past Carin'', about the trials of a woman in the bush during drought, told a story barely dissimilar to that of his own mother. The final stanza goes:

> My eyes are dry, I cannot cry,
> I've got no heart for breakin',
> But where it was in days gone by,
> A dull and empty achin'.
> My last boy ran away from me,
> I know my temper's wearin',
> But now I only wish to be
> Beyond all signs of carin'.
> Past wearyin' or carin',
> Past feelin' and despairin'.
> And now I only wish to be
> Beyond all signs of carin'.

Louisa Lawson eventually succumbed to the strain of her battles with life. She was a patient at the Gladesville Mental Hospital in Sydney when she died in 1920 at the age of 72. She was buried in a pauper's grave.

PIERROT

I doubt that television programs like Big Brother, The Bachelor *or* Temptation Island *will still be showing 50 years from now, and certainly not with the same characters. Yet, you can pick up a newspaper on any Sunday and read about Mr Bumstead in the comic strip 'Dagwood' or Mr Wilson in 'Dennis the Menace' and get the same enjoyment your parents did.*

Why? Because tasteful entertainment is timeless.

Maybe I am getting to be an old so-and-so, but it also seems to me that it is the entertainment without foul language, gratuitous sexual references and graphic personal conflict that stands the test of time and appeals to the most people.

This story is proof of that theory.

THE WIFE OF the park ranger at Ku-ring-gai Chase on the northern outskirts of Sydney was the first to spot his talent in about 1901. She said that Jimmy had limited artistic ability, but he could certainly amuse everyone with his witty sketches. Little did she know how right she was. Jimmy would go on to entertain four generations of people in 20 countries with those 'witty sketches'.

Jimmy Bancks was born in 1889 at Enmore in Sydney. His father was a poor, uneducated Irish immigrant who earned a few shillings a week and a railway cottage next to the tracks by cleaning carriages in the yards at the end of the day. Jimmy was the third of four Bancks children.

For the first ten years of his life, Jimmy moved regularly with the family – from Enmore to Newtown, then to Redfern and finally to Peats Ferry Road in Hornsby. He went to Waitara Convent School then Normanhurst Public School. He wasn't much of a student, but he was always the class clown. Often Jimmy wagged school with his mates, and they spent hours exploring the Ku-ring-gai Chase swimming holes and fishponds.

At 14, and to the relief of his teachers, Jimmy Bancks left school and began studying at the Julian Ashton Art School in the hope of finding a job as an illustrator on one of the Sydney newspapers. But he wasn't good enough and he had to make do with a job as an office boy for a finance company in the city. He kept drawing and submitting his illustrations to publishers, always hoping for a break.

Finally, in 1914, when Jimmy was 25, *The Arrow* newspaper published one of his illustrations. In quick succession, several other journals picked up his work. Three years after his break in *The Arrow*, he was offered his first full-time job as an artist, with *The Bulletin*.

Jimmy was paid the handsome amount of eight pounds a week at a time when the basic wage was three.

But illustrations were not Jimmy's first love – his heart was in comic strips. In 1921, he realised a dream when the Sydney *Sunday Sun* newspaper published the first strip of his comic series called 'Us Fellers', based around a typical Australian boy named Ginger Smith. Within six months, 'Us Fellers' was an outstanding success and Jimmy made some changes. He gave Ginger a dog called Mike, a younger brother named Dudley, a best mate named Benny, a girlfriend called Minnie Peters, a rival named Eddie Coogan and a nemesis by the name of Tiger Kelly. He also changed Ginger's family name from Smith to Meggs.

There was something about Ginger Meggs that struck a familiar chord with boys and families around Australia. He was mischievous and funny, but never law-breaking and never disrespectful to elders. He was lovable and full of fun, but not cheeky.

The editor of the *Sydney Sun*, Eric Baume, loved Jimmy's work, even though Jimmy's years of wagging school came back to haunt him in the form of atrocious spelling. One strip could have as many as 12 spelling errors. Baume fended off a United States attempt to poach Jimmy by giving him a highly paid deal, said to involve a salary larger than the State Governor's.

In 1923, the publishers of the *Melbourne Sun* asked Jimmy to create a cartoon strip for Melbourne readers. He moved to St Kilda and worked out of a studio above Queen's Walk in Swanson Street, where he came up with a series called 'The Blimps', which ran for two years. After that, he introduced 'Mr Melbourne Day by Day' in the *Sun News Pictorial*.

The financial security that came with success allowed Jimmy Bancks to indulge in one of his favourites pastimes – watching cricket. He even travelled to England with the Australian team on one Ashes tour to watch every match.

In 1932, Jimmy married Jesse Taite. Tragically, she and their child died during childbirth three years later. He remarried in 1938 and adopted a daughter.

All the while, Jimmy continued to draw Ginger Meggs, not only for newspapers but also for the famous *Sunbeams Annual* – a top-selling children's book that first appeared in 1924 and was published for the next 35 years.

Jimmy Bancks brought Ginger Meggs to life in comic strips for more than 30 years and created a national icon. Interestingly, some of the most famous features of Ginger Meggs were not entirely of Jimmy's doing. For example, Ginger had red hair only because the three-colour printing process of the day allowed Jimmy to use either blue, yellow or red in addition to black. He figured red hair might go well with the name Ginger.

Jimmy Bancks said that the character of Ginger was based on Charlie Somerville, a kid in the Hornsby neighbourhood who went on to become a prominent local businessman and President of the Hornsby Shire.

Ginger's mum was a mirror image of Jimmy's own mother, whom he described as a 'large, dominating woman', and Ginger's dad, John, was suspiciously like Jimmy's own father – good-natured but ineffectual.

While most of the inspiration for Ginger Meggs came from Jimmy's own childhood experiences, he did take a little licence. For instance, Ginger was famous for his prowess in a back-lane punch-up, whereas, in real life, Jimmy Bancks was hopeless. He only ever had one fight and he got a hiding.

James Bancks died of a heart attack in 1952. But his death was not the end of the story; there's always more.

One of those most downcast at news of his passing was Sydney newspaper baron Sir Frank Packer, who had been one of Jimmy's biggest fans and his regular golf partner. Sir Frank had tried many times to move Ginger Meggs into his papers, but Jimmy insisted on honouring his original deal with the *Sun*. Bancks had been godfather to the older Packer son, Clyde, and taught the younger brother, Kerry, to draw Ginger Meggs.

When Jimmy died, he left an unfinished strip on his desk. His stepdaughter, Sheena, had been given strict instructions that if anything happened to him, she was to ensure that Ginger Meggs continued. With the help of Sir Frank Packer, Sheena arranged for an Australian Consolidated Press artist, Ron Vivian, to continue her father's work. So Sir Frank also managed to fulfil his dream of having Ginger Meggs appear in his papers.

Ron Vivian drew the Ginger Meggs strip until he

died in 1973. Lloyd Piper took over and continued until he died in 1983, and since then the current artist, James Kemsley, has carried the mantle.

Ginger Meggs has had a place in the hearts of Australians for four generations. He even appeared on a 1986 postage stamp. But the red-headed terror has also proved a favourite elsewhere.

His escapades are well known in more than 20 countries, including Holland, Norway, France, South Africa, Spain, Canada, the United States, Bolivia, the Dominican Republic, Honduras, Mexico, Venezuela, Guatemala, Vanuatu, Fiji, Thailand and India. In 1997, Ginger Meggs became the first Australian comic strip to run daily in a major London newspaper when it appeared in the *Daily Express*. In South America he is called 'Arellana'. In France he is 'Pierrot'. But no matter what the name, or what language his fans speak, they always find something to love about the mischievous little boy with the red hair and freckles.

Jimmy Bancks said he owed the success of Ginger Meggs to his family life in Hornsby – he described it as 'a living comic strip'.

PISTOLS AT DAWN

As several footballers have proven recently, alcohol and bravado often go together but are a dangerous mix.

The sight of two drunks in the pub falling about as they try to take their jackets off to settle an argument with their fists can be pitifully amusing. Still, perhaps we should have a system in the pubs and clubs where people with disputes are required to go to a register and sign up for next-day settlement of the matter in the boxing ring. I wonder how many of the six-schooner heroes would turn up and want to get in the ring without Mr Booze in their corner.

This story is about some gentlemen who really should have slept on it.

ONE OF THE sillier European traditions brought to Australia two centuries ago by the British was duelling. Pistols-at-twenty-yards (20 metres) was one way for colonial 'gentlemen' to settle disputes – even though it was illegal. There were some deaths as a result of duels, but most ended harmlessly and some even humorously.

The first recorded duel in Australia in 1788

involved the New South Wales Surgeon-General, Dr John White, and his assistant, Dr William Balmain. They managed to shoot each other, but the wounds were minor. Instead of repeating the duel, they decided to shake hands and resolve their disagreement over a disciplinary matter.

More comical was the duel in Melbourne on 2 January 1840, between Peter Snodgrass and William Ryrie. The pair were drinking in the Melbourne Club throughout New Year's Day when Snodgrass made a derogatory comment about Ryrie's lady friend, who happened to be a notorious barmaid. To the amusement of the other intoxicated members of the club, Ryrie demanded Snodgrass take back the remark or face a beating. Ryrie was tall and skinny, while Snodgrass was heavily built and well able to handle himself. Instead of withdrawing it, Snodgrass continued to make jokes about the woman's chastity.

Someone else suggested that, rather than a fistfight, Ryrie should demand a duel. Both men were lukewarm about the idea, but a French army officer stationed at Port Phillip and visiting the club convinced Ryrie that it was the only way to defend the honour of a lady. Most of those present were amused at the suggestion of this woman being a lady, let alone one with honour.

Unfortunately, while enthusiasm for the duel had mounted, no-one in the club knew how to conduct one. Eventually, they agreed that it involved pistols at dawn. But no-one had any pistols. Ryrie only had a shotgun and Snodgrass a couple of heavy horse pistols.

As both men were about to conclude that the duel was impossible, the club president remembered that a friend had a pair of pistols in a case above his fireplace. He rode off into the late night to find them. When he returned, both Ryrie and Snodgrass were extremely drunk and sharing a joke together. Despite this, the pistols were unpacked and the duel was planned for the following morning at dawn. A young lawyer in the club, Redmond Barry, was appointed adjudicator of the duel, even though he reminded everyone that it was illegal.

Ryrie then pointed out that although they now had pistols, they had no primers, powder or shot. Alas, the duel would have to be cancelled, suggested a relieved Peter Snodgrass.

But no! The French lieutenant said that he could obtain ammunition at the home of the commandant of his military detachment at Port Phillip. It was midnight, but the excitement of the duel took over and Lieutenant Vignolles went off with Redmond Barry to wake the commandant. They returned with the ammunition, and the commandant.

Next someone recalled that the rules of duelling required a doctor to be present. There was no doctor in the club. Lieutenant Vignolles and the commandant were adamant that there needed to be a doctor present. Again the club president rode off into the darkness. When he returned – just in time for the dawn shoot-out to proceed – he was accompanied by Dr David Thomas of Bourke Street.

The crowd made its way to Batman's Hill, not far from the club, and spectators settled with bottles of rum to watch proceedings. William Ryrie and Peter Snodgrass were being railroaded into a duel that neither wanted to fight.

Redmond Barry supervised the loading of the pistols and offered them to Snodgrass then to Ryrie. Next the men stood back to back as their seconds withdrew. As Barry lifted a white hankie and counted out loud, they stepped away from each other. When Barry called 'seven', there was a flash and Peter Snodgrass fell to the ground crying in pain and holding his foot. The toecap of his boot was missing.

Ryrie had not heard anything in his daze and kept striding out until the Melbourne Club president ran to him and told him Snodgrass was shot and the duel was over. Dr Thomas rushed to Snodgrass and, after a short examination, declared to a cheering crowd that Mr Snodgrass would survive the loss of his big toenail.

The duel was declared over and Ryrie the winner. Many of the crowd then proceeded to try their hand with the pistols, shooting holes in the doctor's top hat, which had been placed in a nearby tree. But there's more to this story.

Despite having sustained a splintered toenail, Peter Snodgrass was not deterred from seeking satisfaction with a pistol. Sometime later, he was the one offended at the Melbourne Club and he challenged a young barrister to a duel in Albert Park.

As the pair walked away from each other, a single

shot rang out and Snodgrass fell to the ground. Alas, he had shot himself in the foot, yet again. That duel, also, was cancelled and Peter Snodgrass took his place in history – twice shot in a duel, both times by himself.

Peter Snodgrass's 'accidents' have raised considerable conjecture because he was a crack shot and well trained in firearms handling by his father, who was an army officer. He went on after these duels to lead the hunts for several Victorian bushrangers. Some suggest that he discharged his pistols intentionally in the duels to avoid having to kill his opponents.

Whether it was through compassion or clumsiness, Peter Snodgrass's premature discharge avoided the possible death of the young barrister. As fate would have it, that barrister was Redmond Barry, the very same man who had adjudicated almost exactly a year earlier at Peter Snodgrass's first unsuccessful duel, with William Ryrie.

Of course, Redmond Barry went on to earn his own place in history – as the judge who sentenced Ned Kelly to hang.

PLEASE EXPLAIN!

Not so long ago there was great controversy about the way our history and culture were being presented in the National Museum of Australia. There were claims from the conservatives that the collection had been 'hijacked' and showed a biased perspective on indigenous rights and various social welfare issues.

I thought at the time what a stupid debate it was because all history is subjective – it is merely an account related by someone or some group of people as they believe it happened, as they interpret it, or as they wish to express it.

We put this book together for that very reason: we hope that our stories give you another perspective on Australian history. This one is a good example.

AUSTRALIA'S FIRST GOVERNOR-GENERAL was a Scotsman named John Adrian Louis Hope Linlithgow, Seventh Earl of Hopetoun – better known as Lord Hopetoun. He had been educated at Eton and the Royal Military College at Sandhurst, but had lived a life of privilege and leisure running the family estate in Scotland. Through family connections, he landed an

A 1902 portrait of the Earl of Hopetoun,
Marquis of Linlithgow.

appointment as Governor of Victoria in 1889 at the age of 28. He remained in that role for six years until being recalled to England to serve as Lord Chamberlain in the British Government.

On 15 December 1900, Lord Hopetoun returned to Melbourne, at the age of 40, as the Governor-General Designate for the new Federation. It was a popular choice among the Victorians but other colonies were not so sure. Within two days, the Governor-General Designate would ruffle plenty of colonial feathers.

His first official task was to appoint a Prime Minister. There had not yet been an election and there was no precedent to guide him, so Lord Hopetoun took it upon himself to offer the appointment to William Lyne, Premier of New South Wales – his reasoning was that Lyne was the leader of the largest state of the Federation.

Unfortunately for Lord Hopetoun, William Lyne had also led the opposition to Federation and was extremely unpopular with most other political leaders, especially Alfred Deakin. The 'understanding' among the architects of Federation was that Edmund Barton was to be the first PM. What came to be described as 'the blunder' thrust Lord Hopetoun into controversy both in Australia and in London. Australian politicians from all sides condemned the Lyne nomination and demanded it be withdrawn, threatening that none would serve under Lyne.

Responding to pressure from Sydney, the British Colonial Secretary, Joseph Chamberlain, sent a 'Please explain' telegram to Lord Hopetoun, and later suggested he rethink the Lyne offer. In the face of the controversy, William Lyne returned his commission and Lord Hopetoun offered it instead to Edmund Barton.

Further political tension arose when Lord Hopetoun brought with him from England an official secretary solely responsible for communication with London. This was seen as an attempt to circumvent the Australian executive government.

Even greater problems lay ahead; Lord Hopetoun declared himself too ill to attend the gala dinner on 1 January 1901 celebrating the first day of the new Commonwealth of Australia. By the time he stood alongside the Duke of York on 9 May 1901 for the inauguration of the Commonwealth of Australia, Lord Hopetoun, our first Governor-General, had already lost the trust of most political leaders and many of the public. However, his unhappy posting was not to last long. In May 1902, he resigned in protest at his salary.

Alfred Deakin and several other leaders in the new Federal Parliament, still angry at the Lyne issue, were openly scathing of Lord Hopetoun's love of expensive pomp and ceremony. They intended to curtail his 'extravagant' spending. As a result, the Parliament voted Lord Hopetoun just £10,000 ($20,000) a year to maintain residences in both Sydney and Melbourne *and* to host all official functions. Lord Hopetoun said, quite correctly, that it wasn't enough and that he required more than double this amount. The Parliament refused and so he resigned.

Perversely, later governors-general were paid higher salaries and given a separate allowance to cover official expenses.

But there's always more to the story. It seems unbelievable that the new Commonwealth of Australia was prepared to lose its head of state for the sake of a few thousand pounds. And, as with many things in politics, it *was* unbelievable. In fact, there was another issue behind Lord Hopetoun's demise. It was an issue of principle that would cause debate for the remainder of the century, coming to a head in 1975: immigration.

To the great annoyance of many newly elected Members and Senators, Lord Hopetoun did not believe the vice-regal position existed only for ceremonial purposes. He pointed to the Constitution and the principle of separation of powers. He intended to act as a check and balance on the elected Parliament.

Deakin and his supporters accused Lord Hopetoun of behaving as if he were the 'ruler' of Australia; however, the Governor-General stood firm. To prove his point, he witheld royal assent on a key piece of legislation – the *Alien Immigration Restriction Bill 1901* – the basis for the infamous 'White Australia Policy'. This infuriated the Government and the Parliament. Although he eventually agreed to give assent to the Act, Lord Hopetoun made it clear he would be taking an interest in future developments on immigration.

The rest, as they say, is history. Lord Hopetoun quickly found that his finances had been restricted, making it almost impossible to maintain official residences in Sydney and Melbourne. He left Australia in July 1902, and was made Marquis of Linlithgow by the Queen as compensation for his shortened term in Australia. He was appointed Secretary of State for Scotland in 1905 and died three years later, at the age of 47, never having achieved his real dream, to become Viceroy of India.

The history books might say that our first Governor-General resigned over money. But the popular theory is that Lord Hopetoun was *forced* to resign by politicians who feared he might try to play an active role in the running of the country, or even exercise the ultimate power . . . and dismiss a government!

PORT PIRIE'S FINEST SON

When we were putting this book together I was struck by the enormous wealth of intellect, beauty, talent and courage that Australia has produced over two centuries to the benefit of the rest of the world.

Surely there could be no other country the size and age of ours that has made such a stunning contribution to science, the arts, sports and discovery.

I also realised that in many cases our high achievers are better known outside Australia than they are at home. This story is a perfect example.

HUGH WILLIAM BELL CAIRNS was in his fifth year of medical studies at the University of Adelaide in 1914 when a world war broke out in Europe. He had just been named South Australia's Rhodes Scholar and was bound for Oxford and a stunning career. But this brilliant son of a Port Pirie building contractor had other plans. Without consulting anyone, he withdrew from university and enlisted in the army as a private.

Shortly after he landed at Gallipoli as an ambulance

bearer and began treating wounded with skill equal to the surgeon officers, medical staff realised that this was no ordinary digger. Although he was invaluable to the medical teams on the beach of Anzac Cove, they reported his identity to the high command and Hugh Cairns was shipped back to Adelaide to finish his medical studies.

Dutifully, he obeyed orders to return to Australia, but on the day he graduated he re-enlisted, this time as a captain in the Medical Corps. Within weeks he was saving lives on the battlefields of France as a surgeon.

Hugh Cairns survived the Great War and finally made it to Oxford in 1919 to take up his scholarship. He showed great promise, and in 1926, at the age of 29, was selected for a prestigious Rockefeller Scholarship to work alongside the world's best neurosurgeon, American Harvey Cushing.

On his return to London in 1927, he set up the United Kingdom's first comprehensive department of brain surgery. Hugh Cairns was driven by commitment and passion to learn more about the delicate human brain.

By the time he was 35, he was Honorary Surgeon to the London Hospital for Epilepsy and Paralysis. At 38 he was Honorary Surgeon to the National Hospital for Disease of the Nervous System. And, at the ripe old age of 40, Hugh Cairns was appointed Nuffield Professor of Surgery at Oxford University – the most prestigious surgical teaching position in the Commonwealth.

He was now one of the world's top neurosurgeons, winning awards in England and the United States and pioneering work on the treatment of brain injury and disease. However, he gave up the offer of wealth and fame in order to teach others – he said it was more important for him to pass on what he had learned than to use it for personal gain.

Professor Hugh Cairns was knighted in 1946 for outstanding services to medicine. He died in 1952 at the age of 56.

As impressive as this South Australian's achievements might seem, you haven't yet heard all of the story. Professor Sir Hugh Cairns was one of the world's most eminent neurosurgeons for half a century. Yet some history books recognise him only for the role he played in World War II in treating a mortally wounded patient.

On 10 December 1945, as everyone was preparing for peace, Brigadier Hugh Cairns of the Royal Army Medical Corps was told to prepare for a high-priority mercy flight to Heidelberg in Austria. The Allied Command requested the best neurosurgeon available for a special assignment and Hugh Cairns was the unanimous choice. Cairns and his assistant – another Australian, Lieutenant Colonel Gilbert Phillips – were hurried aboard a military aircraft.

When they arrived in Heidelberg they found an American Army officer in critical condition. He had been involved in a car accident and had suffered spinal injuries. He was paralysed from the neck down. They worked with American military doctors around the clock. For a while it seemed the soldier might survive. They even considered flying him back to the United States. But then a blood clot shut down one of his lungs and he began to develop pneumonia. He remained conscious throughout, talking to the doctors and assuring them he would fight on because this was a 'hell of a way for a soldier to die'. On the tenth day after the car accident, Brigadier Cairns lost his patient to heart failure after the second lung collapsed.

Hugh Cairns had seen a great deal in two world wars, but he was mightily impressed at the courage and good humour that his dying patient had shown in spite of massive injuries. But then this patient was a general, and one with a reputation for exceptional toughness. He was known as the Hero of the Battle of the Bulge and his name was General George Patton.

Hugh Cairns could not save Patton any more than he could save another battlefield warrior injured in a road accident ten years earlier in England. That patient suffered severe head injuries in a motorcycle crash. His name was Thomas Edward Lawrence, better known as TE Lawrence, or Lawrence of Arabia.

THE PRINCE OF PICKPOCKETS

I would hate to be a policeman. They turn up for work each day knowing they are going to have to deal with the worst in life – car accidents, suicides, murders, rapes, domestic violence, violent robbery, vandalism, drug deals and more.

And every day, they do their job knowing that with one mistake, one moment of emotion, one wrong procedure or one wrong word, they could find themselves being investigated, charged, disciplined, dismissed, or even jailed, because of a set of rules that the bad guys don't have to obey.

This is the story of one of the first policemen in Australia. By all accounts he did an excellent job, even though he was rather 'unorthodox'.

WHEN GOVERNOR JOHN HUNTER appointed George Barrington as Chief Police Constable of Parramatta in 1796, it raised plenty of eyebrows. It's not that he wasn't a gentleman – in fact, he was one of the most dapper and refined fellows in the colony – it's just that George Barrington was a criminal. He was known far and wide in Britain as the Prince of Pickpockets.

George Barrington in 1785, before he came to Australia.

When he was appointed Superintendent of Convicts and Chief Constable, he still had a year to serve on a seven-year sentence. Governor Hunter pardoned Barrington and issued him with the first warrant of emancipation in New South Wales.

George Barrington was born in Maynooth, County Kildare, Ireland in 1755. All evidence suggests that he was the illegitimate son of a silversmith named Waldron and a woman named Naith, who was a part-time midwife. His parents gave him a good education at home with the help of a village doctor.

A minister of the Church of Ireland saw George's potential and, when he was 16, he was sponsored to the exclusive Trinity College in Dublin, under a program for disadvantaged youth. But he got into a fight with an older student and stabbed him with a penknife. When he was flogged by the headmaster, he resented the punishment and ran away, stealing the headmaster's gold watch and 12 guineas in the process. He was expelled for his trouble.

George left school and joined a touring theatrical group made up of petty criminals. He began working the county racecourses of Ireland, learning the trade of picking pockets from a man named John Price, who used young boys in much the way that Charles Dickens's character Fagin worked his boys.

In between stealing, George improved his acting skills while with the troupe, starring in some small Irish productions and dreaming of a role at Drury Lane in London. Many times he dressed in clerical robes from the theatre wardrobe while picking pockets so as to avoid suspicion when the robberies were discovered.

In 1773, after John Price was sentenced to seven years transportation, George Barrington went to London at the suggestion of an Irish court after a victim of his crime declined to prosecute.

He found his way into social circles and even picked pockets at Royal Court on the Queen's birthday in 1775. Dressing in fine clothes and carrying himself in the manner of a wealthy gentleman, he spent a great deal of time in the Houses of Parliament, in theatres, at racecourses and in churches around London.

Time and again he was arrested and found in

possession of property belonging to others, but almost every time he charmed his victims out of pressing charges. It was always an 'honest mistake', a 'lucky find' or a 'misunderstanding'. He was so eloquent that his victims usually believed him over the facts.

Eventually, George Barrington's luck ran out and in 1776 he was sentenced to three years hard labour on one of the coal barges in the Thames River. A newspaper reporter at the court described him as the 'genteelest thief ever to have been seen at the Old Bailey'. He was only 21, but was described as tastefully dressed with a gold-headed taper cane, and tassles and Artois buckles on his shoes.

It came as quite a shock to George when he had to mix with vulgar criminals on the hulks. But he was released after just one year of his three-year sentence as a reward for good behaviour. He tried to find work, but within five months he was back on the hulks serving another five-year sentence after being caught stealing watches and wallets at St Sepulchre's Church at Snow Hill in London. His profession was described to the court as 'surgeon'.

This time his health suffered and he became severely depressed. When an escape failed, he tried to commit suicide by stabbing himself with a penknife. No sooner had he recovered from that wound than he contracted tuberculosis. Barrington wasted away and nearly died, but again he survived.

After four years of his sentence, he was released on condition that he leave England and never return. He went home to Ireland, but the police were waiting for him there and he fled back across the sea to England.

In 1783, he was back in the Old Bailey charged with breaking the conditions of his pardon by re-entering England. He managed to convince the magistrate not to send him back to the hulks on the Thames, but rather, to give him 11 months in a prison. No sooner was he released than he was in trouble again.

He went to a box at the Drury Lane Playhouse and tried to steal a £30,000 gold snuff box encrusted with diamonds from the waistcoat of Russian minister Count Gregory Orloff. He was caught in the act, but because the count was a foreign citizen, no prosecution was brought against Barrington.

However, in September 1790, he was arrested for stealing a gold watch from a gentleman's pocket at a racecourse. The victim refused to demand the available death sentence, and the prospect of Barrington walking free, yet again, angered the magistrate, so he sentenced the prisoner to seven years transportation in New South Wales.

But there's always more to the story. When George Barrington arrived in Sydney Town it was obvious that he was a very well-educated and cultured man. Working on the theory that you use a thief to catch a thief, Governor Arthur Phillip made George a policeman soon after his arrival at Parramatta in 1791.

He did so well at the job that only five years later Governor John Hunter promoted him to Chief

Constable. However, while George Barrington did a good job keeping the streets of Parramatta free of pick-pockets and other criminals, he could not control his love of rum. He was forced to retire from public office in 1800 on health grounds; the official papers said he suffered mental illness, but people said it was a drinking problem. Either way, he died four years later.

At about the same time as he retired with his 'incapacity', two books appeared in London shops in George Barrington's name – one was called *A Voyage to New South Wales*; the other, *The History of New South Wales*. From then on, George Barrington was considered one of the colony's first historians and biographers. In 1908, four years after his death, another book was published in his name in London – it was called *The History of New Holland*.

Unfortunately, things are not always what they seem. The available evidence suggests that George Barrington did not write the three books published in his name. Much of the text seems to have been taken from another manuscript by David Collins, a famous magistrate of the early colonial years. To this day no-one knows for certain who wrote the three Barrington books, why they used George Barrington's name, who arranged for them to be published, or who received the royalties.

At the very least, they guarantee that George Barrington, the Prince of Pickpockets, remains controversial, even after death.

THE PROFESSOR

The battle continues to eliminate performance-enhancing drugs from sport. But as quickly as we develop tests, someone finds a way around them.

It is a shame that so many decades of sporting achievement are now under a cloud of suspicion because of revelations about doping; it means that honest athletes whose dreams were ruined by cheats are now left wondering what could have been.

Let's hope that one day naturally gifted athletes might again compete with confidence that the best person wins.

Here is the story of a naturally gifted Australian athlete who had a chance to show what extraordinary feats the human body could achieve.

THEY CALLED HIM the 'Professor' because of his gentle voice, kind nature and dignified manner. And, while William Miller was no academic, most experts believe he was the greatest all-round athlete that Australia, and probably the world, has ever seen.

Miller was born in Cheshire, England, in 1846 and migrated to Melbourne with his parents at the age of five. His father was a champion swordsman, and at 15,

William took up fencing. Within two years, he was more skilful than his father.

At the age of 16, William went to work with the Melbourne and Hobson's Bay Railway Company as an assistant stationmaster. However, he spent a great deal of his time impressing colleagues with feats of strength, including lifting sleepers. By 25, Miller had developed both strength and agility and, in his sport of fencing, he had beaten every opponent in Australia. He was looking for new challenges.

He turned to wrestling, including an unusual form called deep water wrestling; this involved competing 1.2 metres under water. The object was to hold your opponent under until he submitted. Within two years William Miller was the Australian fencing, wrestling and weightlifting champion and State champion in boxing and gymnastics.

But still he was not satisfied. So, in 1874, he went to the United States and became senior physical culture instructor at San Francisco's famous Olympic Club. While there, he tried his hand at prize-fighting. In quick succession, as a professional, he beat the Pacific, East Coast, American and Canadian champions. Although one of his scalps was that of reigning American champ Joe Goss, over 35 rounds, Miller couldn't claim the US title because his application for American citizenship had not yet been approved.

Miller also did a bit of wrestling in the US, winning 55 of 72 bouts and drawing 11. Then there was weightlifting – he outlifted America's best. In one exhibition, 'Professor' William Miller lifted a dumbbell weighing more than 45 kilograms above his head 20 times – with one arm. He also lifted a deadweight iron bar of 704 kilos.

For good measure, the 'Professor' humiliated American track stars. In a 50-hour contest he beat America's champion walker, Duncan Ross, by 48 kilometres (30 miles). In a rematch, Ross pulled out after 64 kilometres (40 miles). Miller challenged Ross's trainer to finish the contest, only to see him carried off the track at the 80-kilometre (50-mile) mark. Miller went on to prove his extraordinary ability by walking 160 kilometres (100 miles) in 22 hours.

William Miller was described by sports commentators of the time as a man built in the form of Hercules. He stood 175 centimetres (5 feet 9 inches) tall, weighed 90 kilograms (200 pounds), had calf muscles measuring 44 centimetres (17.5 inches), a chest of 119 centimetres (47 inches), and forearms of 35.5 centimetres (14 inches).

The 'Professor's' legend continued to grow after he returned to Australia in 1880. It started with a three-match series against Scottish wrestling champion Donald Dinnie. In the first bout, Dinnie broke Miller's left leg, but the Australian continued and forced a draw. The second bout was also drawn, but the third went to Miller.

Then Miller was challenged to a Graeco-Roman bout by the Commonwealth and European champion, Mons Victor. He won that contest, and the following day took on two other challengers and beat them both inside two hours – but only after defeating one of them in a weight-lifting competition!

The Australian wrestling champion, Ned Blackburn, then challenged Miller, who beat him in 45 minutes. So Blackburn and his trainer threw out a challenge and Miller took them on, beating one after the other. William Miller had 108 wrestling bouts in 18 months and won all but one.

Then in 1883, aged 37, he challenged Australia's champion boxer, Larry Foley. In the 40th round Miller knocked Foley down. As the referee applied the count, it was clear Foley was not getting up, and so the excited crowd invaded the ring. The referee could not finish the count and the match was declared a draw. It seemed almost impossible to believe the string of achievements of William Miller, the man they called the 'Professor'. But there's always more to the story.

Miller became a sports coach in Melbourne but in 1903 he was drawn back to the United States of America, where he became physical training instructor to the New York Police Department and later manager of the San Francisco Athletic Club. He also married an American woman named Lizzie Treble. Miller and his wife settled in Baltimore, where he died in 1939, at the ripe old age of 92.

Now, about that lone wrestling bout that the 'Professor' William Miller lost in Australia. It was on 26 September 1885 at Melbourne's Theatre Royal, against an American rated by many at the time as the world's greatest wrestler – Clarence Whistler. Whistler died after the event, from internal bleeding caused by eating the champagne glass from which he toasted his victory over Miller.

PROTECTION, PLEASE

I find it remarkable that recruitment companies in Australia score potential employees according to psychological-profiling criteria that includes age.

If you are over 45, you will score very poorly because you are considered likely to be 'set in your ways and not open to new ideas and technologies'.

Amazing, isn't it? We have gone through decades of protests and court cases to stop discrimination against people on the basis of their gender, their colour, their ethnicity and their religion, but we still allow discrimination based on age. I wonder what happens to recruitment gurus when they turn 45.

Here is a story of a woman who broke the age and gender barriers at the same time.

THE FIRST WOMAN elected to an Australian Parliament was Edith Cowan, who won the West Australian Legislative Assembly seat of West Perth in 1921. Although she lost the next election and failed to regain her seat, she had broken down the gender barriers in Australian politics forever.

Edith Dircksey Brown was born in August 1861,

Portrait of Edith Cowan.

on Glengarry station near Geraldton, north of Perth. She was the second daughter of a pastoralist, Kenneth Brown, and a schoolteacher, Mary Eliza Dircksey Wittenoom. Edith's mother was a gentle and quiet woman who spent much of her time teaching her two little girls to read and write.

When Edith was seven years old, her mother died during childbirth. Kenneth Brown could not cope with the loss of his wife, the pressures of running the property, as well as raising two children, so he sent Edith and her older sister to boarding school in Perth. The two little girls hardly saw their father for the next few years until he remarried and they were allowed to visit the property in school holidays. Feeling abandoned, Edith became withdrawn and took refuge in books, hardly mixing even with the other students at the private girls' school she attended.

One day, however, she met a young and studious lawyer named James Cowan. He was the younger brother of the school principal, and he was also shy and quiet; finally, Edith had met someone whom she trusted enough to confide her feelings. In November 1879, when Edith was 18, she and James married at St George's Cathedral in Perth and set up home at beachside Cottesloe.

James Cowan was Registrar and Master of the Supreme Court of Western Australia, and so Edith spent many days of her early married life sitting in court listening to stories of violence and discrimination against women unfold. In 1890, James was appointed Police Magistrate for Perth; by now he and Edith had four daughters and a son on the way.

With the children at school, Edith Cowan was ready to pursue a burning passion – addressing what she saw as the injustices forced upon women and children by a male-dominated society. With the support of her husband and children, she set out to stir the community into action.

Edith raised funds to establish the District Nursing Society in Perth to provide home-nursing care for financially disadvantaged women. She also formed the Children's Protection Society, finding new homes for unwanted babies born in the slums of Perth, removing children from violent domestic environments and fighting against child exploitation in the workplace.

From 1893, she worked as a volunteer in the House of Mercy in Perth helping young single mothers – this facility was to be re-named the Alexandra Home for Women with an adjoining Alexandra Maternity Hospital. This was the first hospital in Western Australia to admit unmarried women for childbirth.

Edith Cowan was also the driving force behind the Karrakatta Club, which recruited wealthy and influential women for public debates on women's rights and women in the arts, education and literature. She was one of the founders of the West Australian branch of the National Council of Women, and campaigned strongly for the right of women to vote. In 1899 Edith and her colleagues finally forced that change into law in Western Australia. But even though the law allowed women to vote, it prevented them from standing for election to the Parliament.

Meanwhile, Edith had noticed a disturbing trend in cases being heard in court and decided to take action. The sexually transmitted disease syphilis had spread wildly in Australia during the 1890s – to the extent that children as young as eight were being forced into prostitution by brothel owners to satisfy the demand of wealthy clients for girls without the disease. Edith took on the Government, demanding protection for the children. In 1906, the *State Children's Protection Act* was enacted.

During World War I, Edith chaired the Red Cross Appeal Committee, raising money for the families of soldiers serving overseas, particularly the families of those killed or wounded. She noted that the problem of syphilis had re-emerged as soldiers returned from Egypt and France carrying the disease and infecting their wives and girlfriends. Fearing that there would be renewed pressure on young girls, Edith Cowan fought to have laws introduced that imposed prison sentences on any man or woman forcing a girl under the age of 18 into prostitution.

In 1915, when the West Australian Government finally responded to her call for a separate children's court – a campaign supported by her husband and his legal colleagues – it came as no surprise to anyone that Edith Cowan was appointed a Justice of the court.

In 1917 the long battle against venereal disease was also won when laws were enacted to protect women and children by establishing special hospitals to isolate and treat syphilis effectively.

However, it was in 1920 that one of Edith's most dogged fights ended, when the law was changed to allow women to be elected to Parliament. The following year Mrs Edith Cowan stood against the sitting Member for West Perth, TP Draper, who was also the State Attorney-General. Ignoring the urgings of the major political parties, women turned out in force to support Edith and she won by 46 votes after distribution of preferences. Edith Cowan, at the age of 60, and a grandmother, had become the first woman elected to

Parliament in Australia. Even she was stunned by what she had achieved.

Edith encountered daily discrimination and prejudice, even from within her own Nationalist Party, over the next three years as she demanded to be heard on issues such as equal pay for women, fair industrial conditions for nurses, rights for married women to a share of their husband's income, extension of family payments to unmarried mothers, and adequate social support for the poor and underprivileged. One of her proudest moments was the passage in 1923 of the Legal Status Bill that ensured women equal access to professions, including law.

In 1924, the men of the West Australian Parliament conspired to ensure that Edith Cowan was not re-elected. Even her own party was glad to see her go after the trouble she caused by crossing the floor to vote with the Opposition on some issues. Again, in the election of 1927, Edith was targeted heavily by opponents determined to keep her out of the legislature.

Failure to be elected didn't stop her campaigning on her pet issues, and she travelled extensively in Australia and overseas speaking publicly about women's and children's concerns.

Edith Cowan died in Perth on 9 June 1932, aged 71. But that is not all there is to her story.

Edith Cowan was a lifelong campaigner for the rights of women and children, particularly the rights of women in violent relationships and children affected by marriage breakdown and trauma. There was good reason for her passionate and personal interest in families in distress. When Edith's mother died, she was lonely and unhappy at the boarding school in Perth where she and her sister were left, without family support or any of the counselling that children might receive today. Compounding the grief of losing her mother, Edith's father left for the east coast. Distraught at his wife's death, he took to drinking and gambling and completely abandoned contact with his young daughters. When he finally returned to Geraldton and remarried, he took a new wife who had a fiery temper and little interest in children. It was an unhappy marriage and on the rare occasions that the girls travelled home from Perth to see their father, they were often caught in the middle of loud and violent arguments.

In 1876, when Edith was 15, a fellow student at the boarding school showed her a newspaper story reporting that her father had shot dead his second wife after a drunken argument. Young Edith was called from the classroom to the courtroom to give evidence about what she had seen and heard at the property during her infrequent visits.

Kenneth Brown was convicted of murder and hanged. Again, there was no counselling or support for Edith and her sister as they tried to deal with public and peer reaction, as well as with the grief of their father's death and being left as orphans.

Edith Cowan well understood what it was like to be a victim, and she vowed never to stop trying to help others in the same situation, or worse.

RAMPAGING REPORTER

The mistreatment of Iraqi prisoners by American military police drew such a quick and negative response from the Western world because it violated one of the fundamental principles of our society – that two wrongs do not make a right. There is no excuse for mistreating another human being in the manner we saw on television and in newspapers, even if Americans were being subjected to even worse treatment at the hands of their captors.

Societies that live by the principle you should exact an eye for an eye and a tooth for a tooth would say that we are weak and doomed forever to be victims. However, once you begin tinkering with principles, you end up without any.

This is the story of a time the Australian Government began tinkering with principles and got its knuckles rapped by the High Court.

THE FIRST ALARM was raised in June 1934 by a town clerk when he saw a request for a booking of the St Kilda City Hall in the name of the Second National Congress Against War. The letter said that a prominent Czechoslovakian journalist named Egon

Kisch would be speaking against war and fascism. The St Kilda City Council became concerned, and in September wrote to the Chief Commissioner of the Commonwealth Police asking if the organisation booking their hall was 'bona fide and single-minded in its campaign against war as such; or whether it is covertly using an appeal to humanitarianism to propagate Communistic or revolutionary ideals'.

The Director of the Investigations Branch of the Attorney-General's Department quickly ordered that if any communist literature was found in Mr Kisch's possession, it would be considered definite proof of his activities and his undesirability. He should not be allowed into Australia. Inquiries sent to London then revealed that Kisch was a prohibited immigrant in the United Kingdom. It was now automatic – he was also undesirable in Australia.

Egon Erwin Kisch was born in Prague but lived in Germany. In 1933 he was imprisoned by the Nazis but escaped to France and began a global crusade to expose the Nazi agenda. He became known as the 'Rampaging Reporter'.

But he hadn't anticipated the reaction he would get in Britain and Australia. Kisch had been invited to Australia by groups associated with the labour movement and trade unions. That was hardly going to go down well with the Australian Government of Joe Lyons, which was conservative and vehemently anti-communist, especially the Attorney-General, Robert Menzies.

When Egon Kisch's ship docked in Fremantle on

6 November 1934, Commonwealth Police searched his cabin and told him that he was not to disembark because he was an undesirable person under the terms of the *Immigration Act* of 1920.

Assured by the organisers of the Melbourne conference that they would resolve the matter, Kisch obeyed the order and continued on the ship to Melbourne. But the matter was not resolved, and again Kisch was denied permission to land. In protest, as the ship was leaving the Port Melbourne docks on 13 November 1934, Kisch jumped from the deck landing heavily on the wharf and breaking his leg. The ship was recalled to the dock and Kisch was carried back on board by police without being allowed any medical attention.

As Kisch sailed to Sydney, his supporters went to court. Unable to produce details of the warnings from London or any evidence of materials found in Kisch's cabin in Fremantle, Justice Evatt of the High Court ruled that the Australian Government had not established grounds under the *Immigration Act* and that Kisch could enter the country.

When the ship docked, Kisch hobbled defiantly ashore to the cheers of supporters. However, he was immediately escorted away by immigration officers to a nearby police station. There, officials invoked section 3a of the *Immigration Act* – a disguised provision used to prevent Asian and 'coloured' immigration. This section allowed officials to administer a dictation test in a European language to any potential immigrant. Egon

Kisch spoke 11 languages fluently. But the officials decided that his test would be in Scottish Gaelic. Of course Kisch failed the test, and was immediately charged as an illegal immigrant and sentenced to six months imprisonment.

It was only now that Kisch was allowed to see a doctor about his injured leg. Doctors at Sydney Hospital diagnosed fractures and set the leg in plaster.

Kisch's supporters again went to the High Court. In a highly publicised case, Kisch's legal team showed that he had little or no chance of passing the dictation test because Scottish Gaelic was spoken by only one in 600 native Scots, let alone by anyone else.

On Christmas Day 1934, the High Court agreed and decided 4–1 that Scottish Gaelic was spoken by so few people it did not constitute a 'European language' in the terms of the Australian *Immigration Act*. Therefore, Egon Kisch's refusal of entry and conviction were invalid. He was free to enter Australia and conduct his business.

Kisch remained in Australia until March 1935, writing and lecturing on his anti-war beliefs in Sydney, Melbourne and Adelaide. He also visited the coalmines in Newcastle and the prisons in Parramatta, Redfern, Long Bay, Ballarat and Brisbane, campaigning for freedom of speech.

But there's more – as usual – to the story.

Attorney-General Robert Menzies was embarrassed by the Egon Kisch case. He was not involved in the original decision to ban Kisch, but he was responsible for conducting the defence in the High Court. The successive findings of the court allowed political opponents to portray him as an opponent of free speech for years to come.

Yet the embarrassment didn't motivate Mr Menzies to withdraw the dictation test from the *Immigration Act*. In fact, he made no effort to overrule another decision on application for entry by a man named Gerald Griffin. Griffin was an Irish New Zealander with a history of 'very vigorous Unionist propaganda' and who had spent time in Russia. When he turned up at about the same time as Egon Kisch, he was given the dictation test in Dutch. When he inevitably failed the test, he was deported. Despite a delegation from the Trades Hall Council to Mr Menzies pleading for common sense, the Attorney-General refused to back down. Later he made it clear that not only would communists, Nazis and fascists be excluded from entry to Australia, but also people with strong anti-British views.

THE REMARKABLE MACKELLARS

Americans are passionate about loyalty to the Stars and Stripes – they swear allegiance to the flag at school every day, wear it on the sleeves of their business uniforms and display it proudly on stickers in the back windows of their cars.

Australians are no less passionate about national pride and loyalty, with one big difference – when Americans say they love their country, they are talking about a 'nation' that cherishes liberty, freedom and the pursuit of happiness.

When Australians say they love their country, they are talking about the red soil, the white sand, the blue sky, the mountains, rainforests, reefs and the crystal clear water. In the same way Aboriginal people believe the earth is their mother, other Australians consider the physical elements surrounding us to be integral to our national identity.

SIR CHARLES MACKELLAR might have been one of the wealthiest men in New South Wales in the late 1800s, but he was also a one-man crusade for the cause of the poor and delinquent, under-privileged and handicapped children.

The son of a doctor, Charles Mackellar was born in

Sydney in 1844 and attended Sydney Grammar School. When he finished school, he went to work on the family property near Port Macquarie before going to Glasgow, in Scotland, to study medicine in 1866. On returning to Australia in 1871 as a qualified physician and surgeon, he went back onto the land before relocating to Sydney to work in the Sydney Infirmary and Dispensary – now called Sydney Hospital.

Charles had been raised to care about others. Upon his return from Scotland, he was struck by the poverty and despair he saw in the streets of Sydney, especially among children. He set about finding a way to make a difference. This began with his appointment as President of the first New South Wales Board of Health in 1882.

Charles Mackellar worked to improve the living conditions and health of the poor – a scene well removed from the social set in which he moved. With his father's help and encouragement, Charles became an astute businessman; he held directorships of several insurance companies and the Colonial Sugar Refining Company, and was President of the Bank of New South Wales. He built his family a sandstone mansion called Dunara, overlooking Rose Bay, and together they enjoyed Sydney's opera and orchestral music. However, Charles was always concerned by the gap between Sydney's rich and poor.

By 1884 he had become a director of Sydney Hospital, which allowed him to develop medical programs to help the needy. He was also appointed Chairman of the Immigration Board and was a member of the

Pharmacy Medical Board of New South Wales. But in 1885 he walked away from all these senior posts to take a seat in the New South Wales Legislative Council. He soon rose to the position of Vice-President of the Executive Council, and became Minister for Justice in December 1886.

But Charles Mackellar was not a party man and had no interest in playing party games. He spent another 40 years in parliamentary service without holding a ministerial portfolio. Instead, he focused all of his attention and energy on the poor, and on homeless and intellectually handicapped children.

In 1900, Charles Mackellar and his wife, Marion, suffered a crushing personal tragedy when their eldest child, Keith, was killed in the Boer War. On 11 July, a few days before his twentieth birthday, Lieutenant Keith Mackellar was shot dead in a mopping-up operation, almost a month after the war was declared all but over. His family was on the way to London to meet him for a victory celebration. They learned of his death as the ship docked.

Keith Mackellar's 15-year-old sister, his favourite, poured her heartache onto paper with a poem called, 'When It Comes'. The second stanza of that poem went:

So would I like to die, but where?
On the open plain, in the open air,
Where the red blood soaks in the thirsty grass
And the wild things tread my grave as they pass –
There would I die.

Despite his grief, Charles Mackellar continued his fight for social justice in Australia. In 1902 he was appointed President of the State Children's Relief Department, looking after delinquent and 'mentally deficient' children. That year he published a paper that might well find a place on bookshelves today; it was called 'Parental Rights and Parental Responsibility'. The following year he was appointed to the Senate to fill a vacancy, but the regular sittings in Melbourne took him away from his family and from his clinics for the poor in Sydney. He resigned the Senate seat and returned to the New South Wales Parliament.

In 1907, Charles Mackellar published yet another thought-provoking paper on the plight of Sydney's homeless children – it was called 'The Child, the Law and the State'. He argued that there was little good to come from punishing a child for actions that were the product of his or her environment.

Charles Mackellar travelled to London in 1912 to be knighted for his outstanding services to the community. However, in typical fashion, he turned the opportunity into a study tour of Europe and the United States of America to look at how people there treated homeless and delinquent children. His daughter, who spoke five languages fluently, travelled with him in Europe as translator. With the knowledge gleaned on his trip, Sir Charles immediately drafted and sponsored new laws to protect children in New South Wales from violence and exploitation.

In 1916, at the age of 72, Charles Mackellar resigned

as President of the Children's Relief Board. The following year, free of the restrictions of public office, he published in a Sydney newspaper an open letter to the Minister for Public Health entitled 'The Mother, the Baby and the State', in which he pleaded for more assistance for poor and homeless mothers and their children.

On 14 July 1926, Sir Charles Mackellar died. He was 81. But there's more to this remarkable story.

Sir Charles Mackellar sacrificed a great deal to work for disadvantaged and handicapped children. He walked away from a medical career and gave up what could have been an outstanding political career. He was passionate about his cause and totally committed his time and energy to it.

What little spare time he had, he spent with his wife, Marion, his two surviving sons and his daughter at one of the family's several properties near Gunnedah and in the Hunter Valley. Because he could get there easily and quickly from Sydney, his favourite place was their property called Torryburn, near Maitland. It was in these quiet moments that Sir Charles passed on to his children his great understanding of, and love for, the land.

His daughter, Isobel, who so touchingly commemorated her brother Keith's death in verse, was particularly fascinated by her father's words. During one holiday at Torryburn, she witnessed the breaking of a drought and expressed what she saw in a poem she called 'Core of My Heart'. The second stanza of her poem began: 'I love a sunburnt country, a land of sweeping plains . . .'

Of course, when Isobel Marion Dorothea Mackellar finished that poem some time later, she changed the name to 'My Country'. It became required reading for every Australian student – an anthem to optimism in the bush, and a tribute to her beloved father, Charles Mackellar.

SCOTTIE AND THE GENERAL

Jules Verne was convinced that one day we would be able to travel through time. I know plenty of Dr Who *fans who think so too.*

If we could time travel, where would you want to go? Because I am a born sceptic, I am not packing my overnight bag. But if I did have a chance, I would choose to visit Gallipoli in 1915.

Leaving myth aside, I still believe that the military disaster at Gallipoli was a defining moment for our national character. This story convinced me that everything I cherish about the Australian character was present on that battlefield.

IT WAS A brief encounter, a simple exchange between two Australian soldiers in the thick of fighting on the battlefield. The general and the private had never met before and would not meet again. But it was a meeting that would become symbolic of the story of Gallipoli. Scottie, the private, and the general had both landed at Gallipoli in the early morning of 25 April 1915.

Scottie was second man out of his boat as it neared

the beach in the early morning darkness. The first man was killed and so was the one behind him, but somehow Scottie eluded the rainstorm of bullets. Like everyone else, he was stunned at what confronted him – sheer cliffs rising from the beach, withering fire from Turkish guns above, and hundreds of Australian bodies already littering the beach. Scottie had seen plenty of danger as a merchant seaman, a canecutter, a drover, a coalminer and a gold prospector. But nothing could compare with the situation on that beach.

Meanwhile, the general gathered his officers together, assessed the situation, and immediately recommended to his superiors watching from the ships offshore that his men should be evacuated as quickly as possible while there were still some to save. But his request was denied and he was ordered to continue the attack.

By now, Scottie was carrying the wounded to waiting boats. Only 22, he was a big, solid man. One by one he lifted them onto his broad shoulders and carried them to where medical officers prepared them to go out to the hospital ships.

For the next 20 days, both the general and the private ignored their own safety, constantly defying death to make sure as many Australians as possible survived this slaughter. When the general's request for evacuation was denied, he joined his men on the front line to urge them on and let them know that he shared their predicament. Scottie kept carrying out the wounded while dodging enemy bullets and shrapnel.

He wasn't much for discipline and officers, so he ran his own show with just one aim – to save as many lives he could.

Then, on 15 May, with a single shot, a Turkish sniper brought these two men together. As the general scampered from behind a rock, the Turkish sharpshooter put a bullet into his leg, severing an artery. Although mortally wounded, the general ordered that he was not to be carried to medical help on the beach below for fear the sniper might pick off the stretcher bearers. That's how he was, this general – his men always came first.

It was then that Scottie appeared on the scene. 'You'll be all right, Dig,' he said to the general. 'I wish they'd let me take you down to the beach.'

Those simple words of comfort held enormous significance for the general. It was the greatest honour the tough and unruly Australian private could pay an officer – especially a major general – to acknowledge him as a 'digger'. Equally as touching a tribute was this humble private soldier's desire to carry his dying commanding general from the battlefield. The general simply nodded and Scottie went on his way. Three days later the general died from his wounds.

Scottie, too, was killed – shot in the back by a machine gun in exactly the same spot where he and the general had met four days earlier.

But there's always more to the story. The day before his death on a hospital ship off Gallipoli, the general, William Bridges, was knighted for his courage and leadership. He told doctors on the ship how proud he was of the First AIF – the volunteer force that he had recruited, trained and led into battle.

The general's body was returned to Australia, the only time such an honour was bestowed on an Australian soldier killed abroad in World War I. He was buried on the slopes of Mount Pleasant, overlooking the Royal Military College, Duntroon – the officer training college that he established.

Scottie, the private, was buried on the beach at Anzac Cove in a simple grave marked with a wooden cross. There were no knighthoods or medals for him. Although he was recommended for the highest bravery award, the Victoria Cross, by the commanding officer of his unit, and by the Commander of the 4th Brigade, Colonel Monash, the recommendations were turned down because, it was said, he was simply doing his duty as a stretcher bearer. To this day he has received no bravery awards, despite a joint petition in 1967 by the Australian Prime Minister, Governor-General and Chief of the General staff. The War Office in London said it would set a precedent if it awarded the Victoria Cross so many years after the event.

When a photograph of Scottie with one of his donkeys appeared in an Australian newspaper, hundreds of soldiers identified him as John Simpson Kirkpatrick, also known as John 'Scottie' Simpson, the stretcher bearer who carried so many of them to safety at Gallipoli. In the 24 days that he survived at Gallipoli, Private John Simpson made 12 to 15 trips a day through the most dangerous ground, Shrapnel Gully, to carry out wounded.

After his first day of carrying wounded on his shoulders, he rounded up army donkeys on the beach where they had been set free after the initial landing. As a child in England, he had made money giving children donkey rides at the local fair. He loved the animals and they loved him. When he couldn't find feed for his plucky little animals, Private Simpson 'deserted' and set up base with an Indian artillery unit that had brought mules ashore to tow their guns. The Indians were in awe of Simpson's courage and called him 'The Bravest of the Brave'.

When John Simpson was fatally shot, his donkey continued to the beach with the wounded soldier it still carried on its back. After the soldier was lifted down, the small animal turned and walked back along Shrapnel Gully to where Private Simpson lay dead. So was born the legend of 'Simpson and his Donkey'. It's believed that the donkey that was with Simpson when he died was adopted by the Indian soldiers and taken back to India after their evacuation.

A monument to John Simpson and his donkeys stands outside the Australian War Memorial in Canberra. Coincidentally, and appropriately, Scottie's statue stands within sight of Mount Pleasant and his general's grave.

Eight-and-a-half thousand Australians died at Gallipoli.

AWM JO6392

Private John Simpson (right, foreground) carries a wounded soldier to safety at Gallipoli with the help of one of his faithful donkeys.

SCOTTISH MARTYRS

You can learn a great deal about the rest of the world by studying Australian history. Because we have been a melting pot of nationalities and cultures since first settlement, we carry legacies from events on several continents.

For instance, a study of our convict years quickly tells you how badly the English aristocracy behaved towards just about everyone – not just their own, but the Irish, the Scottish, the Americans, the French, the Canadians, the West Indians and the Chinese. There was no discrimination; everyone was treated equally badly.

You'll also find that many of those sent to our penal settlements were not criminals, but political prisoners. This is the story of one such group.

WHEN THE FIRST Scottish Parliament in 300 years convened a few years ago, several of the new MPs spent a moment of quiet reflection before the opening ceremony at a memorial on Calton Hill in Edinburgh. It is dedicated to five men who played a crucial role in restoring self-rule to Scotland – their names were Thomas Muir, Thomas Palmer, William Skirving, Joseph Gerrald and Maurice Margarot.

In 1794 these five men were thrown into rotting prison hulks on the River Thames and made to work on chain gangs in Portsmouth as punishment for their political campaign against English rule in Scotland. After a year they were transported in convict ships to New South Wales. Their crime, said the sentencing judge, Lord Braxfield, was to have 'violated the peace and order of society' by inciting rebellion.

In sentencing Thomas Muir, Lord Braxfield's words were:

> The British Constitution is the best that ever was since the creation of the world. Yet, Mr Muir has gone among the ignorant country people and told them Parliamentary Reform was absolutely necessary for preserving their liberty.

Lord Braxfield went on to tell those in the court what he thought of the campaign for self-rule in Scotland. He asserted that Government in Britain was made up of those who owned land and that they alone had the right to rule. He dismissed the rest of the population – those with only personal property – as 'rabble'.

Two of the five prisoners Lord Braxfield sentenced that day barely survived their time of punishment in Portsmouth, let alone the horrendous six-month passage to Australia. None of the five would see Scotland again after they sailed for Australia.

Within five months of landing in Sydney, 36-year-old Joseph Gerrald, formerly a wealthy owner of plantations in the West Indies, died of tuberculosis. Before he left England, a Government Minister offered to argue his case and stop the deportation, but Gerrald refused, saying he would rather serve his 14 years in the penal colony than compromise his principles.

Nine days later, William Skirving, the quiet university-educated farmer who left a wife and eight children behind when he was marched aboard HMS *Surprise* at Portsmouth, also died – from dysentery.

Next to die was sociologist and barrister, Thomas Muir. Muir was an extraordinary talent who had entered the University of Glasgow at the age of ten and had graduated with a Master of Arts at 17. He studied law under the famous republican John Millar. Thomas Muir escaped from Sydney just 16 months into his 14-year sentence. He made his way to Canada and from there to Mexico and Cuba before being arrested by the Spanish as a suspected spy. The ship taking him to Spain for trial was attacked by British warships and Muir suffered critical head wounds. Friends in France heard of his plight and convinced the Spanish to hand him over; he was taken to Bordeaux, where he eventually died from his wounds.

Thomas Palmer, the Eton and Cambridge-educated Unitarian minister of religion described by a London prosecutor in 1793 as 'the most determined rebel in Scotland', died of dysentery while a Spanish prisoner-of-war on Guam. He had served his seven-year sentence in New South Wales and was trying to make his way home on a British-owned ship that had been captured from the Spanish during war. The ship was blown off course in a storm and, through the worst luck, was forced to take refuge in Spanish-controlled Guam.

Wine merchant Maurice Margarot served all his 14 years in the penal colony of New South Wales before raising enough money for passage to England. He died a pauper in a London hospital on 11 November 1815, without returning to Scotland.

But there's always more to the story. Lord Braxfield was the most senior of five judges who heard evidence against the Scottish Five for 16 hours in front of a jury in 1794. The charges involved the making of inflammatory speeches, distribution of seditious pamphlets and forming of societies such as the Society of the Friends of the People. Most of the evidence was given by English Government spies sent to infiltrate the Scottish movement. They were paid according to how much information they provided, so much of what the court was told was either fabricated or exaggerated.

From the moment the trial began, it was clear that it was politically motivated. There was no criminality – in fact, evidence was given that the five men charged had consistently urged against violence and civil insurrection. There was a groundswell of sympathy for the five and a campaign to have their convictions quashed. But the government stood firm.

When the convicted men arrived in Australia, their

treatment improved. The colonial authorities recognised their standing and education and the fact that they were political prisoners. Unlike the chain gang punishment at Portsmouth, all five were given virtual freedom in the colony in return for a promise not to return to Scotland or continue the democratic struggle. They had been allowed to take with them considerable sums of money donated through a public appeal in Scotland and England. On arrival, each bought a farm and Margarot started a trading business.

Apart from Muir's escape, Margarot was the only one of the five to become involved in trouble in New South Wales. He took part in an Irish uprising at Castle Hill, then outside Sydney, in 1804 and Governor King ordered him sent to Van Diemen's Land and sentenced him to 25 lashes.

There are some surprising asides to the story of the five 'Scottish' martyrs. First, only two of the five – Thomas Muir and William Skirving – were Scottish. Joseph Gerrald was West Indian, Thomas Palmer was English and Maurice Margarot was French.

Second, when Thomas Muir escaped the colony in 1796, he left behind the farm he had bought on the shores of Sydney Harbour. It was called Huntershill, after his father's home in Scotland, and included all of Milsons Point and Kirribilli Point. In other words, the original landlord of our Governor-General's Sydney residence, Admiralty House, and the Prime Minister's Sydney home, Kirribilli House, was a prominent Scottish republican.

SHEARING SUPERSTAR

One of the reasons so many young people left the bush and moved to the coastal cities during the past 40 years was the lack of career opportunity. Every government has promised to tackle the problem of population drift, but none has done so effectively.

When I was jackerooing, young blokes in the bush had only two choices – shearing or droving. Although the money was good, the work was hard and the life was lonely. If you wanted a family life, you had to settle for a poorly paid job as a farm hand, guaranteeing that you'd never have enough money to buy your own place.

It's a shame we have not looked after the bush, because our national identity has been defined in large part by bush legends and heroes – many of them shearers. Here is a story of one of the most famous.

JOHN ROBERT HOWE was born in 1861 on Canning Downs station outside Warwick in Queensland. His family had worked the station for three generations. In sheep country like that there was only one job worth having – that of shearer. So, when John turned 18, he started in the shed at Canning Downs, learning the trade from Chinese workers on the property.

His father was one of the best shearers in the district and had acquired something of a legendary status in 1857 when he drove nine South American llamas all the way from Sydney to the Darling Downs then, on arrival, sheared them.

Young John turned out to be pretty good as well; in his first year out with the shearing teams in Central Queensland he was regularly shearing a hundred sheep a day with the hand shears. Then he met the ringer at Langlo station on the Barcoo River; John tried to be friendly, but all he got back was insults about how slow he was. So, one day John stepped onto the boards determined to prove a point. Only 20 years old, he bet the ringer he could shear the most sheep for the day. John won the bet with a record tally of 211 sheep. Word spread quickly that this skinny young fellow was a 'gun' shearer. Teams around Queensland set out to break the 211 record.

As time went by, John filled out to a solid 89 kilograms of muscle, and improved his skill and endurance with the large hand shears by constantly working a small rubber ball in his hand. He was popular around the sheds and won plenty of money for the others in his team, not only with his shearing, but with his athleticism. He inherited a blinding turn of speed and high jumping skills from his father, who had been a circus acrobat in his youth before turning to shearing. Once, after finishing a full day of shearing, John Howe ran barefoot against a professional sprinter and dead-heated.

In 1892, the manufacturers of the new mechanical shears ran a national competition to find the best shearer in the country. They offered two gold medals – one for the most sheep shorn in a standard eight hours using hand shears, and the other for the most using the new mechanical shears. John Howe wanted both.

On 10 October 1892 at Alice Downs station outside Blackall, he sheared a staggering 321 sheep in seven hours and forty minutes – with hand shears! That is one sheep every 86 seconds. It was a record that would never be equalled. In fact, it took 58 years before anyone could do better using *mechanical* shears. That was in October 1947, when Daniel Cooper junior of South Perth sheared 325 in eight hours at Glenara station in the Langkoop district of Victoria to break his own father's machine record of 316. But there was no doubt who was the best ever hand shearer in Australia.

Of course, John Howe was not content with one gold medal in 1892. A few weeks after the Alice Downs record, John also claimed the other national title by shearing 237 with mechanical blades in a day at Barcaldine Downs.

John Howe retired from shearing in 1900 at the age of 39 and did what most shearers would consider the ultimate – he bought a pub at Blackall. Then, in 1919, John Howe realised a personal dream when he bought his own property, Sumnervale station. Sadly, the following year, he died at the age of 59. But, wait, there's more to the story.

In John Howe's day, shearers worked five days a week in four two-hour runs, in timber and corrugated iron sheds, usually with four stands. Four shearers could take the fleece off about 5000 sheep in a visit. The Queensland shearing season always ran from late winter into early spring but, even so, the temperatures in the sheds would still reach the high 40s.

Shearers traditionally wore a flannel undershirt when they worked – it soaked up the sweat and protected the skin from chafing. But it was very hot. Not only was it hot, John Howe found that the flannel shirt restricted his movement, particularly when it gathered around his large biceps. So one day, in frustration, he tore the sleeves off the shirt and made it into a vest. He then asked his mother to cut the sleeves off all his undershirts.

Because John Howe was Australia's gun shearer, everyone wanted to copy him, and soon shearers everywhere were cutting the sleeves off their flannels in the hope of improving their tally. A clothing company saw the market potential of the idea and quickly produced a cooler, cotton version of the sleeveless shirt just for shearers – it was the forerunner of the blue singlet that became standard attire for shearers, canecutters and workingmen throughout Australia.

The new working-class fad was named after the man who first made it famous – John Howe; although as he was only called John by his mother, everyone else called him Jackie – Jackie Howe.

Jackie Howe, gun shearer, was also one of Australia's first fashion designers.

THE *SHENANDOAH*

If you have ever found yourself caught in the middle of a disagreement between family or friends, you know how hard it is to extricate yourself once you give the slightest hint of sympathy to one or the other. Often you end up being the one out of favour when the others have settled their differences.

It can happen between countries as well as people. When England and Argentina went to war over the Falklands, the United States of America and Australia were almost dragged into the fight. It was only through the involvement of diplomats that processes were slowed down sufficiently to avoid military action.

The Swiss, who are surrounded by traditionally warring neighbours, have got the right idea – don't have any friends or enemies, just Swiss and non-Swiss.

Here is a story about the first time we got ourselves tangled up in someone else's war.

IN A CASE OF SERENDIPITY, it was the eve of 26 January – which we now celebrate as Australia Day – in 1865, when the 790-tonne armed steam clipper *Shenandoah* appeared in Hobson's Bay in Port

LA TROBE PICTURE COLLECTION, STATE LIBRARY OF VICTORIA

The CSS *Shenandoah* sketched at anchor in Hobson's Bay near Melbourne.

Phillip. She had slipped in undetected by the Royal Navy pickets. There was no attempt by the Captain, Lieutenant Commander James Waddell, to disguise their identity – this was a battle cruiser of the Confederate Navy and she was on a search and destroy mission in the Pacific. With the aim of sinking Union trading ships, the confederates had taken to the North Atlantic and later the Pacific with ten armed cruisers. Their plan was make the war as costly as possible for the North so that it would divert resources from the blockade and invasion of the South.

Shenandoah was originally a merchantman known as the *Sea King*. She was bought in London and fitted in

Madeira with eight guns, including four 8-inch cannon and two 32 pounders. Captain Waddell had sailed into Port Phillip asking to carry out some repairs at Williamstown slipway and to take on coal, food and water. His arrival caught the naval port authorities by surprise.

International law required any port to allow a ship requesting assistance at least 24 hours to carry out repairs or re-provision, regardless of the colour of the ensign. However, in this case there were some complicating factors. Queen Victoria had declared England neutral in the American Civil War, with a proclamation that no British subject was to provide assistance in arming or provisioning warships of either side.

While authorities debated what was to happen, the *Shenandoah* began repairs and put ashore 19 prisoners taken abroad when the raider sank, captured and burned 11 Yankee ships shortly before arriving in Melbourne.

Captain Waddell offered to assist colonial authorities by putting back to sea temporarily after every 24 hours in port; that way everyone would abide by the edict from London. Melbourne newspapers called for the arrest of Waddell and his crew. But the people completely ignored the calls, flocking to the bay shore, cheering and waving to the Confederate raider and welcoming the 'Rebs' wherever they went.

The Royal Navy officers of Port Phillip entertained the *Shenandoah*'s officers in their wardroom. The city of Ballarat hosted a ball for four *Shenandoah* officers who travelled by train from Melbourne to see the gold-mines. They arrived at midnight to a brass band and 2000 cheering people.

The Union Government's consul in Melbourne protested to the Governor, demanding the *Shenandoah* be sent packing immediately. For weeks communiqués went back and forwards between Australia and London, and New York and London, and New York and Australia. When the London Admiralty finally issued orders to see the Confederate warship out of the colony, the *Shenandoah* had already completed repairs, bought provisions and, just for good measure, recruited 42 new crewmen from the hordes of volunteers in Melbourne. This was yet another breach of Queen Victoria's rules of neutrality.

On 18 February 1865, the CSS *Shenandoah* sailed out of Port Phillip Bay and back into the Pacific. Melbourne's conduct might have been forgiven in time by the Admiralty, Whitehall and the palace if the story had ended there. But it didn't.

After leaving Melbourne, the *Shenandoah* went on a six-month rampage in the Pacific, capturing 38 Yankee ships, burning 32 and taking 1053 prisoners. Official records indicated that the 1865 value of shipping destroyed by the *Shenandoah* ran to US$6.5 million. But there's still more to the story. Somehow, there always is.

The American Civil War ended just weeks after the *Shenandoah* sailed out of Port Phillip Bay, but no-one could get a message to Captain Waddell to inform him.

Most of the damage she did to Union shipping was after the surrender of Confederate forces in April. The new Government of the United States of America demanded millions of pounds in compensation from the British for the losses sustained because of Melbourne's assistance to the *Shenandoah*. Ultimately, London agreed to liability and paid.

When they realised the war was over, Lieutenant Commander Waddell and his crew surrendered to a British ship that they intercepted on the high seas; they returned under escort to Liverpool docks in November 1865. From there they were returned to the South without trial or punishment.

The *Shenandoah* was sold as part of the recovery of compensation by the American Government. She was bought at auction in 1866 by the Sultan of Zanzibar and wrecked in a hurricane 13 years later.

And Melbourne? Melbourne just kept on loving larrikins. Several former Union and Confederate soldiers, and some of the *Shenandoah*'s crew, settled in Melbourne after the Civil War and are buried in cemeteries around the city.

SOLE SURVIVORS

The four fundamental questions of life are: who am I?, where did I come from?; where am I going?; and why am I here? If you can answer all four you are very lucky, and considered by psychologists to be fulfilled.

Apparently, the most difficult of the four to answer is the last – why am I here? What is my purpose in life?

Sometimes the answer isn't immediately obvious but eventually unmistakable, as this story demonstrates.

AFTER THREE MONTHS en route from London, the safety and calm of Sydney Harbour seemed tantalisingly close for the passengers and crew of the square-rigged sailing ship *Dunbar* as she was pushed north past Botany Bay by a howling south-easterly.

It was 7 pm and the wind was getting stronger. Captain James Green knew it was just 12 nautical miles (22 kilometres) more before he could turn around South Head and into the harbour. But he was sailing blind because driving rain had reduced visibility and they lost sight of land. Captain Green contemplated heading out to sea to wait for the storm to pass, but his crew was keen to make port that night.

Shortly after 11.30 pm, believing they were about six nautical miles (11 kilometres) off the entrance to the harbour, Captain Green ordered the turn to round the Heads. It was to be a fatal order. Because of the storm, the *Dunbar* was actually only two miles (3.5 kilometres) off South Head and still short of the entrance. Disaster was inevitable.

The first warning came with the cry from the bowman: 'Breakers ahead.' Although the wheel was thrown hard over, it was too late. The *Dunbar* was smashed broadside onto the rocks at the base of South Head. As she turned on her side, the lifeboats were reduced to splinters and the rigging wrecked.

One-hundred-and-twenty-one passengers and crew would drown in the boiling seas that night of 20 August 1857. Many of them were whole families, such as the Waller family with six children aged four to 13. Abraham and Julia Meyers and their six children also died.

Rescuers who rushed to the cliffs above the wreck gave up any hope of finding survivors as the storm continued to drive mountainous seas onto the rocks for the next 24 hours. Throughout the following two days, bodies and wreckage from the *Dunbar* washed ashore from South Head to Manly Beach. It was 36 hours before the weather eased enough for people on the cliffs to make out a figure on a rock ledge at the base of South Head. When they finally roped their way down the cliff, they found young Able Seaman James Johnson cold and exhausted, but otherwise unharmed.

He told them how he had been thrown from the deck of the *Dunbar* into the sea, then picked up by a huge wave and hurled into the rock ledge. As the water washed back, he scrambled towards the base of the cliff and climbed to safety on the ledge. James Johnson was the sole survivor of 63 passengers and 59 crew on the *Dunbar.*

But there's more to the story! Able Seaman James Johnson was able to give valuable evidence to the inquiry into the sinking of the *Dunbar*. His detailed account up to, and during, the sinking was largely responsible for the decision to absolve the Captain and crew of any blame.

The only thing James Johnson could not explain was why he alone survived the mountainous seas and sharp rocks that night. He knew there must be a reason that he had lived. But for the moment he didn't know what it was. Nine years later the reason would become clear.

Six weeks short of the tenth anniversary of the *Dunbar* disaster, in July 1866, James Johnson was on duty as lighthouse keeper at Newcastle, north of Sydney. A storm had blown in from the south-east, creating furious seas and blinding spray. It reminded him of the night the *Dunbar* sank.

As Johnson watched from shore, he saw the 550-tonne iron paddle-steamer *Cawarra* pushed onto some rocks called the Oyster Bank, near the entrance to Newcastle Harbour. There were 62 people aboard the *Cawarra* and she was breaking up quickly as she was pounded by the heavy seas.

Without hesitation, James Johnson and two colleagues took to the water in a small boat and rowed out to the Oyster Bank. Before they could reach the *Cawarra*, she was smashed to pieces.

In an extraordinary coincidence with the *Dunbar* disaster, there was only one survivor of the *Cawarra*, and once again it was a young crewman. Frederick Hedges grabbed a plank of wood as he was thrown into the water – this kept him afloat until he clambered onto a harbour buoy.

But the most spine-tingling coincidence of all was that when the sole survivor of the *Cawarra*, seaman Frederick Hedges, was finally rescued, it was by the boat skippered by the sole survivor of the *Dunbar*, James Johnson.

THE SPIRITED MARY WATSON

In this book you will find many remarkable stories – ones that inspire you, amaze you and fascinate you. You will read about women who succeeded against the odds and who endured unimaginable hardship. But you will not find in those stories a woman more courageous than the one we tell you about here.

This is a story of a truly extraordinary young woman.

Today she would be awarded our highest bravery medal. In fact, I would support any campaign to have that medal awarded to her in retrospect.

QUEENSLAND HAS ONLY one monument to a woman other than a head of state and that is the monument to 21-year-old Mary Watson that stands in Charlotte Street in Cooktown.

Born Mary Beatrice Phillips in Cornwall, England, she migrated to Queensland with her parents in the 1870s. She taught school in Maryborough, north of Brisbane, before moving to Cooktown in the Far North. There, she married a retired Scottish sea captain, Robert Watson, and set up house on remote

Lizard Island, 30 kilometres north-east of Cape Flattery. Watson and a partner had set up a sea cucumber processing plant for export of smoked sea cucumber to China.

Robert Watson built a stone cottage for Mary, which – unknown to them – was near an Aboriginal ceremonial site. When Robert Watson and his business partner went to the outer reefs for weeks at a time harvesting sea cucumber, Mary was left on the island with two Chinese servants, Ah Leong, the gardener, and Ah Sam, the houseboy. In 1881, the population of Lizard Island increased from five to six with the birth of a baby boy, whom Mary and Robert named Ferrier.

On 27 September that year, while Robert Watson and his partner were at sea, Aborigines appeared on Lizard Island and set up camp. Two days later they killed Ah Leong with spears as he went to work on the small island farm near their camp. The next day, when Mary saw them on the beach near her cottage, she drove them off by firing the rifle and revolver that Robert had left with her for safety.

But the following day, on 1 October, four of the Aborigines speared Ah Sam in his right side and in the shoulder. Mary Watson realised that the situation was getting worse when she counted ten Aboriginal men near her house. Fearing the worst, Mary took her baby son and the wounded Ah Sam, put them in an empty cut-down, square iron tank that her husband had used to boil the sea cucumbers, packed it with some provisions and paddled away from the island.

They made it to a reef about 6 kilometres from Lizard Island with the hope that a passing fishing boat or coastal ship would see them. But no-one came. The next day was very calm, so Mary Watson paddled the steel tank to an island and went ashore to try to get fresh water because they had exhausted their supply. Unfortunately, there were Aborigines camped on the island, and so Mary had to hide everyone in the mangroves until dark then quietly paddle out to a reef again.

On 7 October, Mary paddled the tank to another island, but again there was no fresh water to be found. By now they had been three days without water and had paddled 65 kilometres from Lizard Island. She cooked some rice and clamfish in salt water and set up camp on the island. They watched a steamer go by, but could not attract any attention, even when waving the baby's white blanket on the end of a stick.

The next day Mary moved to the other side of the island to keep watch for a boat, but still there was no rescue in sight. It was getting cold at night and the wind was blowing strongly, so Mary decided to take shelter and set up a camp. Everyone, including the baby, was now showing signs of physical distress through dehydration.

By Sunday 10 October, six days after they put to sea in the tank, baby Ferrier began to run a very high temperature. Mary gave him some condensed milk to try to fill his little body with fluid, but it seemed to make no difference. Mary herself was now feeling very weak and ill.

On 11 October, Ferrier suddenly improved, but Ah Sam worsened and moved away, preparing to die out of sight of his mistress. Mary, too, was failing quickly. Her throat was parched and swollen and she was weak. Daybreak brought another cloudless sky and she knew that it was only a matter of time before all three of them were dead. Within 24 hours, Mary Watson, her infant son, Ferrier, and Chinese servant, Ah Sam, died of thirst.

But there's always more to the story. When Mary Watson first left Lizard Island, she paddled to the Number One island of the Howick group. Her next stop was the Number Five island. She would have known that these islands were in the main shipping channel. Had she lasted a few days longer, she probably would have attracted attention from a passing vessel or fishing boat.

Mary Watson's story is tragic but inspirational. Her bravery in dealing with the threat from Aborigines, her initiative in using the water tank, her skills and strength in taking it to sea and her survival instincts were truly remarkable for such a young person.

Even more remarkable was that 21-year-old Mary Watson herself was able to tell everyone what happened during those nine days. Through all the harrowing events that beset her, Mary calmly wrote a diary each day. The last entry was on 11 October, so most experts conclude that she died that day or the following day.

It was not until 19 January 1882 – three months after Mary died – that the schooner *Kate Kearney* visited Howick Island and found the bodies of Mary, Ferrier and Ah Sam, the tank and the diary. Poignantly, in the 12 weeks after they died of thirst, it rained so much that the tank was half full of water.

Mary's husband, Robert, had passed the island several times searching for her after he returned to Lizard Island and found them missing. But the tank and the bodies were hidden behind mangroves and were not visible from the water.

Mary Beatrice Watson, her baby and her faithful servant were buried in Cooktown, where a monument was erected to a truly courageous woman.

THE SPOOKS

Most of us accept the right of unions to strike in legitimate circumstances; it is the biggest weapon they have, and at times it has been a strike that has prevented or ended disgraceful injustice or inappropriate work practices.

However, there are some occupations that the community believes should not be involved in strikes, including the military, teachers, doctors, nurses, firemen, ambulance officers and police. But in recent years these professions have become more militant, arguing that they have been left vulnerable to abuse by employers because of the expectation that they will not strike.

If we think that certain professions are essential, we should value them more highly to make sure that they don't need to consider withdrawing services. We can't demand commitment and give none in return.

Otherwise, we might end up with the situation in this story.

BEFORE THE COLONY of Victoria was proclaimed, the Port Phillip district was part of New South Wales and was policed from Sydney. In 1836, New

South Wales Governor Sir Richard Bourke appointed Captain William Lonsdale as the first police magistrate of Port Phillip and gave him three constables – Robert Day, Joseph Hooson and James Dwyer. These three set up the first Melbourne police station on Bourke Street West.

The following year, Sydney sent a police magistrate and three constables to Geelong to quell Aboriginal violence against white settlers. They remained there to patrol the rural districts. By 1837, the Port Phillip police contingent had grown to comprise a chief constable, 11 constables and one 'scourger', who administered corporal punishment. In 1840, a station was opened at Portland, and in 1849 the first police station was opened in Swanston Street.

The inauguration of the new colony of Victoria in 1851 should have heralded a grand new era for the Victoria Police, if not for the fact that it coincided with the discovery of gold. Forty of 50 police constables in the new colony resigned simultaneously to join the gold rush. Retired military volunteers had to be brought in from Tasmania to keep order in Melbourne.

In the years after proclamation of the colony, the Victoria Police gained some autonomy from Sydney. A mounted patrol of 12 troopers was formed, using as their base a police paddock on the site of the present Melbourne Cricket Ground, and a cadet scheme was introduced allowing the recruitment of 800 constables. But the first makings of a new police force came in 1853 when Inspector Samuel Freeman, three sergeants and 50 constables from the London Metropolitan Police arrived under a ten-year contract with the Victorian administration.

They formed an efficient, effective police service that earned respect throughout the colony – a vast improvement on the relationship 15 years earlier when constables Day, Hooson and Dwyer policed Port Phillip. It was hard for anyone to respect those three men, each of whom had been dismissed from the Sydney Police for drunkenness. They only became Victoria's first policemen because no-one else in Sydney would go there.

But there's always more to the story. Melbourne's spring racing carnival of 1923 will be remembered, not for the horseracing, but for the panic and fear that pervaded the Victorian capital because of the Victoria Police. On 29 October 1923, on the eve of the carnival, 29 uniformed policemen refused to go on duty, sparking a strike that was to spread throughout the State and continue for months. Melbourne was a city without law, left protected by a handful of loyal detectives and senior officers, backed up by civilian volunteers and recalled police retirees. The Chief Commissioner, the Premier and the Attorney-General all pleaded with the striking policemen, without success. Even their union urged them to return to work, but still they resisted.

Melbourne traffic was chaotic on the night of 2 November 1923 when not a single policeman turned up for point duty at intersections. The following night, gangs roamed the streets, harassing people and looting shops. The Federal Government sent in troops to protect Commonwealth property, although they were under strict orders not to attempt to enforce law and order.

In retaliation for the strike, the Government of Victoria decided that it would no longer negotiate with the strikers and dismissed them. Now Victoria had no police force at all. Over the next few weeks, under the direction of World War I hero General Monash, a massive recruitment program through city and country areas brought in hundreds of trainees for an intensive course. Five thousand special constables were sworn in to help restore the peace.

The 636 striking Victorian policemen were never allowed back into the force after the 1923 strike. Their protests did result in a royal commission into the affair, but the finding was that their actions were not justified. The whole episode was blamed on one agitator – a Constable Brooks – whom the royal commission said had engineered the strike to gain revenge against his immediate superiors.

In light of recent history, there is a strong sense of déjà vu about the genesis of the strike. The Victoria Police refused duty because four senior constables had been assigned to plain-clothes operations to ensure that police were performing their duties properly. These four hated colleagues were nicknamed the 'Spooks'.

It seems, however, that the internal spying was the

NATIONAL LIBRARY OF AUSTRALIA PIC/7993

Striking Melbourne policemen stand picket in Collins Street in 1923.

final straw for the 1750 policemen, who had been battling unsuccessfully with the Commissioner for more recruits and a pension scheme as well as better pay, leave and uniform allowances. They argued that they should have terms and conditions at least as good as their counterparts' in New South Wales.

SWEET-NATURED PRIMA DONNA

There are endless examples of Australian sportsmen, entertainers, scientists and politicians who were just born at the wrong time and ended up playing second fiddle to another outstanding individual of the era.

Some wait their time patiently and hope for a chance to assume the crown; others give up and fade away. But a few are content to be as good as they can be and take whatever plaudits come their way.

Australia has produced many of these unsung heroes. This is the story of one who found fame despite living in the shadow of the biggest star of the day.

AMY CASTLES WAS just 24 when she gave her first royal command performance in 1906. England's King Edward VII was astounded by her pure voice and her gentle and quiet personality. Over the next 12 years, the young convent girl from country Victoria became the darling of European royalty and threatened to rival the fame of another great Australian soprano of the time, Dame Nellie Melba.

Amy was born in the Melbourne suburb of

NATIONAL LIBRARY OF AUSTRALIA PIC ALBUM 998/30

Miss Amy Castles.

Carlton, not far from Nellie Melba's birthplace of Richmond. She began singing lessons in Bendigo and won her first competition in Ballarat in 1898. Even as a young girl, her immense talent was evident.

At 16, Amy gave a series of concerts in various Australian cities to raise money to study in Paris with the famous Mathilde Marchesi, who had trained Melba. It was rumoured at the time that Melba herself recommended that Amy go to Paris.

In 1899, Amy began studying under Marchesi. However, within weeks, the teacher had made an extraordinary decision; she believed that Amy had been wrongly cast as a soprano. Marchesi declared that she would train her as a mezzo-soprano or a contralto. Amy's voice deteriorated under the strain of Marchesi's demands and when her mother arrived in Paris, Amy was removed from Marchesi's school and enrolled with the famous Belgian baritone, Jacques Bouhy.

Bouhy slowly but surely developed Amy's original soprano voice to such quality that she debuted at London's Queen's Hall at the age of 19. Within five years, Amy was singing lead roles at the Cologne Opera House in Germany.

In 1911, Queen Wilhelmina of the Netherlands invited Amy to perform a royal command season in Amsterdam. Three years later, the Emperor of Austria presented her with a diamond and emerald bracelet after the first Viennese performance of *Madam Butterfly.* Amy was so popular in Austria that she was made Prima Donna at the Imperial Opera House for three years.

Amy Castles was now recognised as one of the world's great sopranos, with a voice that many experts said was the equal of Melba's – and maybe better.

Yet, for all her success, there was one cherished dream that would not come true for Amy Castles – she would never be called to perform at Covent Garden in London, considered the home of English opera. Perhaps when you hear more of the story, you'll understand why Amy was never called.

It was said that Dame Nellie Melba was so influential in London that on her recommendation young performers could get auditions and appointments that would otherwise elude them. One of those who benefited from Melba's patronage in later years was Amy's younger sister, Eileen, who won secondary operatic roles at Covent Garden. But Melba seemed only to help those with lesser talent than hers. She was described by some critics as 'ruthless' in her treatment of potential rivals.

What, then, of the message Melba sent to Amy Castles in 1900 shortly after she left the tutelage of Marchesi to work with Jacques Bouhy? Melba warned that unless Amy returned to Marchesi immediately, she would never be heard of again. Some read those words as a threat, others as friendly advice.

Perhaps Melba really did want Amy to realise the enormous potential she showed when she first arrived in Paris and believed that could only be achieved by the young woman continuing with her own mentor, Marchesi. Or, as some have suggested, perhaps Melba wanted Marchesi to continue to encourage Amy away from being a soprano voice to avoid comparison and competition.

Adoring fans found Amy Castles' failure to perform at Covent Garden inexplicable, given her popularity in the finest opera houses in Europe. Why was Amy never called to 'The Garden'? Could Melba have been responsible? After all, Covent Garden was Melba's European headquarters and the theatre where she carried greatest sway.

Yet, if Nellie Melba was afraid of Amy Castles' voice, she need not have feared her young compatriot. Amy was never inclined to chase Melba's crown. It wasn't in her gentle nature. Indeed, it was at the height of her success that Amy Castles simply walked away from her international fame.

When World War I broke out in 1914, Amy was forced to leave Austria for London. There she devoted herself to entertaining the Allied troops and raising money for the war effort. Later, she returned to Australia to care for her ageing parents. When the war ended and Amy was asked to return to Europe to continue her contract with the Vienna Opera House, she politely declined. Fame and wealth meant little to her compared with the wellbeing of her family.

Amy continued to perform occasionally in Australia and abroad. In 1919 after touring the United States of America, she returned to her hometown of Melbourne for two seasons of grand opera. Amy Castles eventually retired from singing in 1941 and died in 1951, aged 69.

TALL TALES

Our history, our language and our culture are so intertwined that we must ensure generations to come learn about them together.

This story illustrates the significance of all three in understanding where we came from and who we are. For instance, not all our slang is of cockney or Irish origin; some was coined here and is uniquely Australian.

When our elected governments finally treat education as a priority, I hope they don't forget to include Australia in the very multicultural curricula in our schools.

This story is included because it shows what a fascinating and surprising path awaits students who want to explore our history.

THE TERM 'FURPHY' has featured in Australian vocabulary for almost a hundred years. 'It's nothing but a "furphy",' someone might say to describe a rumour or bit of idle gossip passed off as the truth.

It is widely accepted that the term dates back to Australian soldiers in World War I and was associated with the horse-drawn carts with galvanised iron water tanks the Australian Army bought by the hundreds from the Furphy foundry in Shepparton, Victoria. The carts displayed the manufacturer's name in large letters.

However, some historians believe that troops camped at Broadmeadows outside Melbourne in 1914, prior to embarkation for Egypt, began the 'furphy' tradition. Apparently, word of which unit was about to be ordered overseas usually came from the drivers of the Furphy carts, which were used as sanitary vehicles emptying the latrines.

Yet, other experts say the term was coined in Egypt and Palestine in 1915, when the Furphy carts delivered drinking water to the tent lines in training camps. Troopers would gather around to hear the latest news on the progress of the war.

But the most romantic theory is that the term 'furphy' started at Gallipoli, where the Furphy water carts were the most popular meeting place for troops to swap stories and rumours amid the boredom and bloodshed of the trenches. Officers warned the soldiers to put little faith in what they heard at the water carts because they were likely to be mere 'furphies'.

But there is much more to this story than most people know. It involves a man named Joseph Furphy. Joseph was born at Yering Station near Yarra Glen, Victoria, in September 1843. There were no schools and few books in the bush in those days, so Joseph relied on his mother to educate him. When she taught him to read and gave him a Bible and some volumes of

Shakespeare, he memorised them. It turned out that little Joseph had a photographic memory. By the time he was seven, he could recite Shakespeare faultlessly. It would be another 37 years before Joseph would fully appreciate the gift of his memory for detail.

Over the years he worked at everything, from merchant to farmer to wool carrier. But, by the age of 44, Joseph Furphy was penniless and desperate. In despair, he made his way home and joined his brothers in the family engineering business, filling in his spare moments writing. It was then that his recollections of years travelling around the bush came flooding back to him in great detail. His photographic memory had stored an extraordinary library of people, places and events.

With the help of *The Bulletin*, Joseph Furphy became an Australian legend, producing classics including *Such is Life*, *Rigby's Romance* and *The Buln-Buln and the Brolga*. Unfortunately, Joseph Furphy didn't live to see his books published, or to benefit from their success. He died in 1912, in Claremont, Western Australia, 28 years before his writings became popular.

Joseph Furphy was a simple and shy man. When he started submitting his stories to *The Bulletin*, he was too embarrassed to use his real name, so he wrote under the pseudonym of 'Tom Collins'. Now students of Australian language will immediately recognise 'Tom Collins' as a slang term used last century to describe an idle rumour. It started in Melbourne pubs on Collins Street. When someone was spun a yarn, it

A portrait photograph of Joseph Furphy taken around 1900.

was attributed to 'Tom Collins'. Banjo Paterson made the tradition famous in one of his poems.

By coincidence, Joseph Furphy had pre-empted history with his pseudonym. He had linked the name Furphy with rumours and gossip 18 years before Australian troops even set foot in Egypt, Palestine or

Gallipoli, and long before they set eyes on a Furphy water cart.

But to make the coincidence even more extraordinary, the Australian troops who gave the term 'furphy' an association with gossip and rumour would not even have known of Joseph Furphy's stories or his use of the name Tom Collins. Joseph Furphy died two years before the troops assembled at Broadmeadows in 1914, and five years before Gallipoli. His writings did not appear in print until 1917 – more than a year after the evacuation of Anzac Cove.

But there's yet more to this story. When Joseph Furphy was down on his luck and made his way home to work in the family business, he went to Shepparton to the family foundry – the very same foundry that manufactured those water carts, eventually bound for the Middle East and Gallipoli, that would become the centre of folklore as the source of rumours and gossip.

J Furphy and Sons foundry still operates in Shepparton and the original water tanks that Joseph and his brothers made before 1914 were still in production there until 1983. From the first one manufactured until the last, the tanks carried the Furphy family slogan:

Good, better, best;
never let it rest,
till your good is better;
and your better best.

THREE STRIKES TWICE

In every office, every club, every pub, you come across the person who wins the raffle, the jackpot or the lottery not once, but twice, and sometimes three times, to everyone else's one.

Maybe you are one of those people with the luck. I, on the other hand, could throw up a ten-dollar note and it would come down a summons.

I wonder if we each have an allocation of luck to use up through our lives? If that is the case, I can't wait for my turn because I must have most of my original allocation sitting unused. Unlike these fellows.

JAMES HARDY VAUX is the only person known to have been transported to Australia as a convict three times. The first time, in 1801, he was shipped to New South Wales on the *Minorca* after being convicted of stealing a handkerchief. Remarkably, he worked his way into a job as Magistrate's Clerk at Parramatta and became a trusted friend of the emancipist, Reverend Samuel Marsden.

In 1807, Vaux was described as a model prisoner and was rewarded by Governor King with a job as his unofficial secretary. King even took Vaux with him that year on a visit to England. When the ship docked, Vaux took his chance and deserted. A year later he was arrested and convicted of robbery. A death sentence was commuted to transportation for life and he was sent back to Port Jackson under the name James Lowe.

After a number of years in the Newcastle coal mines, Vaux escaped the colony and went to Dublin, using an alias. But he was arrested there for stealing and was sentenced to seven years transportation. He arrived back in Port Jackson for the *third* time in the early 1830s. The last that was heard of him was in 1853 when, at the age of 50, he was again before the courts in Sydney for petty crime. There is no record of what happened to him after that.

But this story is about much more than the demise of James Hardy Vaux. Always a man of surprises, Vaux had written a book while he was working in the Newcastle mines. It was entitled *Memoirs of James Hardy Vaux. Written by Himself.* It was one of the most detailed and colourful accounts of early colonial life and the culture of the penal communities ever recorded.

An English author visiting Sydney saw the manuscript and arranged for it to be published in England in 1819. That is how James Hardy Vaux – scoundrel and convict three times over – became one of our earliest historians and published authors.

Over a century after James Vaux was first convicted, another man was preparing for his day in court. Joseph Samuels believed, like everyone else, that justice was swift in the Australia of the time. When he was arrested in 1903 with four other men for the murder of a Sydney policeman, he expected no mercy. He and another thief, James Hardwicke, were sentenced to hang.

Hardwicke was reprieved at the last minute, but Samuels was driven by cart to Brickfield Hill near the present suburb of Surry Hills on the road to Parramatta and a noose was placed around his neck. The other end of the rope was thrown over the branch of a tree and tied off. In front of a large crowd, the cart was driven from under him. As he fell, the rope snapped around his jaw and broke. He tumbled to the ground, then rose to the boos of the spectators.

He was quickly put back in the cart and another rope was looped around his neck. This time, as the cart went from under him, the knot slipped and Samuels was slowly lowered to the ground until he stood looking in bewilderment at his executioners.

Again, he was loaded into the cart and a third rope placed around his neck. But it also snapped as his weight dropped from the back of the cart.

The angry crowd protested the poor show and demanded Samuels be released. A rider was sent urgently to the Governor's residence to explain what had happened. In the face of public protest, the Governor issued a reprieve.

Samuels recovered fully after receiving medical treatment for rope burns and the bruises from landing on the ground heavily when the ropes broke. He became known as 'The Man They Couldn't Hang'. But don't think that is all there is to this story – there's always more.

When Joseph Samuels survived the three attempts to hang him, the *Sydney Gazette* newspaper suggested he should make the most of his good luck and mend his ways. No-one is absolutely sure if he took that advice. However, three years later in Newcastle, eight convicts stole an open boat and escaped to sea, never to be seen again. The records show that one of the convicts was named Joseph Samuels.

TOO MANY CHIEFS

I've no doubt that some of the stories in this book are going to spark debate and, perhaps, prompt people to tell even more of the story than we uncovered.

That's good and it's why we wanted to present these stories – to promote understanding and discussion of our history and heritage. We Australians just do not know enough about our past. It is not taught sufficiently well in our schools, and our museums and libraries rely on people being motivated to seek the information they hold.

When you read this story you will almost certainly form an opinion about the events it describes, and I can guarantee the opinions will be divided.

IT'S NOT UNUSUAL to find historians disagreeing over versions of events concerning the early exploration and settlement of the Australian colonies. However, there is one issue that provokes passionate debate every time – John Batman's role in the founding of the city of Melbourne.

According to the traditional and romantic account, John Batman, a farmer from Tasmania, sailed up the

Yarra River in his sloop, called the *Rebecca*, looking for grazing land and stumbled across the site for a settlement. '*This will be the place for a village*,' he is said to have proclaimed. The story goes that Batman sat down with elders of the Wurundjeri tribe and signed an agreement exchanging blankets, knives, mirrors, axes and trinkets for 200,000 hectares of land where Melbourne now stands, as well as another 40,000 hectares on Corio Bay where Geelong is now built. It is at this point that opinions begin to differ.

One school of thought is that Batman exploited the traditional landowners and made up the whole story of the treaty; those behind this theory point to Batman claiming to have signed a treaty with the chiefs of the local tribes when the Wurundjeri had no 'chiefs', nor a concept of land ownership, nor the sophistication to make personal marks on a piece of paper. This school says that Batman just wanted to convince the colonial authorities that he owned the land.

Another argument is that John Batman was probably the first white man to acknowledge indigenous land rights and that his treaty was reasonably fair for its era in that, as well as the trinkets handed over at the time, it also included an annual rental in perpetuity for the use of the land.

There is even a theory that John Batman's reference to the site of a 'village' was not on the Yarra, but on a tributary, the Maribyrnong; the maps that Batman made of his cruise were not geographically accurate.

The story that most experts now accept as true is that John Batman was born at Parramatta in Sydney on 21 January 1801. His father was a convict named William Bateman, who was transported for 14 years for receiving stolen goods. Bateman's wife and daughter were allowed to come to Australia at their own expense to join him.

John Batman attended school at Rose Hill and, at the age of 15, became an apprentice blacksmith. When he was 20, he moved with his brother to Van Diemen's Land, where he began farming outside Launceston.

John had a reputation as an adventurer who lived and drank hard. He was a regular customer of the Hobart and Launceston brothels. In March 1826 he captured the bushranger Mathew Brady, earning himself a reward and a commendation from the authorities. Brady was hanged.

He lived with a woman named Elizabeth Callaghan, who had been sentenced to death at the age of 17 for passing a forged pound note in England; her sentence was commuted to transportation. There is considerable doubt that Batman ever married Eliza, as she was known, but she bore him eight children.

Batman knew the Aboriginal people of Tasmania well and during the so-called 'Aboriginal Wars', he negotiated and managed a solution which saw the indigenous people confined to a small area of the island.

In 1834, a Tasmanian grazing family named Henty established the first European settlement in Victoria at Portland. When John Batman heard what the Hentys had done, he also applied for a grant of land in Westernport, but it was denied. So, he got together a group of friends in Launceston and formed the Port Phillip Association to fund exploration of the area around Port Phillip Bay. Batman saw the venture as a way to expand his sheep farming interests.

In April 1835, he hired the *Rebecca* and sailed across Bass Strait, into Port Phillip Bay and up the Yarra – his exploration of the river was the result of pure curiosity. On 6 June, he wrote in his diary that he had signed a 'treaty' with eight 'chiefs' of the local people and he had acquired their 'marks' on the document.

Two days later, he took a small boat upriver. About 10 kilometres upstream, he found a wide expanse of pasture that he thought would be most suitable for grazing sheep. He made some diary notes and sailed back to Launceston to lodge his claim on the land and arrange a larger expedition to settle the area. He was unaware that a Launceston publican named John Fawkner had also heard about the settlement at Portland and sent off an expedition to explore Port Phillip.

When John Batman returned to the site of his new settlement on 2 September 1835, he found the schooner *Enterprize* anchored in the river and Fawkner's expedition camped on the pastures that he had selected. At first Batman argued that he already owned the land through his 'treaty', but the Governor of New South Wales, Sir Richard Bourke declared the 'treaty' invalid because the Aboriginal people had no right to sell land belonging to the Crown. Batman and Fawkner's group then decided to share the land and make application for grant of title.

John Batman set up a farm on what he called Batman's Hill, in the area where the Spencer Street rail yards now lie, and John Fawkner opened the first hotel in the settlement on the corner of William Street and Flinders Lane.

But there's always more to the story. In time, and largely because of the many enemies that John Fawkner gathered in his career as a publican, a newspaper proprietor and a politician, John Batman was officially credited with the founding of Melbourne. But that was long after he died in 1839 at the age of 39.

The four years that John Batman lived with his family in Melbourne were far from happy and prosperous. By now John Batman's many years of womanising in Tasmania had caught up with him and he was dying of syphilis. He lent most of his money to other settlers to encourage them to move to Melbourne. Many didn't pay him back and he had to sell his own land for a pittance to feed his large family. Then his wife, Elizabeth, left him and sailed to England with one of his workers. She returned to Melbourne after John Batman's death and was murdered at Geelong. The final insult came when he asked the colonial government to grant him 40 hectares, including Batman Hill where he had built his home, and they refused.

John Batman had paid a much higher price than trinkets to settle on the Yarra River. He had walked away from 4000 hectares of the best grazing land in northern Tasmania, plus a grand house and a thriving business. Now he had lost his health, his wealth and his wife, as well as one of the things he treasured most – his only son, John. Young John Batman drowned while fishing the waters of the river that his father discovered – the Yarra.

Penniless, crippled and blind, John Batman died leaving his large family destitute in the settlement he had helped establish. It may not resolve the historical debate about whether or not John Batman did the right or the wrong thing by the traditional landowners in settling Melbourne, but it is interesting to note that in his final excruciating days of life, John Batman was cared for and nursed by Aboriginal people.

UNPARLIAMENTARY

Ignore all the excuses, the real reason our parliaments won't allow continuous live broadcast of proceedings is because they are afraid we will see how badly they behave. You only have to sit in the public gallery for an hour or so to see the childish sniping, snoozing on the benches, and the sheep-like process of our party system.

I'm not sure it is even a good idea to allow schoolchildren to visit parliament unless they are warned that this is not the way the community expects adults to behave.

You may find it hard to believe, but there are actually rules of conduct for our parliamentarians intended to maintain that 'good order' you see and hear during the rare broadcast of proceedings.

WHEN THEN Prime Minister Paul Keating addressed certain Members of the House of Representatives sitting opposite him as 'vermin', 'scum' and, in one case, a 'carcass with a coat and tie', he carried on a long tradition of Australian politics – finding new ways to push the boundary of acceptable parliamentary behaviour. He was doing no worse in his day than predecessors who had directed insults across the chamber such as: 'The Member is as uneasy as an old lady upon receiving her first proposal'; 'The Honourable Member has the voice of a bull and the mind of a troglodyte'; 'If there were a tax on brains, the Member . . . would be due for a refund'; and 'If I wished to hear from a backside, I would pass wind myself.'

Since Mr Keating's departure from the scene, there have been several MPs who have added to the glossary of terms considered inappropriate and unacceptable. One Member has been asked on more than one occasion to withdraw and apologise for the use of a common four-letter word. A Minister referred to an Opposition Member as a 'sanctimonious windbag', while an Opposition Member referred to the Prime Minister as an 'a—e-licker' who 'kissed some bums and got patted on the head'. The same person also referred to Members sitting opposite as 'a conga line of suck-holes'.

The Standing Orders of the Senate and the House of Representatives set out the rules of debate for our national Parliament and they are intended to ensure that business is conducted in an appropriately polite and respectful manner without any violence or quarrelling.

Offensive words are not allowed in the House of Representatives, nor are 'imputations of improper motives or personal reflections' on Members. It's much the same in the Senate, except that Senators also must not refer disrespectfully to the Queen, the Governor-General or the Governor of a State.

The definition of what is offensive or unsuitable language is open to considerable debate and interpretation, and so our Houses of Parliament leave the final say up to the Speaker of the House and the President of the Senate. At times this results in accusations of political bias on the part of the Chair. For instance, in 1920, the conservative government of Billy Hughes moved successfully for the expulsion of the Federal Labor Member for Coolgardie, Hugh Mahon. It remains the only case of a Member of the Australian Parliament being expelled.

Mahon was an Irish-born Catholic who campaigned for an Australian republic. He was bitterly opposed to the British rule in Ireland and the oppression of Catholics. At a number of public meetings in Melbourne, he spoke strongly against the British Government and called for Australia to break away from the Empire. When he stood in the House of Representatives and attacked the British Empire and its policy on Ireland, he referred to 'this bloody and accursed despitism'. On 11 November 1920, Prime Minister Billy Hughes cited 'seditious and disloyal utterances' and moved for Mahon to be expelled. Mahon denied the charges but refused to defend himself. The vote was carried and Hugh Mahon was removed from the Parliament. He failed to regain his seat at the subsequent by-election.

Many rulings on unparliamentary language are based on the context in which the word is used rather than the word itself. For instance, in 1970, a Member was merely chastised for saying: 'I never use the word "bloody" because it is unparliamentary. It is a word I never bloody well use.'

Of course, parliamentarians have been trading insults since before Federation and so, from time to time, guidelines have been issued to assist our elected representatives to ensure 'good order'. One such edict was distributed in 1953 by the Speaker of the House of Representatives, who issued a list of 500 words and phrases that he held to be 'unparliamentary' and warned Members not to use them. The banned terms included, 'brutal majority', 'beneath contempt', 'creaking speech', 'dastardly trick', 'dingoes', 'dumb driven cattle', 'gasbags', 'larrikin', 'scab', 'snob', 'squib', and 'tripe'. While these would hardly raise an eyebrow today, the Speaker made it clear that he would act swiftly if these terms were ever again uttered in the House of Representatives. But there's always more to the story.

The 500 words and phrases that the Speaker of the House of Representatives banned in 1953 were but a few of the descriptive terms that had been used in debates during the previous year.

At a time when Australians were looking for 'reds under the beds', the Speaker said he had no trouble at all with accusations in the Parliament that people were 'fascist' or 'communist'. Those terms were not 'unparliamentary' because they simply called for rebuttal and, after all, the Communist Party was a lawful political organisation. But he was appalled at the thought of

Members being described as 'chirping like a tom-tit on a stump'. And he singled out from an earlier debate what he considered the worst example of unparliamentary language – it was the description of a Member as a 'political sausage-skin filled with wind and water, and painted like a Chinese god'.

WATER VENUS

Johnny Weissmuller was the best Tarzan we saw at matinees on the big screen. He couldn't act very well, but with his impressive physique and obvious swimming skills he simply looked the part – even with that American drawl.

Being a US Olympic swimming champion, Weissmuller had no trouble doing his own stunts. He made every rescue look easy as he battled alligators and giant snakes in jungle rivers and lagoons.

Johnny Weissmuller was not the last sporting champion to become a success in movies, but he wasn't the first either. That honour went to an Australian. This is her story.

LONG BEFORE Nicole Kidman, Geoffrey Rush or even Errol Flynn, there was an Australian movie star who stole the American public's hearts. Her name was Annette Kellerman and she came from Marrickville in Sydney.

Between 1909 and 1924, Annette made nine Hollywood films, including the classic *Neptune's Daughter*. Ester Williams starred in the 1948 re-make of *Neptune's Daughter* and four years later played Annette Kellerman in the movie of her life, called *The Million Dollar Mermaid*.

Annette was born into a musical family – her father, Frederick, was a violinist and her French mother, Alice, was a pianist and music teacher – but Annette was more interested in ballet than musical instruments.

Annette's parents encouraged her to swim from the time she was a toddler. She started in the seawater baths at Farm Cove on Sydney Harbour. By the time she was 16, Annette was New South Wales champion in the 100 yards (100 metres) and mile (1500 metres). In those years, women's swimming events were closed to men, so even her father could not witness her early successess.

The family moved to Melbourne in 1902 and Annette was enrolled at a small school in Mentone where her mother was the music teacher. Annette was an average student and spent most of her time giving swimming and diving exhibitions at public baths around Melbourne and underwater ballet shows at the Melbourne Exhibition Aquarium.

In 1903, Annette's father convinced her to turn professional and attempt long-distance swims to advertise herself to potential sponsors. He promoted her as the 'Water Venus' as she set records for 5, 10 and 15-mile (8-, 16-, and 24-kilometre) swims of the Yarra River, thrilling the huge crowds that lined the banks to watch her in daring, figure-hugging one-piece swimsuits.

In 1904 Annette donned a boy's swimsuit and swam 13 miles (21 kilometres) along the Thames River from

Putney to Blackhall near London. The *Daily Mirror* newspaper challenged Annette to become the first woman to swim the English Channel.

She trained for six weeks before setting off with three male swimmers from Dover; however, the icy waters and strong currents forced all three to abandon the attempt. Annette made two more unsuccessful tries to swim the Channel before admitting that she didn't have the strength to overcome the strong currents.

But that didn't mean she couldn't do marathon publicity swims. In 1906 she drew hundreds of thousands of spectators to the Seine River in Paris for a 7-mile (11 kilometre) swim sponsored by a French newspaper. Then she went to Austria to swim against the Austro-Hungarian champion, Baroness Isa Cescu, in a 23-mile (37 kilometre) contest along the Danube from Tulu to Vienna. Annette won easily. In between the marathon swims there were also high diving and water ballet shows in London to sell-out audiences.

But the biggest offers came from the United States of America. In 1906 Annette began performing in an aquatic vaudeville show that toured the major US cities. She was paid more than US$1200 a week – an extraordinary amount for that era. By the time she reached New York, adoring crowds were packing theatres and she was made a headliner at the New York City Hippodrome on a salary of US$4000 a week. Annette Kellerman was now not only the highest paid sportswoman in America, but the highest paid woman.

The media described her as one of the most desirable women in the country. A Harvard University medical school study rated her the 'perfect woman' after an extensive comparison with the bodies of thousands of other women.

Annette's shapely curves and her love of brief swimsuits kept the publicity rolling. In 1907 she was arrested on a Boston beach for indecent exposure when she paraded in a clinging, black one-piece swimsuit. The charges were later dismissed, but the media had a field day.

In 1912, 25-year-old Annette Kellerman married her manager, James Sullivan. It was a marriage that would last 60 years until his death in 1972.

For the three years after her wedding, Annette travelled throughout North America performing in shows and exhibitions and thrilling crowds with 25-metre dives from high towers into small, temporary swimming pools. Then her movie career began to blossom. She made *Neptune's Daughter* in 1915, stunning audiences with dramatic dives from 30-metre cliffs; Annette never used a stunt double. Then came *Daughter of the Gods*, *Diving Venus* and *Queen of the Mermaids*. All were box-office hits. She also made a number of smaller budget films, some of them filmed in Australia.

Annette Kellerman also found time to write three books, including her bestseller, *Physical Beauty*, and a children's storybook. She retired from swimming in the 1920s and opened a chain of health food stores and health spas in Los Angeles and throughout California.

Annette spent ten years in Australia from 1929 building up her business empire. During World War II, she volunteered for work with the Red Cross in Queensland, entertaining the troops. Once the war ended, Annette returned to the United States to develop her business there and to be an on-set adviser for the movie about her life – *The Million Dollar Mermaid*. She returned permanently to Australia in 1970 to live on the Gold Coast. It's an inspiring biography. But there's always more to the story.

After her retirement to the Gold Coast, Annette Kellerman went swimming in the surf every day until shortly before her death in 1975 at the age of 89. Her ashes were scattered on the Great Barrier Reef. It was symbolic of the love affair that she had with the water and the debt that she owed it.

You see, the reason that Annette's father encouraged her to take up swimming in the ocean baths at Farm Cove was as treatment for her crippled and twisted legs. Annette was a victim of polio and for the first 14 years of her life she walked with steel leg braces. Swimming lengths of the Charles Cavill pool strengthened her legs and gave her confidence that one day she might even achieve her childhood dream to dance in a ballet.

Ironically, the little girl who was ashamed of her twisted legs became a sex symbol and a sports superstar. And although she never danced in a ballet, she came very close in 1917, during a fundraising concert in London when she shared the bill with famous Russian ballerina Anna Pavlova.

WHAT'S IN A NAME?

Grace is a wonderful old name that has started to make a bit of a comeback with young parents. It is one of those names that you can't help but say in a gentle way.

I've noticed that some people's names seem to fit their personalities almost as if their parents knew what they would be like and named them accordingly.

Or maybe it's that they go through life being told to live up to their name because that's what their parents had in mind for them. 'Always be kind to people, Charity,' they probably say to the poor child, or 'You must be true to yourself, Faith.'

Anyway, here is a story about a girl whose name could not have been more appropriate.

FIFTY-EIGHT PASSENGERS AND crew were aboard the iron steam schooner *Georgette* when she sailed from Fremantle for Adelaide via Bunbury, Busselton and Albany on 29 November 1876. It was a regular coastal run for the *Georgette* and she carried a heavy cargo of West Australian jarrah timber in her hold.

Just after midnight on 1 December, the ship sprang a leak; she was 32 kilometres out to sea from Injidup and encountering heavy weather. The Captain ordered all crew to the pumps as he made for shore, but the pumps wouldn't work and the water level continued to rise. By four o'clock they were just a few kilometres offshore and passengers had joined the crew with buckets to stop the boilers being flooded, but it was futile. By six o'clock the boilers were extinguished and the *Georgette* was left with only her sails for power. She was being driven steadily towards the beach.

The Captain decided to put 20 passengers into a lifeboat and give them a chance to make for shore. But the boat was smashed against the side of the ship and everyone was thrown into the water. Four crewmen launched a second boat and saved most of the passengers, although two women and five children drowned.

The *Georgette* was now drifting helplessly in the surf at Calgardup Bay, just north of the entrance to Margaret River. Watching the drama from a cliff above the bay was Sam Isaacs, an Aboriginal stockman who worked on the 24,000 hectare property, Wallcliffe. Isaacs rode his horse 20 kilometres to the homestead to tell what he had seen. The only members of the Bussell family at home were Mrs Ellen Bussell and her 16-year-old daughter, Grace.

Grace grabbed some rope, saddled a horse and rode with Sam Isaacs back to the cliffs where he had seen the ship. After searching along the coast they came across a desperate scene. The *Georgette* was on the rocks and breaking apart under pounding from heavy seas. Grace could see women and children struggling in the turbulent surf. They had been crammed onto a third lifeboat, which had capsized. Without hesitation, Grace urged her horse down the sheer cliff face, across the rocks and coaxed it into the wild surf. They swam through two lines of breakers to reach the drowning passengers. With women and children hanging from her saddle and stirrups, and the rope, she towed people to shore, two or three at a time.

Sam Isaacs followed Grace into the surf with his horse and rescued the last of the lifeboat passengers. Over four hours, Grace Bussell and Sam Isaacs had rescued every one of the 50 people on board the *Georgette*. Then, while everyone slumped exhausted on the beach, Grace rode 20 kilometres back to the house to get help and to arrange for food and blankets to be ready for the survivors when they arrived.

The story of Grace Bussell was flashed around the world by the media and she became an instant celebrity. She was declared the 'Grace Darling of Western Australia' in reference to another young woman in England 38 years earlier who, with her lighthouse-keeper father, had rowed to sea to save victims of a shipwreck.

Grace Bussell was awarded the Royal Humane Society Silver Medal in 1878. Sam Isaacs was awarded the Bronze Medal. The Board of Trade also presented Grace with a gold watch, and the State Government gave her father a hundred pounds compensation for feeding, clothing and housing the survivors.

Sadly, the strain of the whole event took a toll on

Sixteen-year-old Grace Bussell.

Grace's mother, Ellen, and she died just weeks after the rescue.

The Captain of the *Georgette* was charged with five counts of negligence, but was found not guilty, although his master's certificate was revoked.

But, as you've probably guessed, there's more to the story. The extraordinary tale of 16-year-old Grace Vernon Bussell's bravery was front-page news in Perth. It was there that a young surveyor, Frederick Drake-Brockman, who came from a famous pastoral family, read the story and declared that this was the woman he would marry. Apparently he saddled his horse immediately and rode 300 kilometres to meet her. Frederick and Grace married six years later and had two sons, Edmund and Geoffrey.

As might be expected of the children of a heroine like Grace Bussell, both became decorated heroes in World War I. Both landed at Gallipoli and fought through the fiercest battles of France and Belgium. Both reached the rank of Brigadier. And both were decorated several times for bravery: Edmund received a Distinguished Service Order and was later knighted; Geoffrey received the Military Cross.

Edmund became a Senator. Geoffrey married an historian, Henrietta Jull, who went on to unlock the secrets of an even more famous Western Australia shipwreck – the *Batavia*. Grace's husband, Frederick Drake-Brockman, became Surveyor-General of Western Australia and opened up the north-west of the State.

Grace Bussell Drake-Brockman died in 1935 in Guildford, Western Australia at the age of 75. The beach where she made her dramatic rescue is now called Redpath Beach, and the rock that the ship struck is called Isaacs Rock, after Sam Isaacs, the brave stockman who helped her save the 50 passengers and crew of the *Georgette*.

WHISKERS

In August 1991, an Aboriginal member of the Northern Territory Assembly stood to deliver an emotional speech. It wasn't about land rights or health, welfare or law and order, but about a white man who lived for many years with the Tiwi people on Bathurst Island.

The man, known as 'Whiskers', had been dead for 30 years, but the Assembly Member wanted to record officially for the first time the feelings of Tiwi people about this man and what he did.

This story is based on what that Aboriginal Member of the Northern Territory Assembly told his colleagues in Darwin.

THE MESSAGE FROM Canberra to the Administrator of the Northern Territory was short and to the point – please explain! The Federal Government had heard what most of Queensland and the Northern Territory was talking about – that a 39-year-old Frenchman named Francis Gsell was buying Aboriginal girls as young as eight on Bathurst Island, north of Darwin, and keeping them as a harem of wives.

Canberra understood that Gsell had acquired as

many as 150 wives. In itself this was unacceptable, but this man was none other than the Administrator of the Bathurst Island Mission; alarm bells were ringing everywhere. When Canberra learned that Gsell had bought a four-day-old baby, the telegraph lines between Darwin and the capital went into meltdown.

But there was a great deal more to this story. The answer back from Darwin was that everything was under control. Gsell was not involved in a flesh trade; he was buying the girls to save them from traditional arranged marriages to old men of the tribe.

Since first arriving on Bathurst Island in 1911, Gsell had watched young girls taken against their will, but he was forbidden from interfering in tribal law. Men were allowed to have many wives. Finally, he found a way around the rules – he bought the girls, then educated them on the mission until they were 18 and could marry a husband of their choosing.

Government officials in Canberra were not the only ones alarmed by the early reports of Francis Gsell's activities on Bathurst Island. The Vatican in Rome was also demanding answers, because Francis Xavier Gsell was not just the Administrator of the mission, he was also a Catholic priest! Father Gsell was summoned to Rome for a meeting with none other than the Pope to answer charges that he had abused his position.

Father Gsell told the pontiff the story of a young girl named Martina, who came to him pleading to be saved from an arranged marriage. An old man from the tribe had come to claim her and she sought protection from Father Gsell. The priest knew that he could not interfere with tribal custom or he would lose the trust of the people, and so he had to stand and watch as she was dragged away, screaming. Five days later Martina returned with spear wounds in her legs asking again for help.

Father Gsell asked the sisters on the mission to look after Martina while he talked with the families involved, all the time stalling as he worked out a plan. Then it came to him that he would buy the girl. He negotiated a price and Martina was saved.

News spread quickly of the sale of the young girl and families appeared from everywhere offering to sell their daughters to him. In one case an old man brought a four-day-old baby to him and offered to sell the infant, who was betrothed to him.

Each girl that Father Gsell bought became his tribal 'wife' under Tiwi custom. Of course, each 'wife' went into the care of the sisters. Father Gsell knew that a girl's family would often still pressure her to choose the husband they had arranged for her. But at least he had guaranteed she would be an adult when she married.

After hearing the story first-hand from Father Gsell, the Pope cleared him of all charges and sent him back to continue his missionary work.

Francis Gsell was born in the Alsace-Lorraine region of France in 1872 and trained for the priesthood in France, then Rome. He was ordained a priest in 1896 and was sent to Sydney with the Missionaries of the Sacred Heart to administer the Papua missions.

In 1905, the Conference of Australian Catholic Bishops strongly condemned the way Aborigines were being treated and their culture destroyed. So, the following year, Father Gsell was asked to go to Darwin to re-establish the church with appropriate respect for the indigenous people.

Father Gsell believed that he would have more success in his missionary work by removing the Aboriginal people from European influence. In 1910, he convinced the South Australian Government to give him 20,000 hectares on Bathurst Island to establish a mission. For the next 28 years, he worked the mission with the Tiwi people. He insisted that the Catholic brothers and sisters working with him respect Aboriginal custom and not impose Christianity. He operated that way throughout his encumbency. While he did not convert a single Tiwi adult to Christianity in his time on Bathurst Island, the community is overwhelmingly Catholic today.

In March 1938, at the age of 66, Father Gsell was appointed Bishop of Darwin. In all, he spent more than 40 years in the Northern Territory – from 1909 until his retirement in 1948. He died in July 1960, in Darwin, at the age of 88.

He was known fondly by Aboriginal communities as 'Whiskers' because of his long white beard. But he was known among the amused Catholic bishops of the world as 'The Bishop with 150 wives'.

Bishop Gsell (right) in Melbourne in 1947.

WHO'S ON FIRST?

Lawrence Hargraves is to blame. If he hadn't been ill, he almost certainly would have beaten the Wright Brothers into the air and Australia would have achieved the world's first powered flight.

But, alas, he had generously shared his ideas with everyone, including the American brothers, and they claimed the record and gave him absolutely no credit at all.

'My ideas are free to the world,' said Lawrence.

But then, having missed out on the world record, Lawrence didn't go ahead and claim the record for the first powered flight in Australia.

This story explains what happened as a result.

IS IT ANY wonder that few Australians know who was the first person to fly an aeroplane in Australia? We have a record for the first flight in a heavier-than-air machine; we have another record for the first powered flight in a heavier-than-air machine; then we have a third record for the first controlled, powered flight of a heavier-than-air machine; and, to top it off, we have a record for the first certified series of power flights. Ensuring total confusion, all but two of the records are contested.

There are few arguments about the first flight of a heavier-than-air machine in Australia – that was made by *The Bulletin* and *Punch* cartoonist George Taylor, in a biplane glider in the sandhills at Narrabeen on Sydney's northern beaches on 5 December 1909. He built the glider from plans drawn by his friend Lawrence Hargraves and with the help of furniture manufacturer Edward Hallstrom.

Hungarian-born Ehrich Weiss claimed the honour as the first man to make a powered flight in a heavier-than-air machine when he flew three times around a paddock at Diggers Rest, 30 kilometres from Melbourne on 18 March 1910. He had brought a French Voisin biplane from Germany by ship in order to claim the record. Weiss and his crew celebrated throughout the day, relieved that they had finally set the record after being grounded for 17 days by bad weather.

But they were soon to receive heartbreaking news. They were not the first – Weiss had been beaten to the record by a 20-year-old South Australian motor mechanic named Fred Custance. While Weiss was grounded in the wind and rain in Victoria, Custance had flown successfully at Bolivar, 16 kilometres north of Adelaide. Custance was flying for the first time in a French Bleriot aeroplane imported by an Adelaide businessman named Jones. Mr Jones had gone to an air show in France and seen the new flying machines; he was so impressed that he bought one, had it crated and shipped it to Adelaide.

Custance had flown for five minutes and 25 seconds, covering more than 1.5 kilometres at a height of about 5 metres. On a second flight – attempting to set an altitude record – Custance crashed from about 16 metres, slightly injuring himself when his head crashed forward into the fuel tank. It seemed that Ehrich Weiss had spent a fortune bringing his plane to Australia only to be beaten by Victorian weather.

However, there was some doubt expressed about whether Fred Custance broke anything except his nose that day in 1910. Mr Jones, the businessman, was an entrepreneur who stood to gain financially from claiming the record. The only witnesses were Jones and a couple of his neighbours. Experienced pilots were suspicious when young Fred Custance said that it was very easy flying – quite similar to running along the ground except for a floating sensation. The Bleriot that he flew was considered one of the most difficult aircraft to fly.

Perhaps Fred Custance answered his critics a few years later, during World War I, when he demonstrated natural flying skills with the Royal Flying Corps in Palestine.

Ehrich Weiss was bitterly disappointed at not being the first person to make a powered flight in Australia. But he settled for an undisputed entry in the record books for the first certified *series* of powered flights in Australia, by inviting journalists and dignitaries to witness a number of long flights at Diggers Rest in Victoria and Rosehill in Sydney during March 1910.

Of course, in keeping with the confusion of this story, you won't find Ehrich Weiss in Australian aviation record books; he used his stage name – a name more befitting the world's most famous magician and escapologist – Harry Houdini. Houdini was in Australia to perform his vaudeville escape act and decided to combine the visit with an attempt on a flying record.

But there's always more to the story, isn't there? Plenty of aviation enthusiasts claim that neither Houdini nor Custance deserve the credit for the first powered flight, because the honour belonged to an Englishman named Colin Defries. On 18 December 1909 – four months before Custance and Houdini – Defries climbed into his Wright brothers biplane on Sydney's Victoria Park racecourse and flew for about 300 metres at a height of around 4 metres. Media present were astounded at the smoothness of the flight, until a gust of wind blew Mr Defries's hat off. He immediately let go of the control to grab for his hat – as a gentleman would – and the aircraft went into a dive. He cut the engine and managed to set the aircraft down with moderate damage – Australia's first recorded crash landing.

Defries was denied the right to claim the record because it was said that he was not in control of the aircraft on landing. But then neither was Fred Custance, who knew all about Defries – it was on his attempt to better Defries's altitude record that Custance crashed.

And what about Carl Wittber? He went out to the farm where Fred Custance was to attempt the record and tried his hand at taxiing the aeroplane during trials. On one run he unintentionally became airborne and flew for more than 36 metres at an altitude of 1.5 metres. That was on 12 March 1910 – five days before Custance and six days before Houdini! Because it was an accident, no-one, especially Mr Jones, sought to have it entered as a claim on the record.

But for many Australians, the most important record is that for the first flight in Australia by an Australian, in an Australian-designed-and-built aircraft. That record was claimed by John Robertson Duigan, a 28-year-old farmer from Mia Mia in Victoria. He and his brother, Reginald, had never seen an aeroplane when they built and flew their own design on 16 July 1910. It was made out of ash and red pine, and held together with piano wires. John rebuilt the engine and flew again in October in front of witnesses to claim the record. He flew almost 200 metres at a height of 4 metres.

John Duigan continued with his flying, winning a Military Cross for gallantry as a pilot in the Australian Flying Corps in World War I.

THE WRECK OF THE *CATARAQUI*

It's said that inside every one of us there is a hero; it's just that not all of us are called upon to reveal it.

Certainly, several of the heroes that I have interviewed over the years – and there have been many – have said with humility that what they did was no more than anyone else would have done in the circumstances.

I guess the only way to prove that would be to put yourself in the same situation, and most of us would hope never to be in a war, a firestorm, a bombing, a siege, an earthquake or any of the other crises that demand heroics. Nor would we wish others to suffer injury, illness or tragedy to test our reaction.

'Show me a hero and I'll show you a tragedy,' it was once said. It would be wonderful if we didn't need any heroes.

IT WAS A foul and dark night when the *Cataraqui* entered a part of Bass Strait known as the Graveyard of Ships on 4 August 1845. She was 106 days out of Liverpool, bound for Port Phillip Bay with 367 passengers and 44 crew.

Cataraqui was a migrant ship – very different from

the convict ships of the day. She carried families of so-called 'able-bodied poor', who were given free passage to Australia in return for working in the colonies. The owners of the migrant ships were paid a bounty for every person they delivered alive to the colonies.

Almost 250 of the passengers came from villages between Bedford and Cambridge and nine villages near Oxford. The remainder were mostly from Ireland. All the families were poor and many had six or more children. In fact, 171 of those aboard the *Cataraqui* were under the age of 14.

The first six weeks of the trip from Liverpool took place in fine weather and calm seas. But, as Captain Christopher Finlay steered his ship into the Indian Ocean from Cape Town, the Roaring Forties began to take hold. During the next four weeks, five babies were born and six infants died as the cold and wet weather made life below decks miserable. The weather worsened as they neared the Southern Ocean, and Captain Finlay could not take bearings on the stars to establish his position. Instead, he had to work on guesses and rudimentary calculations.

As a westerly gale drove mountainous seas over the stern of the barque, making steerage impossible, the Captain decided that he was 60 or 70 miles (110 to 130 kilometres) from the western entrance of Bass Strait and north of King Island. He put the ship into a tight turn and waited for the storm to abate. But his officers insisted they push on to the safety of Port Phillip.

Captain Finlay gave the order at about 3 am for storm sails to be set as he steered for where he expected the entrance to Bass Strait to be. However, within 90 minutes, the *Cataraqui* drove hard up onto rocks on a reef off King Island. Huge waves crashed over the ship, washing 200 passengers, many of them children, and all the lifeboats overboard. The surviving crew and passengers clung desperately to the deck.

At 4 pm – almost 12 hours after hitting the reef – the ship broke in two. Another 100 people were washed to their death in the tumultuous seas. By next morning, only 30 survivors remained clinging to the bow. The water was rising and they had no choice but to make for King Island. Only nine made it through the boiling seas and razor-sharp rocks of the reef.

A former convict named David Howie was the first to find the survivors of the *Cataraqui*. Howie had been with a team of workers collecting seal and kangaroo skins on the island when he saw wreckage floating in the sea near his camp. He followed the trail along the current to the beach, where he found the chief mate, Thomas Guthrie, six sailors, an apprentice and a sole passenger – Solomon Brown. Forty-four crew and 367 passengers – a total of 411 men, women and children – had drowned in what remains one of Australia's worst maritime disasters.

The survivors might also have died had David Howie not had the presence of mind to leave a note at his base camp telling of his search for a wreck. The captain of a small cutter named the *Midge* stopped to take shelter from the bad weather, saw the note and sailed to the reef looking for Howie and a wreck. After three days of attempts, the *Midge* loaded the nine survivors and took them to Port Phillip. They arrived six weeks after the sinking of the *Cataraqui*.

But there's more to the story, as always. Solomon Brown, the only passenger to survive the sinking of the *Cataraqui*, had lost his wife, Hanna, and four children. He settled in Melbourne, but was forever haunted by the drowning of his wife and children in Bass Strait. Three years later, he too drowned – not at sea, but mysteriously in a creek just 40 centimetres deep in a suburb of Melbourne.

Of the surviving crew, only Chief Mate Thomas Guthrie went back to sea. A year after the sinking, he earned command of the ship *Tigress*. In an incredible coincidence, on the first journey under Guthrie's command, the *Tigress* ran onto a reef near Adelaide. Remembering the *Cataraqui* disaster, Captain Guthrie grabbed a rope and swam for shore to set a lifeline for his passengers and crew to pull themselves to safety.

Thanks to that lifeline, all but one person on board the *Tigress* survived. Amazingly, the only person who disappeared that day was Captain Thomas Guthrie, survivor of the *Cataraqui*.

YOUR MONEY OR YOUR LIFE

It has been a point of contention for almost two centuries that England solved its crime problem by sending it to the Australian colonies and then had no hesitation in asking us to send reinforcements every time it got into trouble in a war.

In recent years we got a little of our own back when a couple of our 'dirty rotten scoundrels' made their way to the United Kingdom to wreak havoc on trusting investors and business partners. A case of 'coals to Newcastle', you might say.

But in the early years of New South Wales we also managed to send some of our unwanted types to the United States of America. This is the story of one such 'export'.

ONE OF THE most notorious playgrounds for pirates, thieves and murderers in the late 19th century was 'The Barbary Coast' in San Francisco. Sleazy bars and saloons supplied women, gambling and rough bourbon whisky, usually distilled on the premises.

One of the most colourful Barbary Coast saloon owners was Australian bushranger Frank Gardiner, who had been banished from New South Wales in

King of the Road, Frank Gardiner (depicted at middle right) along with his gang (from top to bottom) Bourke, Hall, Gilbert and Dunne.

1874 as a condition of pardon from a 32-year prison sentence. He went by the name Frank Smith when he arrived in San Francisco from Hong Kong in 1875, but his real identity was soon revealed and he became a celebrity among his patrons.

Frank Smith's true name was not even Gardiner, it was Christie. Francis Christie was born in Scotland and moved to New South Wales with his parents when he was just a small boy. By the time he was 20, Christie was already in trouble with the law, jailed for five years with hard labour for horse stealing in Victoria. He escaped the infamous Pentridge Gaol in Melbourne after five weeks and disappeared into western New South Wales. Four years later he was arrested again for horse stealing, this time under the name Francis Clarke. He was convicted and sentenced to a further seven years hard labour at the Cockatoo Island Gaol.

After his release, Gardiner promised his sisters that he would try the honest life. He went to Carcoar, west of Sydney, and opened a butcher shop. But the boredom drove him mad and he pulled up stakes and headed for the Kiandra goldfields. For the next 12 years he was involved in horse and cattle stealing, armed robbery, assault and attempted murder of police. He was wounded and arrested in one attack, only to be rescued by his gang.

Gardiner became Australia's first professional bushranger with a skilled gang, among them John Piesley, John Gilbert and Ben Hall, and a thoughtful plan of action. Using various names, including 'Jones', and titles such as 'The Prince of the Tobymen' and 'King of the Road', he terrorised the coaches carrying gold and cash from the New South Wales diggings.

In 1862, Frank Gardiner and his gang pulled off the biggest robbery in Australian history to that time. They stopped the armed gold shipment from Forbes to Penrith at Eugowra Rocks and made off with 76 kilograms of gold and cash adding up to about $4 million in today's terms. The gang split after the hold-up, with Gardiner heading to Queensland with a married woman named Kitty Brown. They bought a shop and a pub in the names of Frank and Kitty Christie.

Meanwhile, back in Grenfell, police rounded up many of the gang involved in the robbery – one was even hanged. But they only ever found half the gold and cash. Eventually, in 1864, Frank Gardiner was arrested at Appis, near Rockhampton, after a tip-off from a man most believe was Kitty Brown's husband. Gardiner was sentenced to 32 years hard labour.

He had served 10 years when his sisters successfully pleaded for mercy, and the Premier, Sir Henry Parkes, asked the Governor, Sir Hercules Robinson, to grant a pardon on condition that Gardiner leave New South Wales forever. Frank Gardiner was taken to Newcastle and put on a ship to Hong Kong.

Meanwhile, in Sydney, scandalous accusations were being made about corruption in the pardoning of the colony's most notorious bushranger. Sir Henry Parkes, the Father of Federation, was forced to resign.

There are a few different stories about when and

how Frank Gardiner died. Some say it was in 1890 from the effects of drinking his own whisky. Others say it was in 1903 in a gunfight over a poker game at the Twilight Saloon that he ran for 15 years. Yet others say he died peacefully in 1904 at the age of 74 after a career as a successful rancher and businessman, as husband to a wealthy San Francisco widow and father to twin boys.

It is probably appropriate that Frank Gardiner should be mysterious and controversial in death as he was in life. However, it could be that there's more to this story.

Several historians and researchers now claim that in 1912, two young Californian men arrived in Grenfell claiming to be prospectors and asking permission to make some exploratory digs for two weeks around the area of Frank Gardiner's old camp. Witnesses said the two young men carried a set of plans. After just one week, the pair hurriedly packed up and returned to the United States with bags weighted with what they described as 'rock samples'.

Most believe the two young men were the twin sons of Frank Gardiner, and that they had returned to collect the millions in gold and cash buried near Grenfell by Gardiner 50 years earlier, in 1862, immediately following the robbery of the Forbes gold shipment.

Could it be that Frank Gardiner was still alive in 1912? If so, he would have been 82 years old. We may have to wait a little longer to know the end of this story.

BIBLIOGRAPHY

Ackroyd, Peter, *Dickens*, Mandarin, London, 1995

Adam-Smith, Patsy, *Outback Heroes*, Lansdowne Press, Sydney, 1981

Andrews, EM, *Australia and China*, Melbourne University Press, 1985

Atkinson, Ann, *The Dictionary of Famous Australians*, Allen & Unwin, Sydney, 1995

Austin, KA, *A Pictorial History of Cobb & Co.*, Rigby, Sydney, 1997

Baker, Sidney J, *The Ampol Book of Australiana*, Currawong Publishing, Sydney, 1963

Barker, Anthony, *What Happened When*, Allen & Unwin, Sydney, 1998

Barry, Paul, *The Rise and Rise of Kerry Packer*, Bantam, Sydney, 2000

Bassett, Jan, *The Concise Oxford Dictionary of Australian History*, Oxford University Press, Melbourne, 1994

Bilby, Joseph G, *The Irish Brigade in the Civil War*, Combined Publishing, Pennsylvania, 1998

Blaikie, George, *Great Australian Scandals*, Rigby, Sydney, 1979

Brunsdon, Jyoti (ed.), *I Love a Sunburnt Country*, Angus & Robertson, Sydney, 1990

Cashman, Richard (Senior Consultant), *Australian Sport Through Time*, Random House, Sydney, 1997

Caswell, Robert, *Shout*, Currency Press, Sydney, 1986

Charles, Michael, *Pictorial Memories of Old Parramatta*, Atrand, Sydney, 1995

Clarke, Frank, G, *The Big History Question*, Kangaroo Press, Sydney, 1998

—, *The Big History Question Volume II*, Kangaroo Press, Sydney, 2000

Costello, Con, *Botany Bay*, Mercier Press, Dublin, 1996

Coulthard-Clark, Chris, *Soldiers in Politics*, Allen & Unwin, Sydney, 1996

Crowley, FK, *Modern Australian Documents*, Volume 2, Wren, Melbourne, 1973

Curran, Tom, *Across the Bar*, Ogmios Publications, Brisbane, 1994

Cutlack, FM, *The Australian Flying Corps*, University of Queensland Press, Brisbane, 1984

D'Este, Carlo, *A Genius for War*, HarperCollins, London, 1995

Daniels, Kay, *Convict Women*, Allen & Unwin, Sydney, 1998

De Vries, Susan, *The Complete Book of Great Australian Women*, HarperCollins, Sydney, 2001

Dennis, P, Grey, J, Morris, E, and Prior, R, *The Oxford Companion to Australian Military History*, Oxford University Press, Melbourne, 1995

Faigan, Julian, *Uncommon Australians*, Art Exhibitions Australia Limited, Sydney, 1992

Fitzgerald, Shirley, *Sydney 1842–1992*, Hale & Ironmonger, Sydney, 1992

—, *Red Tape Gold Scissors*, State Library of New South Wales Press, Sydney, 1997

Flynn, Michael, *The Second Fleet*, Library of Australian History, Sydney, 2001

Folkard, Frederick C, *The Remarkable Australians*, KG Murray Publishing, Sydney, 1965

Fortheringham, Richard, *In Search of Steele Rudd*, University of Queensland Press, Brisbane, 1995

Fraser, Bryce (ed.), *The Macquarie Encyclopedia of Australian Events*, The Macquarie Library, Sydney, 1997
—, *Government in Australia*, The Macquarie Library, Sydney, 1998
—, *People of Australia*, The Macquarie Library, Sydney, 1998
Frost, Alan, *Botany Bay Mirages*, Melbourne University Press, Melbourne, 1994
Hall, Robert A, *The Black Diggers*, Aboriginal Studies Press, Canberra, 1997
Hetherington, John, *Nellie Melba*, Melbourne University Press, Melbourne, 1995
Holden, Robert, *Orphans of History*, Text Publishing, Melbourne, 2001
Hornadge, Bill, *The Hidden History of Australia*, ETT Imprint, Sydney, 1997
Hutchinson, Garrie and Ross, John (eds), *200 Seasons of Australian Cricket*, Ironbark (Pan Macmillan), Sydney, 1997
Irvin, Eric, *Dictionary of the Australian Theatre 1788–1914*, Hale & Ironmonger, Sydney, 1985
Jeffreys, Max, *Murder, Mayhem, Fire and Storm,* New Holland Publishers, Sydney, 1999
Jones, Barry, *Barry Jones Dictionary of World Biography*, Information Australia, Melbourne, 1996
Joy, William, *The Aviators*, Shakespeare Head Press, Sydney, 1965
Karskens, Grace, *The Rocks*, Melbourne University Press, Melbourne, 1998
Kemp, Peter (ed.), *The Oxford Dictionary of Literary Quotations*, Oxford University Press, New York, 1998
Laffin, John, *Gallipoli*, Kangaroo Press, Sydney, 1999
—, *The Somme*, Kangaroo Press, Sydney, 1999
Lockwood, Douglas, *Australia's Pearl Harbour,* Rigby, Sydney, 1977
Loney, Jack, *Wrecks on the New South Wales Coast*, Oceans Enterprises, Yarram (Vic), 1993

Lucas, John, 'Making a Statement: Annette Kellerman Advances the Worlds of Swimming, Diving and Entertainment', in *Sporting Traditions*, vol. 14, no. 2, May 1998

Mann, Alan, *The A–Z of Buddy Holly*, Aurum Press, London, 1996

McPhee, Margaret, *The Dictionary of Australian Inventions and Discoveries*, Allen & Unwin, Sydney, 1993

Meaney, Neville, *Australia and Japan*, Kangaroo Press, Sydney, 1999

Meeking, Charles (ed.), *Pictorial History of Australia at War 1939–45*, Australian War Memorial, Canberra, 1958

Monash, Sir John, *The Australian Victories in France in 1918*, Battery Press, Nashville, 1993

Nagle, JF, *Collins, the Courts and the Colony*, University of New South Wales Press, Sydney, 1996

Neal, David, *The Rule of Law in a Penal Colony*, Cambridge University Press, Melbourne, 1991

Newton, Dennis, *Australian Air Aces*, Aerospace Publications, Canberra, 1996

Newton, Dennis, *Clash of Eagles*, Kangaroo Press, Sydney, 1996

Nunn, Harry, *Bushrangers – A Pictorial History*, Lansdowne Press, Sydney, 1997

O'Farrell, Patrick, *The Irish in Australia*, New South Wales University Press, Sydney, 1993

Pearl, Cyril, *Morrison of Peking*, Angus & Robertson, Sydney, 1967

Richardson, Matthew, *The Penguin Book of Firsts*, Penguin, Ringwood (Vic), 1997

Robson, LL, *The Convict Settlers of Australia*, Melbourne University Press, Melbourne, 1994

Rolls, Eric, *Citizens*, University of Queensland Press, Brisbane, 1996

Salter, Elizabeth, *Daisy Bates*, Coward, McCann & Geoghegan Inc., New York, 1972

Sandilands, Ben, *Australia's Unsung Heroes*, HarperCollins, Melbourne, 1997

Scharf, J Thomas, *History of the Confederate States Navy*, Random House, New York, 1996

Tomlinson, Norman, *Louis Brennan – Inventor Extraordinaire*, John Halliwell, London, 1980

Uglow, Jennifer (revised by Maggy Hendry), *The Macmillan Dictionary of Women's Biography*, Macmillan, London, 1999

Vamplew, W, Moore, K, O'Hara, J, Cashman, R and Jobling, I (eds), *The Oxford Companion to Australian Sport*, Oxford University Press, Melbourne, 1994

Wannan, Bill, *Great Book of Australiana*, Rigby, Sydney, 1977

Wigmore, Lionel and Harding, Bruce, *They Dared Mightily*, The Australian War Memorial, Canberra, 1986

Wilson, PD, *North Queensland WWII 1942–1945*, Queensland Department of Geographic Information, Brisbane, 1988

Australia Through Time, Random House, Sydney, 1997

The Australian Encyclopaedia, The Grolier Society of Australia, Sydney, 1963

Colonial Secretary Index, www.records.nsw.gov.au

Prime Ministers of Australia, National Museum of Australia factsheet

Also worth a look are:

www.adf-serials.com

www.aec.gov.au

www.asap.unimelb.edu.au

www.buddyhollycenter.org

www.Catholic-Hierarchy.org

www.cnn.com

www.deakin.edu.au

www.dorsetmag.co.uk

www.geocites.com

www.gg.gov.au
www.gutenberg.net.au
www.kepl.com.au
www.lexscripta.com
www.lion-nathan.com.au
www.literature.org
www.nla.gov.au
www.nsw.gov.au
www.rba.gov.au
www.sa.gov.au
www.scs.une.edu.au
www.sl.nsw.gov.au
www.spartacus.schoolnet.co.uk
www.unsw.adfa.edu.au
www.uq.edu.au
www.visionaustralia.org.au
www.whitehat.com.au
www.worldwideschool.org

ACKNOWLEDGMENTS

Special thanks to the staff at the National Library of Australia (especially the newspaper reading room), the Australian War Memorial Reading Room, the Mitchell Library in Sydney and the State Libraries of Victoria and South Australia.

This book is dedicated to my wife, Dymetha, and my children, Robert and Sarah. Thank you for your faith, your strength and your love.

Christopher Stewart